Implementin
Learning in Early Childhood

This ground-breaking book proves that Project Based Learning (PBL) does work in early childhood classrooms. Most common understandings of PBL in Pre-K through 2nd grade are rife with assumptions, misconceptions, and perceived barriers that have prevented its widespread implementation. *Implementing Project Based Learning in Early Childhood* breaks down these barriers, offering teachers and leaders at various stages of PBL implementation the tools, resources, instructional strategies, and suggestions needed to dispel the myths and discover the truth.

Full of practical approaches and strategies, chapters encourage you to consider your current practices from new perspectives while "Reflect and Connect" sections provide opportunities to think through your questions, make connections to your current practices, and plan your next steps. Educators will gain a deep understanding of PBL in early childhood and build their confidence to engage all students in high quality Project Based Learning from the beginning of the school year to the end.

Sara Lev has worked as an early childhood teacher in public, private, and charter school settings since 2005, and is a National Faculty Member for PBLWorks.

Amanda Clark has worked in public education for over 15 years, is currently Assistant Professor of Education at Central College in Pella, Iowa, and is a National Faculty member for PBLWorks.

Erin Starkey has been in education since 2008 serving as a classroom teacher, district instructional coach and technologist, curriculum writer, and National Faculty member for PBLWorks.

Implementing Project Based Learning in Early Childhood

Overcoming Misconceptions and Reaching Success

Sara Lev, Amanda Clark, and Erin Starkey

Routledge
Taylor & Francis Group

NEW YORK AND LONDON

First published 2020
by Routledge
52 Vanderbilt Avenue, New York, NY 10017

and by Routledge
2 Park Square, Milton Park, Abingdon, Oxon, OX14 4RN

Routledge is an imprint of the Taylor & Francis Group, an informa business

Library of Congress Cataloging-in-Publication Data
Names: Lev, Sara, author. | Clark, Amanda, author. | Starkey, Erin, author.
Title: Implementing project based learning in early childhood : overcoming misconceptions and reaching success / Sara Lev, Amanda Clark and Erin Starkey.
Identifiers: LCCN 2020004821 (print) | LCCN 2020004822 (ebook) | ISBN 9780367198008 (hardback) | ISBN 9780367198015 (paperback) | ISBN 9780429243332 (ebook)
Subjects: LCSH: Project method in teaching. | Early childhood education--Curricula.
Classification: LCC LB1139.35.P8 L48 2020 (print) | LCC LB1139.35.P8 (ebook) | DDC 371.3/6--dc23
LC record available at https://lccn.loc.gov/2020004821
LC ebook record available at https://lccn.loc.gov/2020004822

ISBN: 978-0-367-19800-8 (hbk)
ISBN: 978-0-367-19801-5 (pbk)
ISBN: 978-0-429-24333-2 (ebk)

Typeset in Optima
by Cenveo® Publisher Services

To early childhood teachers,

        and to the children who teach them.

Contents

Meet the Authors

Sara Lev

Sara has worked as an early childhood teacher in public, private, and charter school settings since 2005, where she has also held a variety of leadership roles supporting teachers with social and emotional learning and Project Based Learning. In 2017, she became a National Faculty Member for PBLWorks, where she facilitates workshops throughout the United States. Sara earned her Master's Degree in Early Childhood Education from Bank Street College in New York City. She lives in Los Angeles with her husband and two sons.

Amanda Clark

Amanda worked as an elementary teacher, literacy leader, and instructional coach for 16 years. She earned her Master's and Doctor of Philosophy degrees at Drake University in Des Moines, Iowa. She currently is an Assistant Professor of Education, preparing pre-service teachers to use learner-centered practices and Project Based Learning in their future classrooms. Amanda is also a National Faculty Member for PBLWorks. She lives in Des Moines, Iowa with her husband.

Erin Starkey

Erin has been on her professional journey since 2008 when she graduated from Abilene Christian University. Immediately following undergraduate school, she was part of the Texas State Teacher Fellows program, earning her Master's of Education in 2009 during her first year of teaching. Her experiences include being a classroom teacher, instructional coach, district technologist, curriculum writer, and workshop facilitator. She is currently part of the PBLWorks National Faculty. She and her family reside in San Antonio, Texas.

List of Illustrations

Figures

Tables

Acknowledgments

This book was born out of a workshop session developed and facilitated at a PBLWorks (formerly the Buck Institute for Education) National Faculty summit. Thank you to Becky Hausammann for recognizing a partnership when you saw one, and to John Larmer for connecting us to Routledge. We are grateful to the PBLWorks National Faculty and staff for inspiring us and cheering us on. The many teachers around the country who we met during PBLWorks workshops and support visits were instrumental in the development of this book, notably the early childhood team in Burkburnett, Texas.

Many people aided in the early research and content for the book including Sara Beshawred, Michelle Cantrell, Amanda Narconis, Suzie Boss, Alison Kerr, Hillary Johnson, Dana Roth, and Mari Lim Jones; and at the final stages, Alek Lev, Teresa Dempsey, Sabina Anderson, Erin Gannon, and Kari DeJong, thank you for providing kind, helpful, and specific feedback. Your insights were invaluable.

Sara thanks...

All of my instructors at Bank Street College of Education, especially Alice Mangan, Judy Leipzig and Sal Vascellaro, who had a profound impact on my commitment to teaching young children. You charted a path for me by illuminating what teaching could look like.

The children and families of the first Transitional Kindergarten class at Larchmont Charter School (Hollygrove). To Amy Held, Alissa Chariton, Eva Orozco and the teachers and staff at LCS for supporting the *Outdoor Classroom* project, especially our music teacher Malcolm Moore and art teacher Andrea Ramirez. Laura Garland, thank you for being a thought partner and friend. Thank you to Victor and Audrey Yerrid, Lisa Freeman,

Andrew Zack, and Heather McIntosh for contributing your talent and expertise to the project.

My whole family for your love and interest in this work, especially my parents Gene and Barbara Ridberg. My sons Zachary and Chaplin, thank you for understanding the importance of this project and freeing me up for early morning writing sessions, hours in coffee shops and for your words of encouragement. My husband Alek, thank you for being my partner, editor and overall anchor. Your clarity of vision and thought-provoking questions inspire me to be a better writer and an even better human.

Amanda thanks…

The late Jan Drees, a true visionary for education who used research on learning and brain development to create a school in the heart of downtown where you worked, not where you lived. You were truly an innovator and I am blessed to have worked alongside you. To my colleagues who became my Des Moines family, thank you for sharing your time, talents, and resources. Operating on the cutting edge of instructional strategies was challenging and demanding, but we did it with grace, determination, and collective efficacy. I am thankful for every child who entered my classroom and every family I had the privilege to serve. May all of you stand a little taller, speak a little louder, and find a way to positively impact the world because of our time together.

And to my husband Aaron, who continues to be my biggest supporter. You graciously listen as I work through ideas and have always given me the time and space to follow my dreams. To my family, thank you for supporting every new project my teammates and I dreamed up. It is through your time, talents, and resources that my students had incredible learning experiences. And for every time you told the story of the Downtown School, you helped spread the message of PBL with others.

Erin thanks…

Those who have continually inspired me to be a positive, authentic force in the field of education. Sara and Amanda, the best co-authors imaginable. You amaze me with your brilliance, work ethic, and heart for learners. It has been such an honor to work alongside you to bring Sara's story to life and share the power of PBL with educators and students around the world.

My ACU professors, Dana Pemberton, Julie Douthit, and Stephanie Talley. Thank you for pointing me to PBLWorks in 2009. I wouldn't be here without your guidance and encouragement. Cynthia Evans, my mentor and friend. You've profoundly shaped my work from the beginning. You taught me to create more, do more, and have fun because our learners deserve it! My past, present, and future learners. You will change the world for the better. You are the reason I do this work and I'm grateful to be a part of your journey.

Grandmother and Granddad, Barbara and C. G. Gray, you sought out those who needed you most and I endeavor to bring that same freedom to students I work with. My husband, Seth, thank you for always believing in me and supporting my journey. And, my babies, Lincoln and Margot. Your pure joy and excitement about life and learning inspire me to bring the very best I can to those who may teach you someday.

Introduction

> If there's a book that you want to read, but it hasn't been written yet, then you must write it.
>
> — Toni Morrison

When I tell people, both educators and non-educators alike, that I teach kindergarten, I get one of two responses: "You must have so much *patience*. I could never do that job," or "Oh, you teach the *babies*!" (The latter is typically accompanied by a sweet smile, tilted head, and hands placed affectionately over their heart.) And when I tell people that I use Project Based Learning (PBL) with my four- and five-year-olds, the reaction is nearly universal: "How? They're *so* young." Early on in my teaching career, I laughed off comments like these and didn't think twice about the implied message that my students couldn't engage in Project Based Learning because they were too needy, lacked basic skills, and couldn't work together.

More recently though, I have viewed these comments as opportunities to advocate for young learners, to impress upon adults that children this age are most assuredly not babies; that they are independent, adept communicators who bring a wealth of knowledge, experiences, and skills into the classroom each day. I am passionate and curious about my students, who they are, and who they are becoming. What children say and do means something to me, and the learning we do together surprises and inspires me each day, even in the (admittedly many) moments of challenge.

I feel very fortunate that I was introduced to Project Based Learning at the beginning of my teaching career. The ideas and values that lie at the heart of PBL have shaped my teaching practices from the day I decided to become a teacher, and I embraced PBL because those values aligned with my own; that children are independent and inquisitive, that learning must involve meaningful relationships and happen in community with others, and that children can and should play an active role in the world. After many years as a classroom teacher, my commitment to these values has only grown. I am grateful that my journey has led me here, where I now have the opportunity to support other teachers in learning about PBL along with two colleagues and friends, Amanda Clark and Erin Starkey.

We believe all students, regardless of their age, can engage in Project Based Learning (PBL). Project Based Learning empowers students to learn and discover many lessons about themselves and the world. Children stretch themselves to ask questions, make plans, and follow through on their ideas. It is through Project Based Learning that children not only learn academic content, but more importantly, they begin to better understand themselves as human beings and as learners. They build relationships with one another, with their teachers, and with members of a wider community in which they play an important part. PBL leverages young children's inquisitive nature and interests, and engages children in explorations and discoveries that directly relate to and impact their lives and the lives of others.

Project Based Learning is a pedagogical approach to instruction in which students actively construct their own knowledge over a sustained period of time, collaborating with their peers to complete a public product that answers a driving question or solves a challenging problem. The "project" in the phrase "Project Based Learning" refers to a complete unit of study, one that is thoughtfully designed and implemented over several weeks or even months. This should not be confused with what teachers colloquially call a "project," which is typically a one-off, hands-on activity like a diorama, a poster, or a timeline. Project Based Learning engages children in rigorous inquiry as active participants in the learning process. It integrates essential academic and social and emotional skills and empowers children to take their new learning beyond the classroom.

As National Faculty members with PBLWorks (formerly the Buck Institute for Education), we have the privilege of working with teachers of all grade levels from across the globe. Many teachers come to the introductory PBL workshops energized to learn about Project Based Learning and how they can effectively design a project for all of their students. But some early childhood teachers are not yet convinced that PBL will work in their classrooms. Even though preschool and early elementary teachers attend the same workshops as their upper elementary, middle, and high school colleagues, they frequently sit shaking their heads thinking – and often, declaring aloud – "Sure, I can see it working for older students but *my kids can't do this.*"

When teachers are asked to explain more about what is causing these doubts, they usually reveal that their feelings are connected to their philosophy of education, current instructional practices, or myths about PBL. Teachers often wonder how their students, still emergent readers and writers, can engage in research and project work. They assume they will need to front-load so much content there will be no time for anything else. Teachers are unsure about their children's abilities to work as independent learners and to collaborate with their peers. They struggle to imagine their young students as active members of the learning process, able to reflect, revise, and give/receive feedback on their work. They fear that no assessments in PBL can reliably measure their students' progress, and they are unsure if their children are too young to participate in any type of public sharing of learning.

We understand these concerns, worries, and challenges. We have worked in early childhood classrooms, taught primary grades, and coached preschool and early elementary teachers and school leaders. By drawing on the research about how children learn, our understanding and appreciation for learner-centered practices, and our experiences, we address the issues specific to early childhood PBL so you are prepared to facilitate learning with our youngest students. In the coming pages, we will tackle some of the barriers and assumptions that often hold early childhood teachers back when they want to implement PBL. Each chapter is framed by one of the specific sentiments that we heard from teachers across the country, and we address each misconception chapter by chapter.

This book tells the story of a single project that I facilitated with my own Transitional Kindergarten (TK) students in

Transitional Kindergarten (TK) is intended to be the first of a two-year kindergarten program in California. Children who qualify for TK (those who turn 5 between September 1 and December 2 of that school year) will complete TK and then attend kindergarten the following year. TK classrooms can look different at different schools. They can be stand-alone, TK only classrooms or they can be TK/K combined.

the fall of the 2018–2019 school year, in which my four- and five-year-old students designed their own outdoor classroom space. My classroom was comprised of a diverse group of learners who came from a variety of linguistic and cultural backgrounds. Over the course of the book, you will meet and walk alongside many children (all of whose names have been changed) as they engaged in the *Outdoor Classroom* project. You will discover that school-age students who are in the early childhood stage of development (ages 3–8) are capable, thoughtful, perceptive individuals who can engage in cognitively complex and rigorous project work.

The types of learning experiences and instructional strategies that you will read about provide strong examples of the many ways in which PBL *can* be implemented with our youngest learners. In this book, we provide research to help you overcome the misconceptions present in early childhood PBL. We also purposefully avoid simplistic tips and tricks in favor of practical approaches and strategies, and encourage you to consider your current practices from new perspectives. We offer informal opportunities to engage with the text and more guided moments called "Reflect and Connect," when you might imagine one of us sitting across from you, coaching and supporting as you think through your questions, make connections to your current practices, and plan your next steps. We also created a document to help you identify where the ideas you are reading about fit within a PBL unit. The Stages of Early Childhood Project Based Learning can be found following this Introduction. In addition, we included two appendices for you to access as needed and called for by the text. Appendix A is a completed project planner for the *Outdoor Classroom* project, and Appendix B is a list of additional research articles and websites that will enhance your understanding of the content in this book.

As you read each chapter, we ask that you have an open mind, seek to understand, and try to visualize how PBL can work for *your* group of students in *your* place and *your* time. Knowing that every teaching and learning situation is influenced by a unique set of conditions, our goal is to make Project Based Learning feel attainable so you are prepared for successful implementation in your own classroom. Implementing Project Based Learning may mean changing some of your beliefs about teaching as you align with a constructivist approach to learning and use learner-centered practices to plan, manage, teach, and assess. You may need to let go of some of the practices that have become comfortable for you thus far or make adjustments to some of your tried-and-true instructional strategies.

We know the idea of adding "one more thing" can sometimes feel untenable. But PBL is not "one more thing" to tack on to an already full schedule. It is *the* thing – the vehicle – used to integrate academic skills and content alongside social and emotional skills, to embed purposeful literacy, and to empower young children to take an active role in the learning process.

Remember that there is no such thing as a perfect project. There are always things that can be improved or changed upon reflection, and the *Outdoor Classroom* project is certainly no different. We also know that this project is specific to a particular time and place (a new grade level with an empty classroom) and might not be easily replicated. The point is not to "copy" this project, but to witness how the elements are woven together in a context that was authentic and relevant to *this* group, at *this* time, and in *this* place. One of the most unique aspects of PBL is that it can be (and it *must* be) adapted and related to your school community.

We sincerely hope that you will use this book as a resource and we encourage you to lean on your colleagues, seek additional trainings, dig into the research, and connect with us on social media. We are excited that you are interested in PBL and we want to support you with implementation, regardless of where you are in your journey.

Sara Lev
January, 2020

The Stages of Early Childhood Project Based Learning

Teachers approach Project Based Learning in three stages. First, we develop and plan the project (Stage 1). Then we implement the project with our students (Stage 2). Finally, we reflect on the project (Stage 3). Since this book is divided into chapters organized by commonly held misconceptions rather than by the chronology of a project, it may be helpful to reference this chart when you encounter new terms or unfamiliar elements. This will help you determine where the components of each stage are situated within the context of Project Based Learning.

Foundational Beliefs

Constructivist principles
Learner-centered practices

Stage 1: Project Development

Examine **standards**
Prepare for **intentional integration**
Embed **social and emotional learning**
Use existing curriculum scope and sequence for **parallel integration**
Set up **literacy structures**
Envision potential **authentic public products**
Choose **learning goals**
Create **driving question**
Write **project summary**
Consider **fieldwork**
Plan lessons and experiences for **sustained inquiry**
Develop **assessments**

Stage 2: Project Implementation

Facilitate **entry event**
Elicit and record **need-to-know questions**
Engage in **sustained inquiry**
Notice connections for **spontaneous integration**
Create opportunities for **collaboration**
Incorporate **reflection, feedback,** and **revision**
Revisit **need-to-know questions**
Connect with **expert visitors**
Participate in **fieldwork**
Plan for **celebration**
Document **learning**
Record additions and changes in **project planner**
Present the **public product**

Stage 3: Project Reflection

Talk with **colleagues**
Look back on **project plan**
Think about **successes**
Consider **areas for growth**

Constructivism in Practice

Creating the Conditions for Project Based Learning in an Early Childhood Classroom

Project Based Learning seems too open-ended and unstructured.
Where would I even start?

One of the most common misconceptions early childhood educators have about Project Based Learning (PBL) is that it seems far too unregulated and student-driven to implement with young children. Many teachers assume that PBL is a chaotic free-for-all, and if the teaching is scattered and inconsistent, then the learning must be superficial. This assumption holds primarily true with those unfamiliar with the complex and essential theory that creates the conditions for teaching and learning in a PBL unit: *constructivism*. Constructivism is a learning theory based on the premise that learners generate meaning triggered by interactions with the world around them (Brooks, 2013; Narayan, Rodriguez, Araujo, Shaqlaih, & Moss, 2013; Woolfolk, 2013). Project Based Learning is a pedagogical approach to instruction that combines the theoretical principles of how children learn best (knowledge construction) with the premises of learner-centered practices. PBL is based on the constructivist belief that the most effective form of learning occurs when knowledge is *constructed*, meaning that through social interactions with others, students build upon their existing wealth of experiences and knowledge in order to create new understandings. This differs fundamentally from more traditional philosophies that view children as empty vessels, needed to be filled in by knowing, experienced adults. And the way that teachers accomplish this, traditionally, is by systematically covering grade-level content. Thus, we believe that it is important to begin your Project Based Learning journey here, appreciating the key ideas about constructivism, so that you can create and sustain the conditions for successful PBL in your classroom.

Constructivism offers teachers a value system that guides the choices and decisions we make in our classrooms, just as our personal values guide us in our lives outside of school. Perhaps constructivism is brand new to you, or maybe you remember reading about constructivism in your teacher training program, but you can't quite remember all the tenets of social constructivism. Maybe you have experience with components of Project Based Learning but haven't considered the connection to constructivism. No matter where you are on this spectrum, it is important to have a familiarity with the five basic constructivist principles, defined below, and how they lay the groundwork for the implementation of PBL.

A good place to start in terms of developing a solid understanding of social constructivism is by reading the following statements by Brooks (2013):

> The goal of education rooted in constructivist learning theory is to offer students opportunities to **construct** understandings at the leading edge of their current functioning. These **opportunities** are designed, offered, and managed by a teacher with understandings of how people forge new concepts, including both the **individual** and **collaborative** nature of concept formation.
>
> (p. 271)

Based on this definition alone, it is easy to see why some teachers have the perception that PBL is open-ended and unstructured. Words like "construct," "opportunities," "individual," and "collaborative" are certainly a part of constructivism and PBL. However, without a strong understanding of what they mean in context, misinterpretation is bound to occur, especially when teachers try to use strategies in their practice without fully understanding the theory and research behind them.

Developing a conceptual understanding in tandem with opportunities for practical applications of learning is essential for both students and teachers in Project Based Learning. To effectively, thoroughly, and purposefully implement Project Based Learning in your classroom, it is essential to first have a basic understanding of the principles of constructivism.

Now reread the statement strands by Brooks that have been highlighted in Figure 1.1 , this time reading between the lines to uncover some of the principles of constructivism.

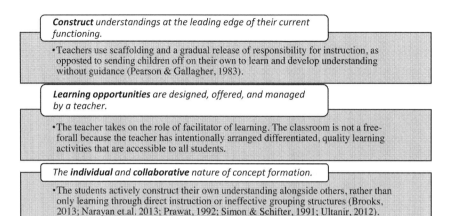

Construct understandings at the leading edge of their current functioning.
- Teachers use scaffolding and a gradual release of responsibility for instruction, as opposed to sending children off on their own to learn and develop understanding without guidance (Pearson & Gallagher, 1983).

Learning opportunities are designed, offered, and managed by a teacher.
- The teacher takes on the role of facilitator of learning. The classroom is not a free-forall because the teacher has intentionally arranged differentiated, quality learning activities that are accessible to all students.

The **individual** and **collaborative** nature of concept formation.
- The students actively construct their own understanding alongside others, rather than only learning through direct instruction or ineffective grouping structures (Brooks, 2013; Narayan et.al. 2013; Prawat, 1992; Simon & Schifter, 1991; Ultanir, 2012).

Figure 1.1 Brooks statement chunked and highlighted

These principles are not merely educational guides; *they are values –* values that will guide your instructional decisions, inspire the classroom culture you create, the experiences you plan, and the conversations you have with children. Teaching through PBL draws on a belief of constructivism and the values we find in the principles. As you approach implementing PBL, consider the fact that our teaching experiences go far deeper than just transmitting content and skills *to* children. Every interaction we have, each lesson we plan is a reflection of what we *believe about* children. Our classrooms are more than just "learning spaces." They are places where the values we hold about children are evident during each interaction, each unit, each minute, and each day. They reflect who we are as educators. And these constructivist principles, as revealed through PBL, allow teachers to approach teaching and learning in ways that empower children, allow them to be a part of their own learning process in community with others, and realize the meaning and relevance of their learning. The projects in which children engage during PBL tell stories about how teachers view children, and also, how children see themselves.

The five principles of constructivist learning theory, shown in Table 1.1, provide teachers with a solid foundation for developing a classroom where PBL can thrive (Driscoll, 2005). More important than memorizing the key features of constructivism – as important as they are – is being able to identify how the principles underscore everything we do when designing, developing, and implementing projects with young children.

Table 1.1 Principles of Constructivism

Principle 1	Embed learning in complex, realistic, and relevant learning environments.
Principle 2	Provide for social negotiation and shared responsibility as part of learning.
Principle 3	Support multiple perspectives and use multiple representations of content.
Principle 4	Encourage ownership in learning.
Principle 5	Nurture self-awareness and an understanding that knowledge is constructed.

The principles of constructivism represent the values and beliefs that guide our instructional decisions as we create the conditions for deep learning. It is our role, as teachers, to take the specifics of each principle and arrange meaningful and relevant experiences where students learn in collaboration with their peers. Conversely, traditional teaching practices rely on the teacher to transmit the knowledge to students and then check to see what they learned. Project Based Learning encourages students to draw on their prior knowledge and experiences to construct knowledge and become independent learners who are capable of taking an active role in their learning throughout a project.

Principles and values such as these can have a profound impact on our teaching. When we strive to hold those beliefs at the center of our work (as Project Based Learning demands that we do), we empower young children to move through life knowing they have a role to play, not just "when they grow up," but as young learners. We want our students to know they can contribute to the world around them *now*, as members of their classroom community, and also as members of the wider community outside of their classroom walls. Understanding the individual principles and where they naturally overlap will help you plan, create, and sustain an environment in your own classroom that fosters student growth through PBL.

In this chapter, we introduce each of the constructivist learning principles with a theoretical lens sharply focused on early childhood Project Based Learning and specifically, on Sara's *Outdoor Classroom* project. We will take you behind the scenes of the planning and preparation that goes into a project and you will see firsthand how the constructivist principles informed Sara's instructional decisions. By focusing on what these principles look like in the context of a project, we hope to deepen your understanding of constructivism and help you make connections to your own teaching, thereby setting the stage for implementing Project Based Learning in your own classroom. Included in each section are also examples for how each principle informs curriculum, instruction, and other classroom decisions in a more general context. We also suggest specific "Quick Strategies" for implementation and applications of the principles as the basis for the rest of the book. Chances are that as you view the principles of constructivism through an early childhood lens, you'll recognize aspects that are familiar to you, even if you are teaching in a more traditional environment.

The *Outdoor Classroom* Project: Constructivist Principles in Practice

Two weeks before the first day of school, Sara visited her new TK classroom to begin making plans for the year. The space was relatively small, but adjacent to that room was an empty outdoor area that had previously been used for storage and as a holding space for children during carpool (Figure 1.2).

Figure 1.2 Two weeks before the first day of school

Sara could immediately see its potential. Knowing that the physical environment of the classroom would reflect her values as a teacher and that her students would need more space to learn, she immediately had a thought: *"This should be our first project."*

Sara's first teaching decision – the idea that four-year-olds would have an instrumental role in designing and creating their own learning environment – embodies all five constructivist principles in one single thought. Sara knew the small indoor classroom would be inadequate for the developmental requirements of four- and five-year-olds in terms of movement and variety, so the outdoor classroom needed to be created for practical use. The empty, adjacent classroom provided a **realistic, relevant**, and **complex** problem for the students to solve. Sara also knew the TK learning goals could be integrated into a project like this one because she had spent time looking at both the foundational skills for the end of pre-school (pre-school learning foundations) as well as the Common Core State Standards for kindergarten in her previous teaching roles as a TK teacher. She knew that the specific grade-level standards, when connected to authentic purposes, could serve as a strong foundation for students' realistic and relevant learning.

This project would require children to take an **active, shared role in their community by negotiating** their wishes and their needs when making decisions together. The *Outdoor Classroom* project would engage children's **multiple perspectives and use multiple representations of content**, as children would need to offer design suggestions based on their backgrounds and prior experiences. They would need to represent their ideas in a variety of ways that would honor their diverse learning community. By beginning the year with this project, Sara would be honoring and valuing students' ideas and experiences all the while learning more about them throughout the project. This project would support children's **self-awareness and an understanding of how learning is constructed** by asking them to take initiative in their learning when considering what they wanted and needed for the space. Collaboratively creating a physical space would provide the children with an opportunity to literally see their learning throughout the entirety of the project. Finally, and perhaps most importantly, the project would give children **ownership over their learning**. The classroom they created would be a place they learned and played each day. Knowing they had a major role in creating the space would foster a sense of pride, ownership, and commitment to keeping the space organized for optimal use.

Although Sara could have designed and set up the space before the children arrived, she decided the creation of the outdoor classroom was an authentic context for teaching social and emotional competencies, as well as academic standards. Sara began developing her project idea and decided *"How can we create an outdoor classroom where we can play and learn?"* would make a strong driving question. Sara also knew that she would be able to integrate some of her content standards around social studies, math, literacy, science, and social and emotional learning (SEL). In her mind, Sara determined the basic structure of her outdoor classroom idea, which helped her design and plan the project as follows: *Students will design an outdoor classroom space. They will meet with an interior designer and create a layout of the space. After deciding on key elements of the space, students will design those areas. Students will learn about shape, size, design, measurement, story, characters, and presentation skills. They will share their space with their families and celebrate their learning.*

In the coming pages, we unpack each of the constructivist principles with a lens on the planning of the *Outdoor Classroom* project to demonstrate how the project itself and Sara's classroom are grounded in constructivism. As you deepen your understanding of the principles, we encourage you to reference the completed project planner included in Appendix A. The project planner serves multiple purposes throughout the design and development phases of a project and is especially helpful when identifying your own learning goals and aligning your instructional practices. While this document includes a high-level overview, it also includes details that tell the story of the project. We will return to the project planner throughout the book, highlighting things for you to notice and consider when planning your project.

Principle 1

Embed Learning in Complex, Realistic, and Relevant Learning Environments

Creating a learning environment where children can engage deeply with relevant content and make connections to the wider community is essential to planning and implementing high-quality Project Based Learning.

The standards and skills associated with emergent literacy, mathematics, the school community, and making scientific investigations are just a few of the early childhood concepts that have developmentally appropriate, authentic applications and connections beyond the classroom. Unfortunately, adults often underestimate young learners' intellectual abilities and try to make the standards more "accessible" to children by teaching skills by way of cute, "kid-friendly" themes like teddy bears, dinosaurs, and nature. However, when we fail to teach skills and competencies as they apply to our world outside the classroom walls, we risk robbing children of their natural capacities to make meaning of the world around them. An appropriately complex learning environment invites students to engage in authentic experiences that require them to solve challenging problems in collaboration with others (Narayan et al., 2013). Project Based Learning asks students to learn through the investigation of a challenging problem or question which consists of many different and connected parts. It provides opportunities for students to construct their own understanding of the content by engaging in creative thinking, critical thinking, and problem-solving (Brooks, 2013; Narayan et al., 2013).

To create and maintain this condition for learning, it is essential to first become familiar with your standards and learning goals (Prawat, 1992). Then ask yourself, *for whom* and *how* and *in what context* are these skills relevant? Young children are more apt to participate in learning when it is connected to their lives, which is why identifying how standards relate is so important. We also recommend that you become familiar with the social and emotional learning skills and competencies children are developing. As you design your project, you will be able to see where these goals and standards might naturally fit within an overall project design. Then plan on integrating them into the project in applicable ways. Fortunately, there are many ways to embed standards and learning goals into realistic contexts when creating PBL units through an integrated approach.

In the *Outdoor Classroom* project, it was essential to present the driving question (the main question that would guide project work) to students and set a clear reason for learning. In this case – as it should be in all cases – the rationale for the driving question was clear. *We need this space to learn and play.* Sara knew the driving question in advance for this project and wanted to make sure the students understood why *they* had to help. And then they needed to know the "why" behind each subsequent decision they made throughout the project – *why* they needed to brainstorm ideas before deciding on a final plan, *why* they needed to map out the plan ahead of time, *why* they needed to draw and design instruments before actually building them. Thus, the driving question that Sara developed – "*How can we create an outdoor classroom where we can play and learn?*" – was a natural offshoot of the "authentic problem children faced."

For young children, breaking down complex problems into smaller parts helps them to problem-solve and feel successful along the way. So, Sara divided the challenge of designing an entire classroom into manageable steps. She asked students how they would want to use different areas of the outdoor classroom and they came up with several ideas, including a puppet theater and a musical instrument area. Sara saw those as two distinct, smaller "chunks" of the larger project design. Sara then created questions under the umbrella of the driving question that included, "What do we need to know to create our musical instrument area?" and "How can we design a puppet theater for our outdoor classroom?"

Along the way, there were many other times where learning was embedded in the project in authentic, relevant ways. Children designed puppets for the puppet theater (first learning about what a "character" was during Literacy, then drawing and labeling their puppets with descriptive characteristics). The class learned that puppeteers open puppets' mouths only on the break between syllables, so children used their puppets to practice their phonemic awareness. To solidify geometry concepts, they practiced identifying and sorting three-dimensional shapes by organizing the new block area in the outdoor space. They met and interviewed an interior designer, a puppeteer, and a musician to help guide their learning. They wrote and read a letter to their school principals proposing their classroom redesign. They presented their outdoor classroom to parents using presentation skills. These examples point to a classroom culture where the learning was relevant, authentic, and embedded within the project.

Sara's intentionality in planning helped children to find purpose in the many skills and competencies they were learning. Letter writing, designing spaces, generating interview questions, and organizing materials are skills that the children could apply to larger contexts long after the completion of this one project. And in the end, the children felt successful because they knew they had answered their driving question, part by part, seeing it through to completion.

Quick Strategies

Embed Learning in a Complex, Realistic, and Relevant Learning Environment

1. Connect standards to authentic contexts.
2. Consider the developmental needs of your children.
3. Identify two or three social and emotional learning goals that are relevant to the project.
4. Design your project around relevant and complex problems.
5. Break down complex problems into manageable parts.
6. Be prepared to explain the "why" to your students.

 # Principle 2

Provide for Social Negotiation and Shared Responsibility as Part of Learning

When teachers implement Project Based Learning, they create and sustain a classroom environment that is built upon respect, developing strong relationships, and giving students tools and strategies to become independent learners. Teachers take on the role of a facilitator of learning, encouraging students to co-construct meaning by sharing and listening to one another's ideas and by learning to disagree respectfully, as well as having a role in the learning process. This is particularly relevant for young children who are new to school and have not yet had to navigate the wider social world on a regular basis. Communication skills such as listening, sharing, turn-taking, and compromising all play central roles in creating an environment built upon cooperative learning, relationships, and interdependence (Hammond, 2014). A classroom that encourages the co-creation of norms and agreements (e.g., Responsive Classroom, EL Education), alongside teacher-facilitated discussions, helps with issues that arise and tends to foster strong collaboration and communication skills in young students. Important social and emotional learning competencies such as self-awareness and empathy are also developed when teachers take the time to get to know their students as individuals, leverage their strengths, and support them in developing relationships with their peers. Young learners quickly discover that they have a shared responsibility in their community and that others are counting on them. Everyone benefits by following the co-created expectations for their classroom environment.

When designing and implementing projects for young learners, it is also important to purposefully plan experiences that support and scaffold the development of children's independence and collaboration skills. Children develop greater independence when they take an active role in their learning – when they are able to carry much of the cognitive load, contribute ideas, reflect upon their learning, and make revisions based on feedback. These elements are key parts of Project Based Learning, as children develop their answers to the driving question through several drafts of a product and learn to give and receive feedback with their peers.

The physical environment of a classroom is also an important component of this principle. Spaces should be arranged in ways that encourage collaborative work and shared responsibilities. Community tables, communal materials, and a meeting area with enough space for children to sit in a circle to have discussions are all essential elements to setting up this condition for learning. Seating should be flexible so that different group formations can take place during learning times. Children should be entrusted with access to their materials and explicitly shown how to take care of them. Opportunities to develop independence using repeated practice with materials at the beginning of the year will make project work time more successful.

Sara spent the first few weeks of school introducing students to routines and structures using the Responsive Classroom approach (Denton & Kriete, 2000). Together they created their class agreements and learned the expectations for the classroom and the school's shared spaces. The moment a teacher asks "What agreements should we make so that everyone gets to learn and play?" children know they have a shared responsibility in the learning that will go on in their classroom. This is very different learning approach than a teacher coming in and posting the "class rules" that were made *for* them, not created *with* them. Sara also focused on developing a community from day one by having the students learn about each other and building relationships through morning meeting activities, collaborative games during recess and transition times, flexible learning partnerships, and open seating during work times. This was all a part of creating and building a culture conducive to PBL in the first few weeks of school. Children immediately got the message: my voice counts and we mean something to each other.

To hook the students into the project, Sara strategically planned her entry event. She invited students to use the outdoor classroom and play with blocks, hoping they would wonder why there were no other materials to use. The space invited students to practice **negotiating a social situation** and **sharing the responsibility** for using the materials and the area safely. When the class came back inside, Sara said, "You know, we can use that space – it's a great space to play with blocks – but there's a problem. Do you notice anything else out there to do?" They said no. Sara responded, "I am wondering – how can we make that outdoor classroom a place where we can play and learn? What else might we need?" This learning experience as the entry event led directly to the driving question for the project. It also led to students generating a list of "need-to-know" questions – the essential wonderings the children came up with in order to answer the driving question.

Entry Event

A first lesson or experience that sparks student interest and that launches the inquiry process.

Driving Question

The question that frames the project work.

Need to Know List

The collection of the students' questions that they want to investigate and learn more about. The things they literally need to know that should guide teachers' instructional planning.

Public Product

The things(s) students create throughout the project to share their learning with a wider audience.

Notice that even though Sara had developed the driving question in advance and could easily have announced, "We have an outdoor space and we want to make it a place to learn and play," she *waited* until the lack of materials with which to learn and play were a part of the students' *shared experience*. It was not abstract; it was meaningful and relevant and felt as though it came directly from the students' lives.

Figure 1.3 The first list of ideas in words and pictures

Throughout the project, there were many opportunities for children to collaborate and share their ideas. The initial list of ideas came from them, which included wanting a puppet theater, a music area, a snack table, "to paint the walls," and a space for books (see Figure 1.3).

When it came to designing the space, the children had to communicate why they thought certain areas should be in certain spaces. After meeting with an interior designer who showed the class how she creates "Idea Boards" at the beginning stages of a project, students created their own boards. After sharing these, children needed to agree on final selections. Then they each created their own floor plan, cutting and pasting images that represented the different areas of the outdoor space in their own chosen locations.

There were further opportunities for **shared responsibility** and **social negotiation**. The class took a trip to a music store where small groups worked together to complete a scavenger hunt for instruments. Children designed original musical instruments and needed to reflect, provide feedback to others about their work, and make revisions to their designs. Each child made one revision to their musical instrument design and shared the reason behind their decision with the class. Children also collaborated on how they wanted to share their project work with their families, eventually planning the entire celebration and family breakfast.

 # Quick Strategies

Provide for Social Negotiation and Shared Responsibility as Part of Learning

1. Co-create a set of agreements and norms with your students. Review these often so that young children remember classroom expectations and begin to develop independence.

2. Arrange your learning space to accommodate partner, small group, and large group experiences.

3. Intentionally create multiple opportunities for your students to experience successful collaboration, including planned practice experiences through games, role-playing, problem-solving tasks, etc.

4. Give students opportunities to take responsibility for classroom jobs, decisions, and their own learning.

5. Partner with children in the learning process, building opportunities for them to give and receive feedback, reflect on their learning and engage in the revision process.

 # Principle 3

Support Multiple Perspectives and Use Multiple Representations of Content

The third principle of constructivism calls for us to use instructional approaches which ensure that the content is presented from multiple perspectives and through multiple modalities. Considering the same topic through different senses may enhance a child's understanding of the content (Driscoll, 2005). In the same way, presenting similar content in three different ways (i.e., read-aloud, video, hands-on experience) enables learners to have multiple entry points. And in general, using multiple representations of content to deliver instruction conveys to students that they can represent their understanding of the content in various ways too. This principle also calls for us to support students as they share their perspectives and make meaning of everything they are learning.

One of the goals in Project Based Learning is to encourage students to have a choice in how they want to represent and publicly share their learning. Traditional classrooms typically offer one approach to completing a task. Every student may make the same spinning butterfly life cycle wheel, color the same fall tree picture, or paint all the apples red for a dramatic play center. In reality though, these learning opportunities become more about following directions than representing students' learning. It is important that we encourage children to think about *how* they best process and express new information and then allow them to tap into their strengths when completing representations of their learning. When students learn to think about their own thinking (metacognition), they feel empowered to develop greater self-understanding and independence in their learning.

When children are encouraged to express their learning using different modalities like clay, blocks, paint, or drawings, they learn what strategies and tools are most comfortable and beneficial for their learning style. "Creating and sharing multiple representations of learning at multiple points in the process allow students to demonstrate and deepen their learning simultaneously" (Krechevsky, Mardell, Rivard, & Wilson, 2013, p. 58). The learning that happens when students watch and observe their peers developing project work in different ways is powerful, especially when discoveries are made. Also, when students are given the chance to make choices in how learning is represented and shared, they understand that learning and representing can look different for everyone.

One aspect of this third principle is students' ability to **support multiple perspectives** in their work. Teaching students how to participate in group discussions and how to respectfully respond to peers are great mini-lessons, not just for the beginning of the year, but also as reminders during project work. When students experience being heard by their teachers and peers, they are more likely to feel valued and appreciated. In turn, they will learn to demonstrate this same level of attention when they are on the listening side of a conversation. Through repeated experiences and practice in developmentally appropriate contexts, young children can learn to appreciate multiple perspectives while becoming aware of their own viewpoints and learn to articulate them.

The cultural and linguistic diversity of Sara's classroom naturally brought multiple perspectives into the project. The students had different opinions about how to design the puppet theater and how to arrange the outdoor classroom space. Creating and sharing their learning from their own **perspective** gave rise to numerous **representations** and rich learning conversations. For example, using pre-cut shapes for the puppet theater as well as giving students the option to invent their own shapes provided an entry point for every learner, regardless of their language skills and background knowledge. Hearing the different perspectives shared in the classroom conversations invited revisions to the designs before the class built the theater out of wood.

Throughout the project, Sara often had her students represent their learning using different modalities. Sometimes everyone used the same materials and at other times, students could choose from different options. As Sara planned her project, she asked herself, "What are the different ways children might access content and then demonstrate understanding?" She often taught through photographs, illustrations, role-plays, blocks, paint, clay, recycled materials, and music. These same materials were also used by the students. The students crafted musical instruments by first drawing their designs, then revising and constructing them using recycled materials like cardboard, wire, and plastic. They created their puppets by first drawing a simple sketch, then using fabric, yarn, and other accessories to build them. In each of these design projects, children pulled from their own experiences and perspectives.

Children with diverse learning abilities and languages were able to work and play together because they could access the content of the project using a variety of modalities. A student who had special needs found a connection through musical instruments and puppets. He was able to cut and glue pictures of the proposed outdoor classroom areas on his first draft of a map of the outdoor space. A child learning English as a second language pointed to and named the areas of the classroom in his home language, and Sara repeated them for him in English.

The public product also included **multiple representations** and **perspectives**. Children invited their families to celebrate in their learning at the end of the project and planned the celebration. They suggested decorating the classroom with balloons and strands of lights. They also wanted to "show parents around all the parts of the classroom." When it came to the presentation, some children volunteered to speak in front of the whole group, some shared the outdoor classroom via their original illustrated floor plan, some dictated descriptions as a part of a slide show presentation, and some chose to walk their parents around the space, sharing the objects and different areas.

 Quick Strategies

Support Multiple Perspectives and Use Multiple Representations of Content

1. Encourage students' ability to listen to understand by beginning with low-stakes, nonacademic topics for discussion. Quick, easy discussions in which students take turns listening, responding, and sharing what *others* say builds empathy and understanding of multiple perspectives.
2. Offer structured parameters on some aspects of project work and multiple options for other aspects.
3. Offer students a variety of materials and modalities in which to demonstrate their learning.
4. Use a gradual release approach by slowly adjusting the number of choices available based on the complexity of the task, stage of the project, and types of decisions students are learning to make.
5. Provide students with frequent opportunities to share their work so they improve communication skills and gain experience in moderating their tone, voice level, and register. Rubrics and feedback protocols are tools that give students specific and helpful areas to improve on.

Principle 4

Encourage Ownership in Learning

Launching the inquiry process through student questions is one of the most essential ways through which PBL inspires ownership in learning. Young children benefit from a scaffolded approach, and there are multiple resources to help you support student questioning skills. The Question Formulation Technique (Rothstein & Santana, 2011), KWL charts, and Reading and Analyzing Nonfiction (RAN) charts (see *Quick Strategies*) are helpful structures to use when modeling how to develop project-related questions and can all be adapted for young children. By posting questions on a co-created anchor chart or sentence strips where students can reach them and interact with them daily, students feel empowered by what they are asking and learning throughout the PBL unit. When young children drive their learning through self-generated questions, they have ownership over both the learning process as well their mastery of content and skills.

There are several additional structures that can help scaffold student ownership in project work. Learning stations, workshops, and centers offer a variety of experiences which encourage students to question and make their own meaning of what they are learning. Reflective journaling through student sketches, dictation, and playing with words builds students' self-confidence in their questioning and writing skills. In turn, sharing those journal entries gives students buy-in to higher quality work as well as practice taking turns and effective listening and speaking. Learning from peers, rather than relying on the teacher, helps students take responsibility for their own learning. Interactive project calendars, team contracts, and co-created task lists can also be great scaffolds to equip learners with the ability to embrace this condition for learning.

Encouraging students to take ownership over their learning also means coaching students to find out how they learn best and teaching them how to recognize when they are learning or when learning breaks down. Young children need guided practice as well as scaffolding when making decisions. Embedding mini-lessons that scaffold decision-making helps young children learn how to make informed choices. These decisions range from seemingly simple choices like where to sit on the carpet, what kind of writing tool to use, or what to play at recess, to more complex decisions, like what questions take priority during investigations or with whom to partner during an activity. When teachers continuously make these decisions for children (i.e., always assigning children seats and partners or telling them what questions to ask) they rob them of the opportunity to learn *how* to make choices. Making decisions within given parameters or adhering to certain guidelines can enable students to make more decisions through planning documents or by dictating their ideas. In order to build a culture of independence and inquiry, students should be given different amounts of autonomy over decisions within projects and as the year progresses.

When we honor their contributions and validate their ideas, young children are supported in owning their learning. Ownership over learning does not mean that every child is working on something different while simultaneously needing help from the teacher. It also does not mean that students have full reign over the classroom or that the teacher does not plan for instruction. Ultimately, the teacher carefully and intentionally works behind the scenes *and* alongside students to craft learning experiences that guide students toward the target skills and content for the PBL unit. We want to leave room for students' genuine curiosity to grow. If we desire curious and autonomous learners, we must have a plan in place to help make that happen.

From the moment Sara asked children "What does this space need?" she invited her class to **take ownership of their learning**. She sent a message that the space could not be created without their ideas, and that there was a lot to learn in order to make the space work. Sara also set the conditions for children to expand their understanding based on their current and previous experiences. She carefully planned ways to honor the ideas children had and then built on them by first asking for their thoughts, ideas, and understandings. Questions like *Had they seen a puppet theater before? Where? What was it like? What instruments had they seen and played? What colors did they think would work in the space and why?* revealed that children certainly had ideas about what would make the outdoor classroom a place they wanted to spend time. Ignoring those ideas and simply delivering the content would have not only robbed the students of ownership in the work from the beginning, it would have vastly limited the creativity and variety that they ultimately brought to the project.

Throughout the project, Sara intentionally supported students' growth while drawing on their prior knowledge. When thinking about the music area for the space, she asked children what instruments they already knew about. It turns out they had a wealth of knowledge and experiences, and were able to suggest a variety of instruments, including "your voice." The next step was to build on their knowledge so children could decide what instruments they wanted in their space. Sara borrowed a number of instruments from the school music teacher, which the children explored and then discussed the differences and similarities they noticed. Sara developed the project in this way because she knew she wanted students to design their own instruments. In order to do that, however, she needed children to build more knowledge and learn about the different aspects of the instruments, including the sound, what they were made of, and the way instruments were played. Children collaborated to play the instruments and shared with one another what they noticed. As children began to understand the aspects of instruments on a deeper level, they were able to make informed decisions about the instruments for their classroom as well as their own designs.

Along the same line, Sara often asked her students "How do you think we can learn more about this?" throughout the project. This was another way for children to have **ownership over their learning** – for them to contribute to *how* learning would take place. A student actually said, "We could visit a music store." Even though Sara had already thought of this as a possible field experience, she didn't announce it until a child in her class made the suggestion. Other ideas were offered, including going to see a concert or having someone come visit. She knew it wouldn't be possible to follow every suggestion, but it was important to honor each by at least acknowledging its validity.

As the project ended, children took **ownership over their learning** by planning out the final presentation and celebration for families (Figure 1.4).

Figure 1.4 Outdoor classroom family celebration

Sara usually has an idea for the public product before starting the project but leaves room for children to make decisions as well. She asked them, "How do you want to share your learning?" Children decided on all of the things they wanted to include in their celebration. This included making invitations for their parents, decorating the space, and showing their families their puppets and instruments. They truly *owned* their learning from start to finish, from project plan to project celebration.

Quick Strategies

Encouraging Ownership in Learning

1. Harness students' questions throughout the project.

   a. KWL and KWHL (Know/Wonder/How/Learn) charts honor what children already know and help them capture their thoughts and questions in an organized way.

   b. RAN – Reading and Analyzing Nonfiction charts encourage students to consider what they think they know and what they want to know. They help children identify misconceptions and mark new learning. Post-it notes make student questions visible and interactive.

   c. QFT – The Question Formulation Technique helps to generate, structure, and prioritize student questions. Teachers use images, quotes, or videos as a "Question Focus" to help drive learning forward. Then children list (or dictate) as many questions as they have, without stopping to edit them. After sharing and charting the questions, the teacher supports the children as they select "priority" questions to start investigating.

2. Offer students a choice for the next steps. A structure like a Plus/Delta, a two-column chart where students reflect out loud on the *plusses*, or strengths, of the project, as well as the *deltas*, things that need to change, for the next project empowers students by letting them share real challenges and real successes from their points of view.

3. Provide space for wonder. Wonder Boards/Wonder Walls are physical spaces children can interact with to write or draw what they are wondering about. This could be related to the project or lead to future projects.

Principle 5

Nurture Self-Awareness and an Understanding That Knowledge Is Constructed

Children develop the skills to understand their own thinking and learning when given the opportunity to engage in metacognitive actions like making plans and following through with them, monitoring their thoughts, and evaluating their work (Woolfolk, 2013). Children need multiple opportunities to build knowledge and reflect on their own growth when they are engaged in sustained inquiry. Teacher modeling, explicit instruction, and repeated practice also support young children as they become aware of learning patterns within themselves. Engaging in project work is a natural way for students to begin to develop the skills needed to internalize when they are learning and when their learning breaks down. Learning is constructed by harnessing opportunities for students to reflect on their thinking, feelings, actions, and decisions. Children begin to understand *how* knowledge is constructed and the role their thoughts and emotions play in that process. They can then apply that new awareness to future learning experiences.

Project Based Learning offers young children a unique opportunity to follow their learning from start to finish in a project. When beginning a project, we might say, "This is a question that is *so big,* we need to do a project together to find out the answer." We walk alongside them, guiding them through a learning journey. We coach when we help students practice for a presentation. We mentor when we role-play how to critique the work of a peer. We model when we use an alphabet chart to find the beginning sound for the word the student is trying to write. We learn right along with our students, acknowledging those moments when we aren't sure of the answers ourselves. Since the fifth principle asks teachers to become *facilitators* of learning as opposed to directors or the "authority" (McCombs & Miller, 2007; Wurdinger, Haar, Hugg, & Bezon, 2007), we create the conditions for learning and allow students to construct their own knowledge. We guide students through the learning process by providing structures and scaffolds along the way.

We can cultivate students' understanding that learning is a process and that knowledge is constructed by modeling our own thinking throughout the day. Students discover that learning is a process when they are regularly invited into that process. To return to the example of children choosing their own seats, teachers might "think aloud" as they model for students how to make a decision about seating. They could articulate a thought process like "Hmm…do I want to sit up front? Or in the back? What color carpet square would I like? Is there enough space for my body in between these two friends?" Modeling thinking processes out loud for children helps to put language to potential thoughts as they go through the learning process. In addition, when we use explicit language about learning, like "focusing attention," "ignoring distractions," or "growth mindset," young children begin to understand that learning requires a set of skills – skills that even adults continue to practice. It is important to remind children that we will support them in developing the tools they need to be a learner when they become frustrated or overwhelmed. As teachers, we cultivate positive attitudes and growth mindsets in our students so they learn to recognize and say when they need help. We encourage them to draw on their schema, previous experiences, and current understandings to construct knowledge. We honor their feelings about school and learning, and leverage successes and frustrations to honor where they are with their learning and to plan future lessons.

With support, children can become more aware of what impacts their ability to participate in and reflect on their learning. If we foster the intrinsic connection between academic, social, and emotional learning, then we create the optimal conditions for Project Based Learning. The Collaborative for Academic, Social, and Emotional Learning (CASEL) defines self-awareness as "the ability to accurately recognize one's own emotions, thoughts, and values and how they influence behavior…the ability to accurately assess one's strengths and limitations, with a well-grounded sense of confidence, optimism, and a 'growth mindset'" (casel.org). Young children are beginning to develop this self-awareness as they navigate their new school landscape. As teachers, we have an opportunity to help children become aware of *how* they experience learning and *what* they bring to learning each day. We believe these skills are at the core of our work with young children as we guide them toward becoming independent learners.

As Sara began to plan the *Outdoor Classroom* project, she was just getting to know her students and beginning to develop an understanding of their specific needs. The first six weeks of school involved building community through games, songs, and other activities. The children needed to build trust with one another and with their teacher; they needed to feel a sense of safety and belonging. In these moments (and moving forward through the year), Sara saw herself as a coach who helped her students develop and practice new skills as they knew what to expect on a day-to-day basis. For example, when a child is feeling frustrated by taking on a new challenge or attempting something for the first time, we must take a moment – or more – to listen and understand the source of frustration. We mirror that child's feelings to model the skill of naming and expressing the feelings. Then, we offer a tool or a suggested strategy. For example, *"Luca, you seem really frustrated because you feel like you don't know how to draw a triangle. That can be upsetting. What I do sometimes when I'm drawing something new is, I just think about one part of the shape – one line at a time. I picture the way the lines are going. Which line do you want to start with? Then I will help you to think about the next one."* When students reflect on their growth and experience the feeling of pride, we can name this by saying, *"In the beginning of the year, you didn't know how to do that! And now you do. How does that feel? You look like you feel really proud."*

It was important to Sara that children were not asked to do anything that felt very unfamiliar in this time period or asked (or pushed) to do things they may not yet be able to do. So Sara was careful to regularly provide choice for students in order to observe what they determined was "just right" for them. For example, she knew that not all of her children entered school knowing how to write their names independently. Rather than having students trace their names or copy them from a card, when it was time to write names on papers, Sara offered choices; a child could write her whole name (in whatever way she knew how), one letter of her name, or she could ask a teacher to write it for her. It was essential that children immediately felt a sense of confidence in this new environment, no matter what they could or could not yet do.

> Giving students choice communicates that wherever you are and whatever you are capable of is just where you should be.

Sara made the learning process visible for her students in a variety of ways. She charted the questions students were asking when they wondered about different musical instruments, were preparing to meet a professional puppeteer, or when they were curious how they would make a "Music Area" in the outdoor classroom. She intentionally revisited this Need to Know list each day and returned to the students' questions. Crossing off the questions that had already been answered helped the children understand what was left to do. She modeled her own thinking and questioning process so that children could see how learning takes place. Project Based Learning has the potential to invite children into the learning process in numerous ways, but as teachers, we also have a role to play. It is our responsibility to ensure that children know *what* they are learning and *why,* and then help them to also see *how* that learning takes place so that they understand how knowledge is constructed.

 Quick Strategies

Nurture Self-Awareness and an Understanding of How Knowledge Is Constructed

1. Scaffold children's social and emotional learning by embedding SEL into your curriculum. This can happen through the use of an explicit program, capitalizing on authentic moments that take place during the day, or with an integrated approach.

2. Make the learning process explicit by modeling "think-alouds" such as "I wonder" statements.

3. Facilitate productive struggle by recognizing when and how to support students. Consider when to jump in to provide an answer or "help" and when to offer guidance and support instead of a solution.

4. Capitalize on processes that make students' learning visible. Reflective journaling and revisiting the need-to-know list are concrete ways for students to *see* their learning throughout a project.

Reflect and Connect

It is helpful to understand each of the constructivist principles separately and how they naturally intersect and overlap. These core values inform how we establish norms and routines, design and develop lessons, and facilitate learning with our students. As we end our first chapter, take a few moments to reflect on what you read about constructivism and how it serves as the foundation of implementing PBL successfully in your early childhood classroom.

- *What did you notice?*
- *What connects with your current practice?*
- *What stretched your thinking?*
- *What do you still wonder?*

Overcoming the Misconception

When implementing Project Based Learning with young children, where do we begin? We don't just start with a plan book, carefully making sure we cover standards, orchestrating daily lessons, choosing relevant discussion topics, and administering assessments. But that doesn't mean that PBL is open-ended and unstructured. All of these elements will come, but we must first begin with a *belief system* that informs the way teaching and learning should happen in our classroom. We need to understand a specific set of values, namely, the principles of *constructivism,* which are at the core of every part of Project Based Learning. Without a solid understanding of how constructivism informs the teaching and learning within a project, PBL seems chaotic and ineffective. But these five principles provide the framework and the structure for how learning takes place in PBL. Once you see that there is most assuredly a structure to Project Based Learning, the plans you make will have direction, purpose and meaning for both you and your students.

None of these principles can stand alone, as evident by the amount of overlap in the individual descriptions of each principle as well as the application in Sara's *Outdoor Classroom* project. Inviting students into the learning process through scaffolded instruction, encouraging them to share their perspectives, and situating learning within a meaningful and relevant project are just some of the big ideas that are at the heart of Project Based Learning. As you read on, you will continue to see how the principles of constructivism inform the way that children learn through PBL. Children learn from social interactions and hands-on, minds-on experiences, and this gives us, as teachers, a clear purpose for designing and developing Project Based Learning units. The values emanating from this belief system encourage us to engage our youngest students, in community with others, in the learning process.

References

Brooks, J. G. (2013). Constructivism: Transforming knowledge of how people learn into meaningful instruction. In B. Irby, B. Brown, R. Lara-Alecio, & S. Jackson (Eds.), *The handbook of educational theories* (pp. 271–275). Charlotte, NC: Information Age Publishing, Inc.

Denton, P., & Kriete, R. (2000). *The first six weeks of school. Strategies for teachers series.* Greenfield, MA: Northeast Foundation for Children.

Driscoll, M. (2005). *Psychology of learning for instruction* (3rd ed.). New York, NY: Pearson.

Hammond, Z. (2014). *Culturally responsive teaching and the brain: Promoting authentic engagement and rigor among culturally and linguistically diverse students.* Thousand Oaks, CA: Corwin Press.

Krechevsky, M., Mardell, B., Rivard, M., & Wilson, D. (2013). *Visible learners: Promoting Reggio-inspired approaches in all schools.* San Francisco, CA: Jossey-Bass.

McCombs, B., & Miller, L. (2007). *Learner-centered classroom practices and assessments: Maximizing student motivation, learning, and achievement.* Thousand Oaks, CA: Corwin Press.

Narayan, R., Rodriguez, C., Araujo, J., Shaqlaih, A., & Moss, G. (2013). Constructivism–Constructivist learning theory. In B. Irby, B. Brown, R. Lara-Alecio, & S. Jackson (Eds.), *The handbook of educational theories* (pp. 169–183). Charlotte, NC: Information Age Publishing, Inc.

Prawat, R. (1992). Teachers' beliefs about teaching and learning: A constructivist perspective. *American Journal of Education, 100*(3), 354–395. doi:10.1086/444021.

Rothstein, D., & Santana, L. (2011). *Make just one change: Teach students to ask their own questions*. Cambridge, MA: Harvard Education Press.

Woolfolk, A. (2013). *Educational psychology* (12th ed.). New York, NY: Pearson.

Wurdinger, S., Haar, J., Hugg, R., & Bezon, J. (2007). A qualitative study using project-based learning in a mainstream middle school. *Improving Schools, 10*(2), 150–161. doi:10.1177/1365480207078048.

Learner-Centered Teaching Practices

I need to keep control of my classroom so that learning can happen.
Giving students so much choice feels too chaotic.

In Chapter 1, we unpacked the five constructivist principles that create the conditions for Project Based Learning in your early childhood classroom (Table 2.1).

We explored these principles in practice when we shared Sara's *Outdoor Classroom* project, providing opportunities for you to think about why and how you could establish a constructivist environment in your classroom to start you on your journey toward implementing Project Based Learning. The next step on this journey is to develop a solid understanding of what a learner-centered classroom looks like, sounds like, and feels like within a constructivist framework. According to McCombs and Whisler (1997),

"Learner-centered" is the perspective that couples a **focus on individual learners** (their heredity, experiences, perspectives, backgrounds, talents, interests, capacities, and needs) with a **focus on learning** (the best available knowledge about learning and how it occurs and about teaching practices that are most effective in promoting the highest levels of motivation, learning, and achievement for all learners) (p. 9).

The term "learner-centered" challenges the belief held by many teachers that it means children *dictate* instruction, and that following children's interests and questions will veer the class off course of expected curricular content. But as Panitz (1999) writes, "student centered, also called learner-centered, means that students *provide input* into what the class does and how they do it" (p. 11). A learner-centered classroom is not

Table 2.1 Principles of Constructivism Review

Principle 1	Embed learning in complex, realistic, and relevant learning environments.
Principle 2	Provide for social negotiation and shared responsibility as part of learning.
Principle 3	Support multiple perspectives and use multiple representations of content.
Principle 4	Encourage ownership in learning.
Principle 5	Nurture self-awareness and an understanding that knowledge is constructed.

a learner-*controlled* classroom, nor does it mean every child has their own individual learning plan. Lessons are differentiated because we acknowledge the developmental needs of the learners. In a learner-centered classroom, it is the students' academic and social and emotional needs, ideas and related questions that are quite literally "at the center" of the instructional decisions. Project Based Learning fits here; at the juncture between the theoretical constructivist principles that inform our values about how children learn best (knowledge construction) with the premises of learner-centered instruction.

The structure of PBL is one in which teachers facilitate learning experiences where students are empowered in their learning from start to finish. These values and teaching practices inform every phase of a project. We saw this in Sara's *Outdoor Classroom* project. She launched the project when the students were in the outdoor space and used the student-initiated ideas and questions to start the inquiry process. The other phases of the project were also learner-centered, as the children developed the knowledge, skills, and dispositions to create a public product that was shared with family members and guests. Throughout the entire project, the children's development, needs, and interests were the center of teaching and learning, while still holding students accountable for academic content (Pierce & Kalkman, 2003).

Early childhood classrooms offer a perfect opportunity to build learner-centered environments because teachers understand the importance of building relationships with their students and "recognize the needs and strengths of the whole learner—social, emotional, and physical, [and] academic" (Pierce & Kalkman, 2003, p. 127). Early childhood teachers also understand that "learner-centered teaching promotes playfulness *and* introduces children to inquiry and academic skills and knowledge" (Diamond, Grob, & Reitzes, 2015, p. 7). In short, the learner-centered classroom focuses on the needs of the individuals while maintaining a focus on teaching that invokes learning.

Premises of a Learner-Centered Model

In their book, *The Learner-Centered Classroom and School*, McCombs and Whisler (1997, p. 9) suggest that the learner-centered model for education is built on five premises:

1. Learners are distinct and unique.

2. Learners' unique differences include their emotional states of mind, learning rates, learning styles, stages of development, abilities, talents, feelings of efficacy, and other academic and nonacademic attributes and needs.

3. Learning is a constructive process that occurs best when what is being learned is relevant and meaningful to the learner and when the learner is actively engaged.

4. Learning occurs best in a positive environment, one that contains positive interpersonal relationships and interactions, that contains comfort and order, and in which the learner feels appreciated, acknowledged, respected, and validated.

5. Learning is a fundamentally natural process; learners are naturally curious and are interested in learning about and mastering their world.

These learner-centered premises differ strikingly with a traditional, content-centered classroom where the teacher is often the center of authority and might focus more on students staying "on task" and "compliant" rather than children engaging in relevant, rigorous learning experiences. However, a learner-centered classroom does not lack order and structure. On the contrary, teachers who maintain a learner-centered environment must take time to establish norms and routines that create a classroom culture where students develop independence, confidence, and competence. In a traditional, more teacher-centered model, tests, benchmarks, and data often drive instructional decisions. In contrast, in a learner-centered classroom, the teacher is responsible for selecting strategies that engage children in the learning process. "The learner-centered model focuses equally on the learner and learning. The ultimate goal of schooling is to foster the learning of learners; and learners learn best when *they* are an integral part of the learning equation" (McCombs & Whisler, 1997, p. 14). We believe the practices associated with Project Based Learning allow the teacher to focus on the individual learners while maintaining a focus on overall learning. The primary characteristics of a learner-centered classroom, compiled from the works of multiple sources (Diamond et al., 2015; Hammond, 2014; Helm & Katz, 2016; McCombs & Whisler, 1997) and our experiences can be found below.

Characteristics of a Learner-Centered Early Childhood Classroom

The goal of learning...

- is to develop a conceptual understanding of the content, making connections between subjects and applying knowledge to new and novel situations.
- is to develop and enhance the students' social and emotional skills and dispositions as well as cognitive growth.

The classroom environment...

- gives students ownership over the space, often allowing the students a choice in where they sit and encourages circle seating for discussions.
- offers flexible seating with clipboards available for students to create their own workspace on the carpet or floor.
- reflects the children's learning. The anchor charts, Project Walls, artwork, and other student-generated materials all relate to what is happening in the classroom.
- is community-based. School materials are shared by everyone in the classroom community, often located in numerous bins around the room for easy access by everyone.

The teacher...

- is the facilitator of learning who provides opportunities for students to engage in dialogue with peers.
- encourages exploration while balancing curricular goals and student interests.
- utilizes culturally responsive teaching practices.
- encourages productive struggle while building rapport and trust with all students.
- designs rigorous learning experiences that allow for inquiry and investigation.

The student...

- creates his/her own understanding throughout the learning process by actively acquiring knowledge and skills through exploration, asking and answering questions, and inquiry.
- contributes ideas, perspectives, and thoughts during learning experiences.
- reflects on learning processes, sets goals, and participates in monitoring and assessing progress.
- constructs meaning in collaboration with peers.

The curriculum...

- is comprised of multiple resources and perspectives.
- finds direction and depth with a project, often developed through student interest and/or questions, building on students' current level of understanding of the topic.
- is viewed as a road map for a year-long journey rather than a linear or hierarchical plan to get students from Point A to Point B.

The instructional materials...

- vary by project type, desired project outcomes, student needs, and relevance.

- are selected based on the experiments, observations, direct instruction, manipulatives, simulations, and play connected to, or driven by, student inquiry.

Problem-solving...

- decisions are democratic and discussion-based.
- opportunities allow students to practice and demonstrate problem-solving strategies in both academic and social situations.
- is supported by the norms and agreements that teachers and students co-create.
- is a process that is rooted in restorative practices.
- teaches the students to be assertive, encouraging them to look for multiple ways to resolve any issues that arise.

The assessment practices...

- are more formative in nature.
- encompass content knowledge and learning processes.
- include teachers' observations, anecdotal notes, discussion participation, student presentations, and portfolios.
- allow the teacher to adjust lessons, check for understanding, give learners feedback, and provide scaffolds and support to ensure all students achieve success with the learning goals of the project.
- encourage students to self-reflect.

Reflect and Connect

As you consider these characteristics of a learner-centered, early childhood classroom, pause and consider:

- Which practices are similar to those you already use?
- What beliefs and assumptions do you hold?
- What resonates with you?
- What might you have to let go of?
- Where might you need to grow?

In this chapter, we articulate what a learner-centered classroom looks like, sounds like, and feels like so that you can begin to envision these practices at work in your own classroom. First, we invite you to *see* the physical characteristics of a learner-centered environment from the inside out. Then we ask you to imagine *hearing* the sounds in the classroom. Next, we ask you to experience how it *feels* to teach and learn in a learner-centered classroom. By highlighting these elements, you will be able to build a strong foundation for implementing PBL with your students.

What Does a Learner-Centered Classroom LOOK Like?

As you enter a learner-centered classroom, what do you *see?* What are children doing, and with what types of materials? Children are actively engaged in investigations, moving freely around the room, working independently and in small groups or partnerships. They are utilizing a variety of materials to express and represent their learning through art, drama, science, writing, data, and charts. Children are playing, engaging with one another in real-life scenarios, using authentic tools, or talking to experts. The students interact with content fluidly and effortlessly. Teachers might be facilitating a discussion, conferring one-on-one, supporting experiments, or supervising learning centers.

You might also take note of the classroom's *physical space*. For students to effectively have ownership in their learning, the physical environment should be one that fosters independence and reflects children's abilities, backgrounds, and experiences. Our classrooms are a public statement of the values and beliefs held by both our school as an institution, and by the teachers themselves (Tarr, 2004). The physical space reflects the mindsets operating within a classroom and therefore has a significant impact on the culture that is created and sustained each day. If, as discussed, we believe that young children can share in the responsibility for taking care of their materials, then we leave the materials out for them to access, rather than keeping them in a closet and taking them out only at teacher-directed times. Likewise, if we hold and explicitly scaffold the expectation that children can make their own decisions about the type of environment that helps them learn best, then we create opportunities for flexible seating in the classroom.

The elements of a learner-centered classroom include items such as wall displays that have either photographs or charts documenting and sharing the learning with the larger community. These displays communicate the class discussions, ideas captured during the inquiry process, and other transcribed conversations about learning that come directly from the children. Class agreements and norms are posted in child-friendly language and students' work displays a diverse range of skills and abilities. A teacher who is designing a learner-centered environment may purposefully leave her walls relatively blank at the beginning of the year awaiting children's work, rather than "decorating" with commercially produced materials. The teacher thinks carefully about what is on display and treats the "environment as a third teacher" (Edwards, Gandini, & Forman, 1998) purposefully choosing charts, books, art, and aesthetics that reflect the backgrounds and cultures of the children in the room. These intentional decisions empower children to have greater ownership in their learning and see their classrooms as safe, inviting, and comfortable.

When high-quality PBL is happening in a classroom, thinking and learning is often made visible on a Project Wall that houses a variety of project pieces like key vocabulary, the Need to Know list, and various project artifacts all within students' reach. Learner-centered classrooms often have flexible seating to accommodate different student groupings. During a project-specific work time, you may see children moving freely around the classroom or working on different project tasks and products. You might also see project work integrated into a content block (when the nature of the project is aligned with that academic area). For example, if children are working on writing an informational text as part of their public product, they may be working on it during their writing block. The teacher frequently moves around the room, supporting students' needs as they collaborate on project work and conferring with individuals to ensure understanding of each required task.

Look closely at the classroom pictured in Figure 2.1. What words would you use to describe the space? See if you can find some of the elements of a learner-centered environment.

Do you see how the texts are placed at the students' level? The books in the display easel tie directly to the project and reflect various perspectives and backgrounds. Did you find examples of flexible seating options on the floor and at the community tables?

Did you notice how the anchor charts, materials, and resources are at the students' eye level and within their reach? Now, reflect on your own classroom. How would you describe the current setup? What is most accessible for your learners? What might need to change to make the space be more learner-centered?

Figure 2.1 A learner-centered classroom

What Does a Learner-Centered Classroom SOUND Like?

What *sounds* might we hear as we walk into a learner-centered classroom? Ideally, we hear children talking; they are debating and inquiring and brainstorming among themselves, with their teachers, and with anyone who might come into the room. A learner-centered classroom is one where questions are valued and honored and where multiple perspectives are routinely heard and validated. In a learner-centered classroom, we also might hear encouraging language like "What questions do you have?" as a way to send a message that *all* questions are valuable, and that teachers expect students to ask meaningful questions. This may be one of the most radical departures from a traditional, teacher-centered classroom, but it's also one of the most important: *learning* is not always equated with *keeping quiet*. *Engagement* is a better indication of learning, and this may sound like quiet, focused attention, but it also might not.

This is a classroom in which teachers use questions to help children drive their own learning. Questions are not just heard at the end of a lesson (i.e., "Ok, any questions?"), but are used to *initiate* the learning. In this classroom, teachers use questions like *What do you notice?*, *What are you wondering?*, and *Why do you think that?* They strive to ask questions that move the children beyond recalling and remembering. And these questions are crucial to Project Based Learning; at the beginning of a PBL unit, children generate a list of questions that launch the project. These questions guide the learning process forward as children seek to find answers needed. Future PBL lessons may be focused on one of these key questions.

Children participate in a variety of learning structures throughout the day. They collaborate and share ideas while constructing a building during choice time, discussing theories while investigating a topic or generating more questions. They sit in a circle, sharing ideas about a particular topic related to the project work or a classroom need. You may also hear children providing feedback to their peers, offering kind critiques and helpful suggestions. Students may be sharing their reflections on what they are learning at various points of a project, not only at the end. These types of discussions are essential in helping move a project forward.

Imagine you are listening to the following math conversation (Table 2.2). As you read through the two versions of the exchange between a teacher and a student, compare the questions used and the responses given first in the traditional classroom and then in the learner-centered one.

What do you notice about the teacher's use of questioning? How does it impact engagement? Content understanding? How does this differ from other possible responses in the same situation? How might you effectively using questioning to increase engagement and deepen content understanding?

Notice that in the exchange from the traditional classroom, the teacher swiftly answered the student's question, showed him/her how to count and how to write the number 7, and then told him/her to copy it. In the learner-centered classroom, the teacher used questioning strategies that encouraged the child to think. In a learner-centered classroom, children become empowered, lifelong learners because they understand that they are actually constructing their own knowledge, rather than having the knowledge directly imparted from their teacher.

Table 2.2 Traditional vs Learner-Centered Classroom

Students are counting a set of objects on the rug. Their task is to count the objects and to record the amount in a math journal. The student (S), age 5, is working on counting strategies and one-to-one correspondence with the teacher (T).

Traditional Classroom	Learner-Centered Classroom
S: *How many beads are there?*	S: *How many beads are there?*
T: *7.*	T: *What do you think?*
S: *7?*	S: *I don't know.*
T: *Yes. Let's count them.*	T: *How do you think we can find out?*
S: *Ok.*	S: *I could count them.*
T: *Watch the way I count them and then you do it. (Teacher lines up the beads, counts one by one, touching each bead.)*	T: *Great. How do you want to count them?*
S: *(copies what teacher did)*	S: *I can line them up (or group them, or sort them by color, or pull one away at a time to count, or create a design and count).*
T: *You counted 7 beads. Now draw the number 7.*	T: *(articulates S's strategy). You lined them up! (or... you put them in two groups – a group of three and a group of four! etc.) How many did you count? Can you record the number 7 in your notebook?*
S: *I don't know how.*	S: *7. How do I make a 7?*
T: *I will draw a 7 (or make it out of dots) for you and you trace mine.*	T: *Where might you find a 7 in our classroom? Could that help?*
S: *(traces the number 7)*	S: *(thinks, then points to the calendar)*
T: *Good job!*	T: *Oh – so do you want to use the 7 in our calendar pocket chart to help you? You remembered that numbers make up our calendar each month, and you can always look at those numbers and pull out the cards when you need some help remembering how to write a number on your own.*

In an early childhood, learner-centered classroom, we also expect to hear peals of laughter, squeals of excitement, and exclamations of "Can I show you what I made?" – the sounds of learners deeply engaged in meaningful experiences. At times there might also be crying, arguments, and social conflicts. *"Can you help me?"* or *"I can't do this!"* or *"He's not listening to my ideas!"* are commonly heard because a learner-centered approach requires a high level of collaboration, engagement, and independence from learners. When young children get to navigate new and challenging situations, these experiences can lead to intellectual, social, and emotional growth. When these moments do occur, teachers can stop and use these 'teachable moments' to draw students' attention back to classroom agreements, team contracts, and norms established early on.

What Does a Learner-Centered Classroom FEEL Like?

Teachers *and* children are strongly invested in the experiences and learning that happens in their classroom each day. Therefore, it is important to consider what a learner-centered classroom feels like for both the teachers and the children. In a learner-centered classroom, there is an almost tangible sense of excitement going on in the room as the children engage in all phases of the inquiry process because the students recognize their questions will be honored and explored or investigated further. The excitement for learning continues to spread when students uncover new ideas and discover the answers to their questions. All of these feelings commingle and create a "buzz" for learning. There is an investment in the unknown that leads to energy and enthusiasm for all involved. Teachers often feel invigorated at the opportunity to design their own PBL units, rather than following premade curricula. The chance to collaborate with colleagues to plan a unit they are passionate about and know their students will be interested in is refreshing. There's no getting around the fact that young learners have a lot of energy and this energy can often feel chaotic to a teacher. But "teachers who see [young learners'] energy as a *resource* rather than an impediment can build on their drive for learning and mastery" (Diamond et al., 2015, p. 15). This high energy, when focused and channeled, can lead to tremendous growth for students and provide inspiration for teachers.

An understandable offshoot of the myth that this type of classroom is chaotic is that it is also *unsafe*. Once again, it's imperative to state that the safety of students is always our top priority. But in a learner-centered classroom, we extend this notion of safety to ensure that *students feel safe to express themselves*. We want them to take *creative* risks and feel unafraid to make mistakes.

This safety and risk-taking apply to the social world as well, as children learn to engage in relationships and challenging problems. In a learner-centered classroom, time is taken to develop the necessary social and emotional skills, and there is a recognition that these skills are intertwined with and as important as "academic" skills. This time becomes especially important when working on a PBL unit, as children must collaborate to see an often-lengthy project through. Many teachers notice that time spent creating this environment of trust and resilience early in the year actually allows more time for learning because they aren't having to constantly intervene in social conflicts as the year goes on. When students are equipped with these skills, and feel emotionally safe, they can more independently navigate these social situations.

Children also feel a sense of *agency* when engaged in PBL because they contribute meaningfully to discussions. Providing children opportunities for self-directed play and exploration of academic content in open-ended contexts develops the children's confidence. They begin to develop a sense of trust in their own interests and abilities. Giving children the chance to draw on their own backgrounds, experiences, and knowledge also enables them to feel that their life is valuable and rich. Teachers can easily help students develop confidence that they have something meaningful to contribute and build upon in so many ways by responding to their questions, integrating their ideas and facilitating accessible and developmentally appropriate experiences.

Learner-centered classrooms also feel *relevant*. The learning takes place in the context of the students' lives in what is meaningful and purposeful to them. An engaging project that has adult-world applications helps students see their work as important, not only in the context of a classroom, but to the outside community as well (Larmer, 2016). Student learning fits into a larger mosaic that makes sense because the children see a purpose to the learning experiences. They feel motivated to take part in the variety of learning opportunities throughout the day.

Finally, there is a sense of *joy*, for both teachers and students, that comes from everyone participating in a learning community where they are valued, respected, and have a sense of belonging. The content and the approach to learning is purposeful, authentic, and culturally relevant. Learning is *fun*. And then all who enter the community begin to feel this joy each morning as they enter school wondering, "What will we do today?!"

The following vignette was written by early childhood teacher Sara Beshawred. Notice the ways in which Sara creates a positive classroom environment that feels learner-centered:

"Mostly Kid Space"

When we say to students, you are safe here, you are welcome here, and you are accepted here, mistakes and all, we communicate not only that there is room for mistakes, but an expectation that they will happen and lead to learning. We communicate that in this place, you are loved. When we communicate that students will have voice and choice over what they read or write with or where/how/ if they sit, we send the message, you are loved.

In an easily accessible space, we have materials for making small repairs – we call it "The Help Desk." On it, you will find paper towels, wipes, bandages, tissues, and a basket of marker caps. The Help Desk solves many of our daily kindergarten mistakes, from spills to paper cuts to lid-less markers. And the most important part – students can help themselves. We cultivate independence when we guide students and create structures for them to be successful in accessing and using materials.

We ask students to be their most authentic selves in a space that reflects that. Our work, photos, and thinking are what bring our environment to life as we honor, work through, and grow from mistakes by making our thinking visible.

From works in-progress, to our child-curated gallery of our best artwork, as one visitor once remarked, "You can feel the children in the room, even when it's empty."

We know that young children's engagement and investment increases when they feel ownership over a space. If you ask the students about our classroom, they will tell you readily that it is "mostly kid space with just a little teacher space." And by that I mean that the majority of the room is created for students, and in many parts, with their input. You will see student-created labels on clear, easy-to-access bins, quotes and charts of student thinking, from our very own alphabet to our growing number line.

We must also have a space for ongoing work; in our room, we call it the Saving Shelf. It is where we can save structures, artwork, toy creations, knowing that they will be safe until we are ready to continue (or discontinue) working with them. I think there is comfort in knowing that even though the work is stopping, that doesn't mean that the ideas have to – for my students who have anxiety around having to stop working and clean up, it really helps to know that their work will be safe and they know where to access it in order to return to it.

Community visitors in our classroom have remarked that our space is "so cozy and warm and loving. There is an exuberance you can feel, and the students are so engaged. It's clear that students have so much agency and voice here. I wish I could learn and spend all day here! It feels so warm." In the words of my kindergarteners, "It feels awesome and exciting, like when you do something that feels happy for you. That's what our classroom feels like."

Sara's classroom is an excellent example of how a learner-centered classroom feels, specifically the ideals conveyed by McCombs and Whisler's (1997) fourth premise.

Pause and read, noticing how the bold words create a space that will foster learning and invite the children into the learning process.

Learning occurs best in a positive environment, one that contains positive interpersonal relationships and interactions, that contains **comfort** and **order**, and in which the learner feels **appreciated**, **acknowledged**, **respected**, and **validated**.

All of the premises of learner-centered classrooms offer an excellent starting place for identifying what a classroom looks like, sounds like, and feels like. We encourage you to reread the premises and the characteristics of a learner-centered classroom, noting where the ideals overlap with how you create the conditions for learning or how you approach teaching and instructional decision-making.

Just as we give our learners voice and choice in the classroom and encourage them to regulate their own learning, we pause here to give you choices of where you want to go with your own learning as it relates to the big ideas in this chapter. You can choose one, two, or all three choices, depending on your current professional goals.

Choice 1: Transitioning from constructivist theory to learner-centered practices

If you need more examples of transitioning from constructivist theory to learner-centered practices, we challenge you to identify the underlying learner-centered premises in each of the stories and examples of the Outdoor Classroom *project in Chapter 1. Did you notice how everything Sara did for the project revolved around the learner? Sara used learner-centered practices when she identified the learning goals and student outcomes for the individuals in the class and the* group as a whole. The way Sara approached the outdoor space was learner-centered in that the students were involved in nearly every decision or the focus of every decision. From the questions the students asked during the various learning investigations to designing, building, and painting a puppet theater, to planning the learning celebration, the students were at the center of Sara's instructional decisions.

Choice 2: Making changes to the physical classroom environment

If you are ready to consider the environment in your current classroom and where you may see evidence of the characteristics of a learner-centered classroom, then close your eyes and visualize your space. Does it look learner-centered? Does it sound learner-centered? Does it feel learner-centered? If you answered yes, then we challenge you to select two elements from the Y-chart shown in Figure 2.2 that would enhance the teaching and learning in your classroom. If you

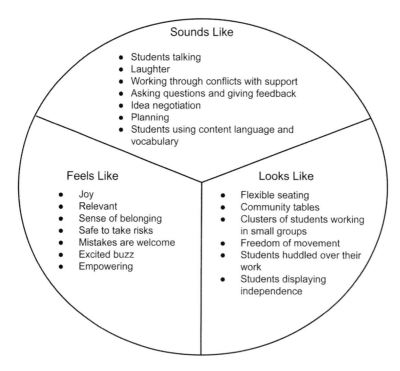

Figure 2.2 Learner-centered classroom looks like, feels like, and sounds like

answered "no" to any of the prompts, then we challenge you to find that same section of the Y-chart and select one element to try and put into practice, or if you have your own idea, feel free to bring in that element.

Choice 3: Going in-depth regarding the learner-centered principles

If you want to read more about the 14 learner-centered principles developed by the American Psychological Association (APA), we encourage you to select an additional reading from the learner-centered resources section in Appendix B. The texts listed include the original framework developed by APA and multiple books on the subject by experts in the field. The principles are arranged into four primary categories: (1) metacognitive and cognitive factors, (2) affective and motivational factors, (3) developmental and social factors, and (4) individual difference factors. Developing an understanding of what each principle means within the context of each category will help you establish and maintain a classroom that is learner-centered.

References

Diamond, J., Grob, B., & Reitzes, F. (2015). *Teaching kindergarten: Learner-centered classrooms for the 21st Century*. New York, NY: Teachers College Press.

Edwards, C., Gandini, L., & Forman, G. (Eds.). (1998). *The hundred languages of children: The Reggio Emilia approach – Advanced reflections*. Westport, CT: Ablex Publishing.

Hammond, Z. (2014). *Culturally responsive teaching and the brain: Promoting authentic engagement and rigor among culturally and linguistically diverse students*. Thousand Oaks, CA: Corwin Press.

Helm, H., & Katz, L. (2016). *Young investigators: The project approach in the early years* (3rd ed.). New York, NY: Teachers College Press.

Larmer, J. (2016). It's a project-based world. *Educational Leadership, 73*(6), 66–70.

McCombs, B., & Whisler, J. (1997). *The learner-centered classroom and school: Strategies for increasing student motivation and achievement*. San Francisco, CA: Jossey-Bass Publishers.

Panitz, T. (1999). Collaborative versus cooperative learning: A comparison of the two concepts which will help us understand the underlying nature of interactive learning. Retrieved from: https://eric.ed.gov/?id=ED448443

Pierce, J., & Kalkman, D. (2003). Applying learner-centered principles in teacher education. *Theory Into Practice, 42*(2), 127–132. doi:10.1207/s15430421tip4202_6.

Tarr, P. (2004). Consider the walls. *Young Children, 59*(3), 88–92.

Project Planning
An Integrated Approach

Before I could start a project, I'd have to teach my kids too many things to get them ready.

Early childhood teachers often believe they have to prepare their students for Project Based Learning (PBL) by teaching them everything they will need to know for the project before it begins. They worry that students won't be able to participate in PBL because they lack the skills and knowledge necessary to be successful, so they try to get their students ready for the project by pre-teaching skills in isolation and front-loading the academic content. When teachers discover their already packed schedule doesn't allow time for teaching the skills for a project ahead of time, they often abandon the plan. Some teachers avoid using PBL altogether because they realize that it is impossible to add anything else to their day. However, successfully implementing Project Based Learning requires us to take a different approach to curriculum planning – specifically, an integrated approach, where the standards and learning goals are viewed as interconnected parts of a whole rather than as isolated skills and knowledge. Using an integrated approach means we teach through the project instead of in advance of the project. When content is integrated, children are able to effectively develop new skills and knowledge, because they see the relevance and broader application of what they have learned.

> The teaching of discrete skills in a linear sequence is rejected by constructivists, as is the notion that demonstrated success on basic skills is a necessary prerequisite to more advanced learning and higher order thinking.
>
> (Harris & Graham, 1994, p. 234)

Constructivist learning theory calls for students to create their own knowledge through interactions with others. If we spoon-feed students by telling them what they need to know to be able to do the next thing in their learning, then we take away their opportunities to think for themselves, problem-solve, and make decisions. Rather than pre-teaching basic skills and front-loading the content, teachers instead can intentionally weave together academic and social and emotional learning competencies into the initial project design. An innovative approach to instructional planning should move students beyond learning and regurgitating facts to a strong conceptual understanding of the content (Erickson, 2002). At the same time, teachers must remain open and flexible as new pathways emerge during the unit. By its very nature, PBL doesn't allow for all content to be predetermined. A project unfolds as students ask questions that lead to the discovery of new knowledge that may not have been expected or included in the original project plan. Therefore, teachers must embed both preplanned and spontaneous lessons into the project accordingly.

In a constructivist learning environment, students make authentic, relevant connections to learning and then retain and apply that knowledge moving forward (Fullan, Quinn, & McEachen, 2017). When we use an integrated approach, the topic becomes the tool for understanding conceptual ideas. It encourages students to identify what they need to know, making the content meaningful and the timing of the learning relevant (Applefield, Huber, & Moallem, 2000). Integration encourages students to take ownership of their own learning, acquiring multiple ways to access knowledge that leads to the development of lifelong learning strategies, interpersonal skill development, and opportunities to demonstrate understanding in multiple modalities (Duke, Halvorsen, Strachan, Konstantopoulos, & Kim, 2016; Langa & Yost, 2007). In addition, content integration supports children as they make meaningful connections between new knowledge and existing schema. Studying one topic within the context of another subject provides opportunities to study each discipline with depth and integrity (Erickson, 2002). Successful implementation of Project Based Learning supports children's development of social and emotional competencies while learning academic content *throughout* a project.

This approach to learning is much like the way a child learns to play a sport. Consider that when a child expresses an interest in, for example, softball, you don't sit her down and teach her the mechanics of throwing, batting, fielding, and all the rules of the game before she plays. When she gets ready to first throw a ball, you don't take time to explain grip, trajectory, and release point; you just give her the ball and say, "Go ahead and throw it." You may model it first, but really, a child just tries it – she *plays*. The mechanics of throwing and batting, the challenge of catching a pop-fly, along with other aspects of the game are gradually *integrated* into conversations and practice sessions. It is under the guidance of a more skilled player (i.e., the coach) and through practicing with peers that young athletes learn the fundamentals, strategies, and rules needed to play the game. Good coaching is a combination of observation, scaffolding, assessment, goal-setting, and building on what players can already do *as they practice and play a game* – rather than being given all of the skills and knowledge ahead of time. We've all seen the Nike slogan "Just do it." We've never seen a T-shirt that says, "Just master each individual skill required for success before engaging in an athletic activity."

Although there are skills that can (and should) be improved upon in isolation, the real and authentic opportunities for learning happen on the field. Integrating curriculum so that learning happens through both social experiences and practice is a solidly constructivist perspective, one that we believe is essential to planning high-quality projects. Implementation of integration at the highest level requires this balance of practice and play with the right amount of coaching and support. Coaches teach and isolate skills during practice, but they also integrate learning opportunities into games played on the field. Similarly, the classroom teacher can also use an integrative approach in the classroom (the "field"). "In its broadest sense, curriculum integration embraces not just the interweaving of subjects but of any curriculum elements that might be taught more effectively in relation to each other than separately" (Ackerman & Perkins, 1989, p. 79).

As we mentioned in Chapter 1, constructivism is about students co-constructing knowledge in a social environment through meaningful and relevant learning opportunities. This means that we must identify what we are going to teach and design a project that honors students' current developmental levels and learning goals. Therefore, we don't pre-teach certain skills to get the children "ready" for the project. Instead, we determine how the *project* can teach the skills, making for authentic learning that will resonate with learners and transfer to other contexts. If, as you choose learning goals for a project you notice that the majority of the selected standards seem out-of-reach for your students, consider doing that project at a later point in the year when your students are ready.

A Vision for Integration in PBL

Implementing PBL with young children requires an integrated approach that helps students understand the relevance of what they are learning. Integration also illuminates connections to scenarios that exist beyond the school walls so that children have the agency to apply their learning to broader contexts. Rather than compartmentalizing each subject, content integration mirrors the way that learning actually happens in the world. When adults are "confronted in real life with a compelling problem or puzzling situation, we don't ask which part is mathematics, which part is science, which part is history, and so on. Instead, we draw on or seek out knowledge and skill from any and all sources that might be helpful" (Beane, 1991, p. 9).

In addition, integration encourages students to identify what they need to know, making the content meaningful and the timing of the learning relevant (Applefield et al., 2000). We drew from constructivist principles and the work of numerous educational pioneers to build our understanding of integration in an early childhood classroom (see Figure 3.1).

It would be natural for teachers to want to teach their students how to do everything in advance of a project. That's how most of us have been trained in our teacher preparation programs; to teach students what they need to know and once they have learned the material, we somehow use it or take a test. There are two issues with this mindset. First, any attempt to front-load skills for a project would most likely take more time than is feasible. Children need plenty of opportunities to engage with content *in the context* of a project and experience related and relevant content *alongside* the project as it naturally emerges. Second, front-loading all of these skills in advance of a project would likely lead to teaching skills in isolated ways, which often feels inauthentic and leads to a "taught it, got it" mentality rather than seeing learning as a progression.

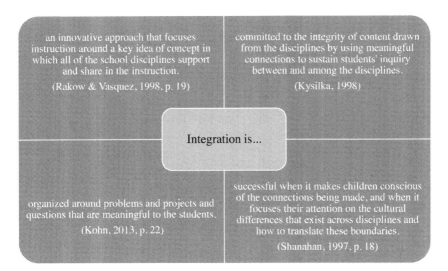

an innovative approach that focuses instruction around a key idea of concept in which all of the school disciplines support and share in the instruction.
(Rakow & Vasquez, 1998, p. 19)

committed to the integrity of content drawn from the disciplines by using meaningful connections to sustain students' inquiry between and among the disciplines.
(Kysilka, 1998)

Integration is...

organized around problems and projects and questions that are meaningful to the students.
(Kohn, 2013, p. 22)

successful when it makes children conscious of the connections being made, and when it focuses their attention on the cultural differences that exist across disciplines and how to translate these boundaries.
(Shanahan, 1997, p. 18)

Figure 3.1 Defining integration

Keep in mind that integration is *not* the same as planning a thematic unit. Thematic units, where all of the learning activities are tied to a central theme, are not synonymous with Project Based Learning. Teaching through a thematic unit is an interdisciplinary approach where everything from the bulletin boards, math problems, centers, games, and snacks coordinate with a central idea. If "we are merely 'coordinating' facts and activities to a topic, we fail to reach higher-level curricular and cognitive integration" (Erickson, 2002, p. 63). Although teaching through a thematic approach may be helpful for students to see the relationship between ideas, or understand the concepts of the theme, the teaching is often superficial and artificial because it is not grounded in a challenging problem or question.

Read the example below comparing a thematic approach to teaching insects with a Project Based Learning unit (Table 3.1). Notice the intentional alignment in both approaches. Think about how coordinating materials, lessons, and authentic learning experiences under a driving question yields deeper learning. Specifically notice how Project Based Learning:

- *promotes an understanding of the connection to the world outside the classroom*
- *encourages students to use language that accurately reflects scientific terminology*
- *engages children with actual specimens and scientifically accurate resources*

Table 3.1 Thematic Approach vs PBL Unit

INSECTS	
Thematic Approach	*Project Based Learning Unit*
A thematic approach to bugs often starts with a read-aloud of Eric Carle's *The Very Hungry Caterpillar*. During science time, the students learn about the life cycle of the butterfly and possibly other bugs or creepy crawlies. The students may assemble life cycle wheels and make butterflies out of bow-tie pasta or clothespins and coffee filters. The teacher might have insect-shaped manipulatives for counting collections or centers. A question of the day board might ask the students if they like/dislike certain insects. The children might make "ants on a log" for snack while listening to songs about insects. During writing time, students might write a story from the perspective of a bug.	**Driving Question:** **How can we protect monarch caterpillars in their natural habitat?** During this unit, the students discovered that some of the monarch caterpillars they were rearing in jars in the classroom were able to complete the full metamorphosis while others made a chrysalis but never emerged. The students identified they needed to know why some of the caterpillars were dying. To answer this question, the students learned about different parasites and diseases from books, videos, and an expert visit. With support from students at a local university, knowledge about where the larvae and food source were found, and what the students learned in the classrooms, the children were able to determine their caterpillars were getting sick from bacteria infecting the milkweed, their food source. It was essential that the students answered this question in support of the overarching driving question.

Planning a thematic unit is similar to planning a theme party for children or adults. From the invitations to the food, drinks, and decorations, everything coordinates. While it is fun to participate in a thematic party, when it is over, we are often left with a costume to stash in the closet and a trinket or photograph to admire. We want the learning that happens in our classrooms to be long lasting and impactful, not forced and artificial. We want our students to make strong connections for themselves within the content of the project so the learning transfers across disciplines and projects seamlessly. As you plan for integration, it may be helpful to pause frequently to assess whether your ideas align naturally to the driving question or whether or not you are making superficial connections for the students.

Planning for Integration

In a typical classroom, planning for day-to-day instruction is usually done in a very linear way, often by looking at the entire unit and designing a sequence of lessons that will cover the content in order. For some teachers, there is no need to create lesson plans because the "planning" that is done involves reading a textbook or looking over the pre-written scope and sequence notes in the teacher's manual. We recognize that some teachers have found success with interdisciplinary planning within their own classroom or across content areas in the upper grades. Sometimes this works and other times teachers "try to do too much at once. What they need to look for are some, not all, natural overlaps between subjects" (Brandt, 1991, p. 24). Trying to put too many disciplines, or standards within a discipline, often results in frustration and teachers abandoning innovative approaches to planning.

The vast difference between this more traditional type of planning and integrated PBL unit planning is worth pausing over. Some of these differences are obvious. Where a traditional unit may have detailed outlines, calendars, homework, specific standards, and an end project, a PBL unit relies much more on student input and experience and the project develops in a more organic way, albeit closely developed and guided by the teacher. However, a project that integrates multiple subjects takes time and substantial planning, but the time invested does lay the groundwork for multiple weeks of teaching and learning (Langa & Yost, 2007). With so many benefits to intentional integration, it is worth the time spent up front planning effectively.

In order to integrate instruction throughout the life of the project, teachers must begin with a holistic understanding of the general topic, specific content, and intended learning outcomes. This involves devoting time to systematically investigate the curricular expectations for the unit (Keeley & Tugel, 2019). Spending time thinking about a project before actually planning helps determines if the topic is meaningful and relevant to the students and viable for the time and place. Understanding the concepts and the content will make it easier to facilitate the learning. Teachers developing a project should first:

- identify some potential misconceptions students may have about the topic
- read blogs about the exact topic and related concepts
- explore children's books, identifying quality fiction and nonfiction texts
- watch videos

Layers of Integration

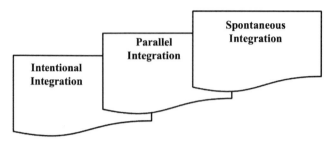

Figure 3.2 Layers of integration

- observe students
- attend workshops or lectures
- look through teacher resource materials
- talk through ideas with teammates or other thought partners
- concept map or web of ideas

Drawing on the ten models of integration from Fogarty (1991) and taking her suggestion that "teachers should go and invent their own designs for integrating the curriculum" (p. 65), we created our own learner-centered, inquiry-based approach to planning. Our three-layered approach allows students to connect their learning to broader contexts while considering multiple perspectives (Figure 3.2). And through authentic investigations, experiences, and problems, it guides students to understand how the varied elements of the content they learn are, in fact, interrelated. In this chapter, we will walk you through our approach to integration, and highlight how Sara used this approach to integrate content and social and emotional competencies in the *Outdoor Classroom* project rather than front-loading the skills ahead of time.

The *Outdoor Classroom* Project: An Integrated Approach to Planning

Sara launched the *Outdoor Classroom* project during the third week of school. In the early planning stages, she thought about the observations she had been making of her students, their skills and abilities, and what she knew about each child's development. She focused on what they *could* do, their interests, and the learning opportunities that lay ahead. Because, for example, many students demonstrated basic number sense and could consistently count a set of ten objects accurately, Sara was confident they could do some basic measuring as they designed spaces in their outdoor classroom. Similarly, most children could identify the letters in their names and write their names with minimal support, so Sara knew they could do some labeling of a floor plan and identify captions that showed areas of their designs. And the majority of her students could use drawing materials (crayons, markers) independently and could collaborate to build elaborate Lego and block structures; these were skills Sara planned to leverage for the upcoming project.

Then Sara considered the potential skills and abilities the children would need to design the adjacent classroom space. Children would most likely need to:

- envision and suggest different areas and represent those areas clearly on a map or floor plan
- label the floor plan so others could understand their ideas, using initial consonants
- create some type of written proposal to the school leaders asking for permission to design the space
- interview experts about the design process and record their questions and observations
- design, create, or build new areas of the classroom, potentially using shapes, lines, or two-dimensional (2-D) and three-dimensional (3-D) materials

To begin, Sara purposefully designed her project with specific, relevant content and skills that would be woven into the project (**intentional integration**). Then she taught some of the essential content and skills *alongside and separate from* her project as a way to scaffold, deepen, and build out some of the new knowledge as the project unfolded (**parallel integration**). And finally, she drew upon curricular connections that naturally and spontaneously emerged throughout the life of the project (**spontaneous integration**). These individual layers create the fabric for a project by ensuring that relevant content and skills are intentionally planned and structured while leaving room to draw learning out of unexpected opportunities.

Integration in Early Childhood PBL: A Three-Layered Approach

Layer 1: Intentional Integration

In the *Outdoor Classroom* project, Sara chose key learning goals in social studies, geometry, literacy, and social and emotional learning. All of these learning goals were related to clearly specified outcomes within the final products, which she envisioned to be the outdoor classroom design and its presentation. The connection between the learning goals and products was clearly understood by the children in the class. Sara planned for students to design and create a floor plan for a new, empty physical space where they could learn and play.

Intentional integration takes place when teachers consider the natural links between different subject matters at the outset of a project and plan for them, carefully designing a project that capitalizes on connections and deep learning opportunities in authentic ways (Fogarty, 1991). Every PBL unit we design begins with intentional integration (Figure 3.3), where we plan the content and skills we wish to embed in an authentic context from multiple academic disciplines. In PBL, these integrated learning goals are directly aligned to the driving question, daily instruction, and the culminating products of the project. Formative assessments are used throughout the project to intentionally measure growth in the specific learning goals, and all of the planned

Layers of Integration

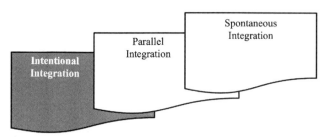

Figure 3.3 Intentional integration

assessments support children in the successful creation of the public product. So when planning a PBL unit, it is essential to make sure that all of the integrated learning goals are significant – meaning they are important, encourage deep learning, and lend themselves well to a project because they require ample amount of time for students to learn (Larmer, Mergendoller, & Boss, 2015).

It is often helpful to link the standards together in your mind, effectively creating a story for the project. This will help you imagine product ideas that naturally incorporate different standards in an integrated and authentic way. Throughout the project, it should be clear to you and your students *why* and *how* these skills are connected. It is our role as teachers, then, to combine the learning goals into meaningful instruction, going deeper within and across content areas with and for students. Figure 3.4 presents some ideas for you to consider as you plan for intentional integration.

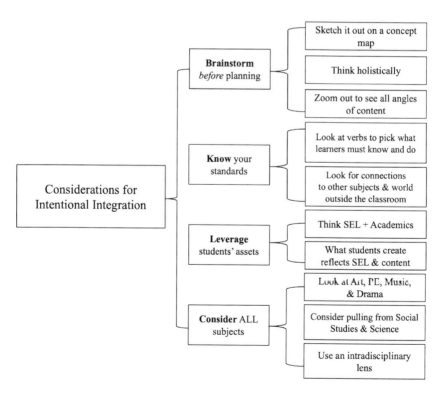

Figure 3.4 Considerations for intentional integration

Layer 2: Parallel Integration

> In order to effectively sequence and differentiate foundational literacy skill instruction, the instruction will need to happen alongside the project. While you may be able to pull it within the project periodically, you won't always be able to do so. At the elementary level, that might mean that during your literacy block, you have a few dedicated stations for word work, spelling, and phonics. The other couple of stations could involve reading and writing for the project.
>
> (Horton, 2017, para. 3)

Teachers can add a second layer of integration (Figure 3.5) into the project plan by identifying specific disciplinary units that support the project goals that could be taught separate from project time. These academic content areas (for example literacy and math) are taught alongside, or *parallel to,* the PBL unit. For example, a parallel unit on nonfiction writing might be taught alongside a project so that students gain more practice writing nonfiction texts which are essential to the creation of their public product. Children can work on important skills and strategies related to nonfiction writing that directly transfer to their project work. The teacher may use project content during direct instruction, interactive writing lessons, and on anchor charts, and the students would use these models and lessons to create their own texts on topics related to the project. Utilizing this layer of integration gives children additional time and focused instruction on one particular learning goal for the project. Parallel integration provides time

Layers of Integration

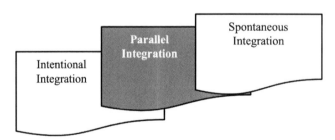

Figure 3.5 Parallel integration

for students to develop content-related skills and strategies in a meaningful way that can be applied to the project and beyond.

Teachers might also lead a parallel unit to support specific social and emotional skills that are relevant to a project. For example, if the students were going to need to complete several drafts of a design or layout, an SEL unit about "mindsets" might run parallel to the primary project so the students could learn about perseverance in the face of challenge. Stand-alone SEL lessons may introduce or reinforce the concept of "fixed" and "growth" mindsets because this knowledge is directly applicable to the project.

If you have flexibility around your scope and sequence, you might move a unit of study in a particular subject area earlier or later than previously determined to overlap with the project. If your scope and sequence is set and unchangeable, then as you first plan your project (intentional integration), build out your project with that set sequence in mind and teach those corresponding units of study during your formal academic learning periods. Regarding both academic content and SEL, parallel integration enables students to interact with a topic in meaningful ways and gives teachers more time to unpack new skills and expand upon concepts introduced in the project through additional learning experiences and opportunities.

Sara planned to integrate geometry into the *Outdoor Classroom* project. However, her geometry unit was originally scheduled for later in the winter, not the fall when the project would begin. Because Sara did have flexibility over *when* she taught her geometry unit, she moved it earlier in the year to coincide with her project so that the math content would be most meaningful to children and they would be able to directly apply the newly developing skills that the project required (Helm, 2008). She used her preexisting, established math time and formal math curriculum to teach specific geometry lessons that covered content the students were expected to learn. For those children who needed practice identifying shapes, Sara had them create shapes out of a variety of hands-on materials. During her scheduled math time, Sara gave children opportunities to explore geometry concepts using clay, toothpicks, popsicle sticks, rubber bands, and geo-boards. She had targeted conversations with each student to assess their ability to name and create different shapes in whatever medium he or she chose, offering children multiple ways to demonstrate their understanding of the concepts. Because Sara was able to realign her schedule, children had additional time to develop their understanding.

Meanwhile, her students used project work time to explore geometry as it related to project needs; mainly, representing the outdoor classroom floor plan and then designing and helping to build the puppet theater. Later in the project, the geometry they previously learned continued to play an important role in children's original musical instrument designs and in how they organized their new space. Children had to learn how to draw their instruments (2-D shapes) and then construct them, using recycled materials (3-D shapes). Students also decided to sort, shelve, and label all of the different 3-D unit blocks as they organized the outdoor classroom (Figures 3.6 and 3.7). Each of these expectations encouraged a direct, authentic rationale as to why they needed geometry in order to be successful in the project work. The parallel instruction that took place enabled children to deepen and solidify their learning of geometry concepts – those that were needed for the project, and then beyond.

In the case of the *Outdoor Classroom* project, if Sara had not had flexibility to shift her geometry unit, she could have used the project as

Figure 3.6 Students sorting, drawing, and labeling 3-D unit blocks for storage in their outdoor classroom

Figure 3.7 3-D unit blocks sorted and labeled on the shelves

an opportunity for students to experience and explore the geometry content that would be more formally taught later in the year. She would have simply focused the project goals on literacy, social studies, and social and emotional learning, rather than geometry when it came to assessing student progress and learning. We will address more specific needs and considerations of assessment in Chapter 8, but for now, as you begin to think through these integration options, focus your assessments on the standards or key learning goals that fit within the context of the project, rather than trying to force integration that does not naturally occur.

Sara's phonics curriculum was also running parallel to the project, as students were learning to recognize the letters in their names during their formal phonics instruction time. Specifically, they focused on recognizing the initial letters of their names. This work served the same purpose as in the case of geometry; children began connecting the work they were doing during their phonics block to what they needed to know to complete the project. For example, when it came time to label the floor plans of the outdoor classroom, children connected the new locations of the outdoor classroom to the letters in their friends' names. Children looked at an initial plan and saw the words "Block Shelf," "Puppet Theater," and "Book Area." Many children immediately noticed and exclaimed "B! That's the first letter in Ben's name!" and "P! That's the first letter in Penny's name!" As with the

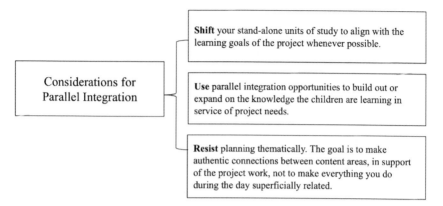

Figure 3.8 Considerations for parallel integration

math, parallel integration enabled children to deepen their practice and their understanding of significant learning for the project.

Parallel integration serves two primary purposes. First, it enables teachers to scaffold, support, and extend children's understanding of key concepts which are necessary elements of the project, giving more time and focused attention to the material. Second, this approach enables children to see how the content they are learning directly relates to the broader, authentic, and meaningful context of the PBL unit. And if we think back to the misconception that launched this chapter – that content needs to be taught prior to projects – you can see how a PBL classroom allows for authentic learning of content all through the day; some content is integrated, and some is parallel, but all of it directly relates to the concerns of the project at hand. Figure 3.8 presents some ideas for you to consider as you plan for parallel integration.

Layer 3: Spontaneous Integration

> Identifying real-world contexts whose features help direct students' attention and thinking in mathematically productive ways is particularly helpful in building conceptual bridges between students' informal experience and the new formal mathematics they are learning.
>
> (Fuson, Kalchman, & Bransford, 2005, p. 231)

The third approach to integration happens when children or teachers discover key knowledge and skills naturally and unexpectedly as a project unfolds. When this takes place, teachers draw out or highlight the new knowledge and then weave in that specific curricular content as it makes sense or as students need to know them for the project. These spontaneously discovered ideas and connections are often quite exciting for both teachers and students. They reinforce the idea that learning is a process, and that unexpected connections arise for both teachers and children.

Spontaneous integration occurred when a professional puppeteer visited the class and explained that puppeteers focus on the syllables of a word so they know when to open and close a puppet's mouth. The children had been learning about syllables during their formal phonics time. After hearing this, Sara jumped at the chance to use puppets to reinforce the children's phonemic awareness related to syllables. She decided that since they were also beginning to explore music, she would use drums and shakers to teach syllables as well, thus deepening a connection between rhythm, sound, and phonemic awareness. It took the puppeteer's visit (learning new information from an expert) along with Sara's observations of instruments to inspire these curricular connections.

Spontaneous integration can also take place when *students* independently notice and draw out curricular connections and bring those ideas into the project (Figure 3.9). When a designer first came and told the children about some of her tools and showed them a roll of measuring tape, a child pointed out the numbers on the tape. Many children then wanted to see what that child meant, and there was an inherent curiosity about the numbers and what they were for. At that point, a child asked if he could see the tape and "measure the classroom."

Layers of Integration

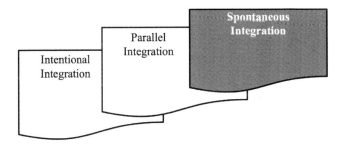

Figure 3.9 Spontaneous integration

Sara went and got rulers and measuring tape so children could explore numbers and measure the outdoor space as they made their designs.

There is also a hybrid version, where something spontaneous occurred to Sara during the project, but she waited to see if one of the students would make a suggestion, rather than bringing it up herself. After children had suggested a puppet theater for the outdoor class-room, Sara got in touch with a parent who offered to design plans and donate wood so that the class could build a puppet theater together. After the parent emailed Sara his drawn plans, Sara noticed a natural connection to geometry that she hadn't considered before. While she had planned to integrate shapes in the outdoor classroom floor plan, she hadn't considered how geometry might play into the puppet the-ater when the children first suggested that as an idea. At that point she decided she would have children design their own individual puppet theaters (to give the parent some ideas) using a variety of cut-out paper shapes (Figure 3.10). Before telling the class her idea, Sara thought she

Figure 3.10 A child uses shapes to create her own puppet theater design

would see if any of the children would make the connection to geometry. Sara simply showed her class the parent's puppet theater design and asked children to share what they noticed. Immediately, a child said that he saw "rectangles and squares" in the design. Another student said, "There were lots of shapes in my puppet theater." Then, Sara wondered aloud if they might be able to design their own puppet theater given they had already learned so much about shapes.

In fact, we believe that spontaneous integration is so beneficial to PBL, we also recommend occasionally taking something that has been *intentionally* planned and treating it as *spontaneous*. Note if children make these connections for themselves and then *make it look as though* the connections came from them. The benefits gained by you announcing your plans are minimal compared to those gained by a student whose initiative has made an impact on the class. In Sara's *Outdoor Classroom*, for example, Sara planned to bring her students to a music store to conduct fieldwork, but she withheld the announcement, and when one of her students made the same suggestion, Sara treated it as *spontaneous integration*. Not only would the class get the benefits of the trip, but the student would feel pride in her idea, and the class would further understand that they have some control over their own learning. In addition, as much as you can, name ideas after children following their comments or suggestions. For example, reference "Molly's idea to make a puppet out of shapes" or "Ginnia's suggestion to visit a music store." Each time you do this, children hear that they, along with their peers, have ownership over the project, even if you had the idea all along.

In PBL, we should be mindful of the language of the standards while identifying the broader applications that these learning goals have to the students' lives inside *and* outside of the classroom walls. This depth of understanding on our part and heightened awareness to making connections within and across disciplines allows us to lift up these connections in authentic and fun ways. Even more exciting is when children discover and share these connections, and we are able to honor those observations and let *children's* ideas move the project forward or in unexpected directions. These spontaneous connections inspire creativity, engagement, and joy for both children and teachers. Figure 3.11 presents some ideas for you to consider as you look for opportunities for spontaneous integration.

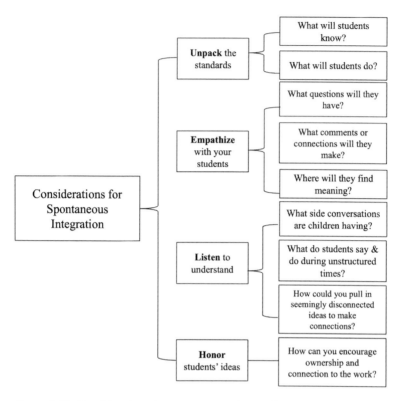

Figure 3.11 Considerations for spontaneous integration

Planning for Layers of Integration for Your Project

As you begin planning and implementing projects, you will start to see how and when to integrate content and skills. Sara knew there were some topics she wanted to teach (mapping skills, taking initiative in learning) and planned for them intentionally to be taught within the project. She knew some would be taught within separate lessons, running parallel to the project. She was also open to making her own observations of students, reflecting on the project, and making additions and changes as necessary. Sara also left space for her students to surprise her by bringing up connections they noticed.

In terms of her daily schedule, Sara built in opportunities for Project Work Time during her allotted social studies and science blocks. She also utilized other times in her schedule where it made sense in terms of project learning goals. For example, children did a character study during reading and worked on their letter about the outdoor space to the principals during writing. Sara was able to integrate project experiences into those times of day because the project content was closely aligned to her established curriculum.

Table 3.2 gives a snapshot of all three levels of integration from the *Outdoor Classroom* project. Sara's school allows teachers to rearrange the units and academic content topics as long as all content standards are addressed.

Take a moment to pause and reflect on how integration helps students connect what they are learning to why it is important. Consider what freedom you have in terms of your scope and sequence or when you introduce content and concepts. What constraint(s) might you need to work within? We understand that you may not have the same autonomy that Sara did with arranging and rearranging the content into projects. You may also not have as much autonomy in terms of weaving in spontaneous integration opportunities. We encourage you to look at the suggestions found in Table 3.3 for how you might successfully navigate content integration based on the expectations at your school.

Planning an integrative curriculum for a project is a labor of love at the heart of successfully implementing Project Based Learning. It takes time and energy to thoughtfully consider the big ideas, concepts, and processes that you want to embed in the project from the conceptual level, along with the day-to-day lessons. Our hope is that the resources we provide will help you visualize and understand how integrating the content and social and emotional learning skills could work conceptually. Regardless of how challenging it might seem, your work will pay off in terms of the level of engagement and authenticity both you and your students experience throughout the project.

Once many of these big project decisions are made, it's time to dig into planning the day-to-day lessons and activities. There are numerous

> Long term achievement gains are more likely when teachers teach for understanding of transferable concepts and processes while giving learners multiple opportunities to apply their learning in meaningful and authentic contexts.
> (McTighe & Willis, 2019, p. 23)

ways to provide hands-on, minds-on learning experiences and practice opportunities for your children, and we will begin to explore those
in our next chapter. Fieldwork and field experiences, guest speakers,
investigations, videos, and read-alouds should all be considered to find
the right fit for teaching your students. We suggest you pause and take
a look at Sara's project planner for the *Outdoor Classroom* project in
Appendix A. Notice in Section 2 how Sara integrated multiple academic
and social and emotional learning goals. The calendar is broken up
into lessons and experiences that include notes on scaffolds and differ-
entiation. We think this will guide you as you develop your own daily
learning targets and lesson ideas. When you are ready to plan your
own project, a blank copy of this planning document can be found at
pblworks.org.

Table 3.2 Integration in the *Outdoor Classroom* Project

Area of Focus	Standards	Project Ideas	Layer of Integration
Social and emotional learning	SED 5.1 Take greater initiative in making new discoveries, identifying new solutions, and persisting in trying to figure things out. (Preschool Learning Foundations CA Dept. of Education Volume 1)	Students make and execute plans from their initial ideas.	Intentional
History and social studies	K.4 Students compare and contrast the locations of people, places, and environments and describe their characteristics.	Students will create floor plans/maps of the layout and describe the layout through pictures and words.	Intentional

(continued)

Table 3.2 Integration in the *Outdoor Classroom* Project (Continued)

Area of Focus	Standards	Project Ideas	Layer of Integration
Math (Geometry)	CCSS K.G.A, K.G.B. 1–6 Identify and describe shapes; analyze, compare, create and compose shapes.	Students use a blank map of the outdoor classroom space and use paper shapes to map out the classroom.	Intentional
		Use Geometry Unit – "Make a Shape, Build a Block" from Investigations, 2008.	Parallel
		Utilize shapes to design a puppet theater, organizing the block shelf with shape labels and names.	Spontaneous
ELA: Reading	CCSS.ELA-LITERACY. RF.K.1.A-1.D Demonstrate understanding of the organization and basic features of print.	Use interactive writing to write a letter to the principals asking permission to design the space.	Intentional
	CCSS.ELA-LITERACY. L.K.1.A Print many upper- and lowercase letters.	Conduct a name study, where the children study one another's names to discover how many letters and syllables they each have so they can connect something known (their own name) with the unknown (other names and future words).	Parallel

(continued)

Table 3.2 Integration in the *Outdoor Classroom* Project (Continued)

Area of Focus	Standards	Project Ideas	Layer of Integration
ELA: Reading (*continued*)	CCSS.ELA-LITERACY. RF.K.2 Demonstrate understanding of spoken words, syllables, and sounds (phonemes).	Children practice phonemic awareness (syllables) through instruments and puppets.	Spontaneous
	CCSS.ELA-LITERACY. L.K.2.D Spell simple words phonetically, drawing on knowledge of sound-letter relationships.	Use *Words Their Way* Phonics Curriculum.	Parallel
	CCSS.ELA-LITERACY. RL.K.3 With prompting and support, identify characters, settings, and major events in a story.	Use character study in Reader's Workshop to support puppet creation and stories.	Spontaneous
ELA: Speaking/ Listening	CCSS.ELA-Literacy.SL.K.1 Comprehension and collaboration. CCSS.ELA-Literacy.SL.K.4 Presentation of knowledge and ideas.	Prioritize student discussions of project plans throughout. Students will plan the final celebration of learning.	Intentional
ELA: Writing	CCSS.ELA-LITERACY.W.K.3 Use a combination of drawing, dictating, and writing to narrate a single event or several loosely linked events, tell about the events in the order in which they occurred, and provide a reaction to what happened.	Students create original stories during writing that inspired puppet shows.	Spontaneous

(continued)

Table 3.2 Integration in the *Outdoor Classroom* Project (Continued)

Area of Focus	Standards	Project Ideas	Layer of Integration
Science: Engineering design	K-2-ETS1-1. Ask questions, make observations, and gather information about a situation people want to change to define a simple problem that can be solved through the development of a new or improved object or tool. K-2-ETS1-2. Develop a simple sketch, drawing, or physical model to illustrate how the shape of an object helps it function as needed to solve a given problem.	Children designed original instruments (2-D drawings and 3-D prototypes) for their music area.	Spontaneous

Table 3.3 Integration in Various School Settings

If...	You Might...
You are bound to a set scope and sequence...	look at all of the key learning goals in a particular time frame, for example an 8- to 10-week window. Use the standards that are naturally occurring in your curriculum documents to design a project. If you discover the project you are designing actually fits better within another 8- to 10-week window, move the project to align with those standards instead.
You have to teach content that does not align with the project...	consider teaching this topic separate from the project. There's no need to force standards into products if they don't fit. For example, if you are teaching place value and that topic doesn't integrate into the project, perhaps teach place value as stand-alone content. Then tailor your products and assessments to align with the standards that *do* naturally fit in the project.
You have some flexibility with the scope and sequence...	shift your units of study to align what students will need to know to answer the driving question with your learning goals.
You have full autonomy over the daily schedule...	experiment with eliminating "chunks" in your day. For example, let go of math time or a literacy block, and let your project goals drive each of the learning periods in your daily schedule. You might consider calling these periods "Project Work Time" and they might encapsulate all of the different integrated content areas that make up your project.

Overcoming the Misconception

The world is not compartmentalized into separate math, reading, and science areas, yet the educational system, for the most part, isolates curricular areas into discrete parts, which often become the parts of a school day (Beane, 1991). While some content can be learned by teaching skills and developing knowledge in isolation, this approach does not mirror the way we experience life. Whenever we can, we must develop learning opportunities in our classrooms for children to experience the integration they see in the world. When we do this, teaching and learning can suddenly feel very free. When we stop to notice, as children often do, that nearly everything – every academic area – is actually interrelated, and we thus integrate learning, our curriculum becomes richer and more purposeful.

References

Ackerman, D., & Perkins, D. H. (1989). Integrating thinking and learning skills across the curriculum. In H. H. Jacobs (Ed.), *Interdisciplinary curriculum: Design and implementation* (pp. 77–95). Alexandria, VA: ASCD.

Applefield, J. M., Huber, R., & Moallem, M. (2000). Constructivism in theory and practice: Toward a better understanding. *The High School Journal*, *84*(2), 35–53.

Beane, J. (1991). The middle school: The natural home of integrated curriculum. *Educational Leadership*, *49*(2), 9–13.

Brandt, R. (1991). On interdisciplinary curriculum: A conversation with Heidi Hayes Jacobs. *Educational Leadership*, *49*(2), 24–26.

Duke, N. K., Halvorsen, A., Strachan, S. L., Konstantopoulos, S., & Kim, J. (2016). Putting PBL to the test: The impact of project-based learning on 2nd-grade students' social studies and literacy learning and motivation. *Unpublished manuscript*. Ann Arbor, MI: University of Michigan.

Erickson, H. L. (2002). *Concept-based curriculum and instruction: Teaching beyond the facts*. Thousand Oaks, CA: Corwin Press, Inc.

Fogarty, R. (1991). Ten ways to integrate curriculum. *Educational Leadership*, *49*(2), 61–65.

Fullan, M., Quinn, J., & McEachen, J. (2017). *Deep learning: Engage the world change the world*. Thousand Oaks, CA: Corwin Press.

Fuson, K., Kalchman, M., & Bransford, J. (2005). Mathematical understanding: An introduction. In M. S. Donovan, & J. D. Bransford (Eds.), *How students learn: History, mathematics, and science in the classroom* (pp. 217–256). Washington, DC: The National Academies Press.

Harris, K. R., & Graham, S. (1994). Constructivism: Principles, paradigms, and integration. *The Journal of Special Education, 28*(3), 233–247.

Helm, J. H. (2008). Don't give up on engaged learning. *YC Young Children, 63*(4), 14.

Horton, A. (2017). Effective Foundational Literacy Skill Instruction and PBL, Part 2 [blog]. Retrieved from: https://newtechnetwork.org/resources/effective-foundational-literacy-skill-instruction-pbl-part-2/

Keeley, P., & Tugel, J. (2019). *Science curriculum topic study: Bridging the gap between three-dimensional standards, research, and practice.* Thousand Oaks, CA: Corwin Press.

Kohn, A. (2013). How to rock the boat: Do you think that just because you're a new teacher you can create meaningful changing your classroom? Alfie Kohn begs to differ. *Educational Horizons, 91*(4), 21–25.

Kysilka, M. L. (1998). Understanding integrated curriculum. *Curriculum Journal, 9*(2), 197–209.

Langa, M., & Yost, J. (2007). *Curriculum mapping for differentiated instruction, K-8.* Thousand Oaks, CA: Corwin Press.

Larmer, J., Mergendoller, J., & Boss, S. (2015). *Setting the standard for project based learning.* Alexandria, VA: ASCD.

Loepp, F. L. (1999). Models of curriculum integration. *The Journal of Technology Studies, 25*(2), 21–25.

McTighe, J., & Willis, J. (2019). *Upgrade your teaching: Understanding by design meets neuroscience.* Alexandria, VA: ASCD.

National Research Council (2004). *How students learn: History, mathematics, and science in the classroom.* Washington, DC: National Academies Press.

Rakow, S. J., & Vasquez, J. (1998). Integrated instruction: A trio of strategies. *Science and Children, 35*(6), 18–22.

Shanahan, T. (1997). Reading-writing relationships, thematic units, inquiry learning… In pursuit of effective integrated literacy instruction. *The Reading Teacher, 51*(1), 12–19.

Research Redefined
Sustained Inquiry in Early Childhood PBL

PBL seems to involve a lot of research.
My students are too young to research on their own.

Early childhood teachers often share that they don't think Project Based Learning (PBL) will work in their classrooms because their children are too young to engage in research. Perhaps it is because most of what is considered as research in schools includes a lock-step process of reading books and finding information, taking notes, and writing a report or essay. Research, especially in the upper grades and continuing through high school and college, is thought of as a way to learn something or find out more. It is not uncommon for teachers to assign individual students a specific hero, habitat, or country to "research" during science or social studies class. It stands to reason that people think Project Based Learning is heavy on research because they know students are continually seeking answers to their questions. And if engaging in PBL requires research, then it is not surprising that early childhood teachers believe they can't implement PBL in their classrooms. However, from a PBL lens, this view of "research" is too narrow and a slight misrepresentation of the true meaning of the word. A Merriam-Webster (2019) dictionary search produced three meanings for the word "research," including (emphasis added below):

1. a careful or diligent search
2. a studious **inquiry** or examination, especially **investigation** or **experimentation** aimed at the discovery and interpretation of facts
3. the collecting of information about a particular subject

Project Based Learning incorporates all three meanings of research. We expect our students to engage in careful and diligent searches for information about a particular subject through investigation and experimentation. We want them to discover and interpret facts and findings in such a way that they need to conduct more research to answer new questions. When we pose a challenging problem or driving question, we invite students to wonder and think and ask questions and seek answers. It is through these student-generated questions that we invite children into the learning process, specifically the *inquiry cycle*, wherein questions lead to answers that demand further questions and further answers. Unlike a traditional school assignment where students conduct research first to learn new information, Project Based Learning uses research as part of a recursive process of sustained inquiry.

> Sustained inquiry is an active, in-depth process that is student-driven, iterative, and extends throughout a project (PBLWorks.org).

PBL teachers arrange for research first by helping children enter a cycle where they generate questions (inquiry) and then by letting those questions guide students' exploration and discovery of answers (investigations and experiments) to a key problem or driving question (see Figure 4.1). These purposeful learning opportunities allow young children to experience age-appropriate research through discussions, interviews, fieldwork, and hands-on classroom experiences. As we scaffold students through the process of sustained inquiry, teachers encourage and guide children's curiosity, which further extends students' investigation and exploration. These experiences inspire and empower children to research deeper into a subject and take an active role in constructing new knowledge through meaningful social interactions within authentic contexts.

Young children *can* engage in research when teachers expand their understanding of the concept to include three specific elements (1) **inquiry**, (2) **investigation**, and (3) **experimentation**. Children readily engage in these research opportunities by way of firsthand, authentic experiences that lead them to discover, interpret, apply, and learn. With the right amount of scaffolding and support, students *can* look into, probe, or explore to find out new information or collect data to answer their questions and to learn more about a project topic.

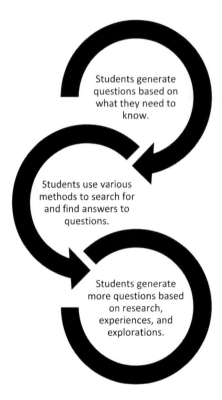

Figure 4.1 The process of inquiry in a project

Expanding Our View of Research for Early Childhood PBL

In PBL, "research" begins when students ask questions relating to a particular topic or driving question, the jumping off point for project inquiry. By definition, inquiry requires students to engage in active learning by generating their own questions, seeking out answers, and exploring complex problems. In PBL classrooms, teachers use the multiple entry points of the inquiry cycle to engage students in the learning process and extend this to include multiple options for research. The goal is to *sustain* the inquiry throughout the entire project, thus encouraging students to dig deeper into the content, constructing meaning for themselves and then equipping them to apply new learning to a broader context.

According to Banchi and Bell (2008), inquiry-based learning opportunities can be categorized into one of four levels of inquiry: confirmation, structured, guided, and open. In the first three of these levels, the teacher typically knows the outcome for the inquiry and provides the question to be answered or problem to be solved. The teacher often presents students with pre-designed recording sheets and the exact materials for the inquiry-based lessons. The teacher also typically models how to conduct the inquiry-based investigation for the class before releasing students to replicate the investigation or engage in a similar experience. The fourth type of inquiry, *open inquiry*, most closely aligns with the vision of Project Based Learning because "students investigate questions that are student formulated through student designed/selected procedures" (Banchi & Bell, 2008, p. 27). In confirmation inquiry, structured inquiry, and guided inquiry, questions are asked to provoke thinking, but the teacher often knows the answers in advance. In *open inquiry*, questions are still used to provoke thinking, but the answers are unknown and warrant investigation.

Investigations and Experiments

Investigations and experiments in PBL are conducted throughout a project, but in a different way than they are in more teacher-centered learning environments where students often conduct research to learn more about the topic or to provide evidence to support a conclusion (Holland, 2017). In these situations, the teacher gathers the materials, follows the step-by-step directions to set up the experiment, makes the recording sheets, and then leads the whole class through the investigation. The teacher takes responsibility for ensuring the experiment "works" so the students experience what is supposed to happen. For example, students might investigate what happens when they place bean seeds in the dark to see if they will grow, or put celery into colored water to see what happens to the stalk and the leaves, or they might investigate where the items in the classroom recycling bins end up at the end of the day. The teacher may also use the term *investigate* synonymously with "look into," "probe," or "explore" as a way to make traditional classroom experiences feel different, fun, or novel, like "Let's investigate how to use a ruler." In a social studies research project, this might look like the teacher pre-writing a list of questions, and by doing so, the teacher ensures that the "content is covered" and everyone is learning the same thing. For example, when children research their family histories using questions like "*What was life like when you were a kid?*" and everyone makes a family tree using teacher-created formats. The results of these teacher-driven, homogenous "investigations" are 20 nearly identical products that display students' ability to follow directions, but do not allow students to follow their own curiosity.

In PBL investigations, however, the teacher may or may not know the outcome in advance and walks alongside the students as they make plans for what, when, and how to investigate as a form of research. A teacher may have some ideas of what experiments students might do at the start of a project but might wait for students to generate their own questions as to when or why those experiments may be introduced. In this case, a teacher plans an experiment *in response to* a student question. For example, if a student asks, "How does water swirl up to help a plant grow?" the teacher might introduce the celery/food coloring experiment so that students can observe water moving up the stem of a celery stalk and into the leaves. Or students might take weekly measurements of the height of different types of plants through direct comparisons, rulers, or snap cubes. They might use the data to determine how to stagger the plants in three rows, so all plants are visible during their peak growing season. Researching in this manner, through investigations, mirrors the work that adults do at their jobs, in their homes, and as citizens in their community.

Project Based Learning asks students to actively engage in three elements of research in this sustained inquiry process – inquiry, investigation, and experimentation – and *for young children, this is no different.* Early childhood teachers play an essential role in this process by facilitating conversations and questions so that their students actively guide and take part in the inquiry process. By the same token, teachers design and plan for learning experiences that place students squarely in the center of investigating concepts and experimenting with their own theories. This work leads students to ask more questions and develop new knowledge. Project Based Learning creates the ideal conditions for student-driven research to flow within the sustained inquiry cycle throughout a PBL unit.

The goal for this type of learning is to...

- apply new knowledge and social and emotional skills to new and novel situations (the why).

The conditions for this type of research happen when...

- the teacher takes on the role of a guide or facilitator and encourages exploration
- the students construct and acquire new knowledge through observation and questioning (the who).

The conditions for this type of research are set when...

- the curriculum and instructional materials represent multiple perspectives and are inquiry-driven, hands-on experiences (the what).
- the instructional methods draw on community resources and student social interaction (the how).

When all of these conditions are in place, children are empowered to deeply engage in meaningful research. In this chapter, we take you through all aspects of sustained inquiry so you are equipped with a deeper understanding of "research" and the tools needed to implement inquiry with our youngest learners. We share Sara's thought processes as she planned the *Outdoor Classroom* project, marked by the questions she considered when arranging learning opportunities in her classroom.

The *Outdoor Classroom* Project: Sustained Inquiry

As the *Outdoor Classroom* project began, Sara had many thoughts and ideas swirling around her head as to how to make the project engaging enough to sustain her students' interest over a few months. She asked herself: What will my role be? How will I encourage student ideas and initiative? How will I support my students who are English language learners and make sure the project is accessible to all students? What kinds of opportunities will there be for fieldwork? Expert visitors? How will student questions drive this process? How will students apply these new skills and know-ledge beyond the classroom? These questions helped Sara stay grounded in learner-centered practices during the planning process and ensured that her students could engage in meaningful sustained inquiry.

 The Why

The Broader Application of Sustained Inquiry

The purpose of engaging children in sustained inquiry throughout a project is to mirror the way that learning happens outside the classroom, ideally preparing students to be college, career, and civic-life ready (National Council for the Social Studies, 2013). Consider how we learn to do a new job as adults. Typically learning the responsibilities and skills of a job involves reading, observation, talking to experts, and plenty of hands-on practice, and not simply reading about what to do in a textbook. Inevitably, what is learned through these first investigations leads to more questions, and more research. Rarely, if ever, does this end in a "test." In fact, it doesn't really end at all. Throughout a job, and a career, inquiry and investigation are ongoing. Bringing this sort of sustained inquiry into the classroom, even – or especially – at an early age, is one of the most important and relevant lessons a student can learn.

When we learn a skill such as playing an instrument or a sport, we go through the same sustained inquiry process of investigation, reflection, and analysis as we watch others, read more, and practice the skill. Traditional school, patterned after the needs of the industrial era, is the *only place* in which we are told we should *"learn"* just by reading information in a book and then regurgitating it. Why do we think that "learning" best happens this way, when little in the actual, current adult world points to this type of learning?

When our students investigate relevant content and conduct research using hands-on methods throughout the inquiry process, the goal of learning comes sharply into view. Project Based Learning gives children the capacity to learn and apply not only the *content* they may learn in other contexts, but also the learning *processes* that connect learning to the out-side world. When given these tools, young children can question, explore, hypothesize, theorize, and test and then analyze to integrate new learning.

This empowers them to go out into the world knowing *they* have the tools to investigate, think critically, form opinions, and eventually, make choices that will impact their communities.

 The Who

The Role of Teachers and Students in Sustained Inquiry

The role of the teacher is that of a guide – a facilitator of learning – rather than a director (Helm & Katz, 2016; Musa, Mufti, Latiff, & Amin, 2011; Walker & Leary, 2009). Teachers establish a safe space so that children can investigate freely, engaging in open-ended exploration, trial and error, questioning, and theorizing (McDonald, Mohr, Dichter, & McDonald, 2003). If a child makes an incorrect assumption, the role of the teacher is to lead him toward finding a correct answer rather than correcting his thinking outright (Chouinard, Harris, & Maratsos, 2007). For example, as a part of a project to create and manage a bakery, children were engaged in dramatic play during choice time. They were acting out shopping in a store using a cash register. Sara observed one child working behind the cash register, and several children "buying" food items. They gave the cashier some money and the cashier put the money in the register. Then, the customers reached into the register to get their money out to purchase more items. Following choice time, Sara facilitated a discussion around how money is spent in a store.

Sara: *During choice time today, I noticed you were pretending to be customers in a bakery. What happened when someone wanted to buy something?*

Elaina: *Well when Daisy bought the muffins, she gave Sam money. He put it in the cash register.*

Sara: *Then what happened?*

Sam: *Then Daisy took the money back.*

Sara: *What do you mean?*

Daisy: *I took the pennies back from Sam. I just got them out of the cash register.*

Sara: *Why?*

Daisy: *Because I had no money left.*

Sara: *Sam, what did you think about that?*

Sam: *I had a lot of money in the register so it was ok.*

Eden: *But you can't do that. You have to leave the money there. That's stealing.*

Miles: *Yeah, like when we buy food at the grocery store you can't have the money back. Or else you have to give the food back!*

Observing the children during choice time and listening to them share about how they think monetary transactions work gave Sara a chance to uncover the assumptions the children held and identify the teachable moment. When the children all had a chance to share their personal observations (having been in different types of stores before), Sara asked the children to think about how they might learn more about the role of cashiers and customers, and a student suggested visiting a bakery.

A facilitator of learning structures the classroom to invite curiosity, creating a culture in which *all* questions are valued, and communicates to students that *together* we can find solutions to our problems and answers to our driving questions. A facilitator uses the power of observing student work and listening to ideas and thoughts to develop a sense of what the students know and are able to do both with and without scaffolds. Facilitators use formative and summative

Involving students in the development of the driving question certainly is an option for older students, and with the appropriate guidance and scaffolding, younger children can do this as well (Lev, 2018). If you are newer to PBL, we recommend that you come up with the driving question without student input. As you grow more comfortable and familiar with PBL, encourage children to participate in the driving question formation, taking care to include children's thoughts and ideas to create a question that will drive your project forward, keeping the language of the question open-ended, engaging, and aligned to learning goals (Larmer, Mergendoller, & Boss, 2015) With guidance and support, young children can co-create the driving question, which increases their investment in and ownership over the project.

techniques to monitor students' progress and guide learners. Sometimes this means taking on a mentoring or consulting role, offering students suggestions, alternative materials, or additional resources. Other times, the teacher takes more of a coaching stance, turning student questions back on the learner and asking them to consider alternative perspectives. PBL facilitators embrace the iterative process of inquiry and orchestrate learning experiences in ways that support and enhance the development of academic and social and emotional skills of all learners simultaneously (Kloppenborg & Baucus, 2004).

How Will I Plan for and Encourage Exploration and Peer Interaction Throughout This Project?

Teachers of young learners often wonder how much of the inquiry process is expected to be driven by the teacher and how much is decided by the students; so it is essential to have a clear understanding of the role of each. We know that in order for young learners to remain deeply engaged in a project there must be plenty of opportunities for them to take ownership and have a say in the learning process. Teachers must stay open to children's interests and questions, while at the same time holding onto curricular objectives and learning goals. Like the framing of a house, there is a clear structure, but there is freedom *within* that structure to build and design so that children's ideas and questions can directly inform the project. How *much* freedom teachers allow depends on their comfort level with learner-centered practices in general, as well as the children's PBL experience.

How Are Students Going to Be Actively Involved in Acquiring Knowledge?

Immediately following the entry event (where children first visited the outdoor classroom and Sara introduced the driving question for the project), Sara asked students for their ideas about what they would like to have in their outdoor classroom. She stayed in her role as facilitator, intentionally asking probing questions to guide students rather than telling them what to do or how to do it. She did *not* tell them what she thought was the best idea or what she thought was possible. Thinking about what the students wanted to know and what she had intentionally identified as teaching points, Sara began to fill in the framing of her project with more detailed lessons, materials, resources, and experiences.

She thought of several potential field trips but did not make plans until the students could explore, question, and talk about the possibilities. Sara wanted to make sure students' interests drove the inquiry, so she intentionally let students' questions and her observations of their interactions between each other be the deciding factors for their experiences. She also wanted to make sure she planned for plenty of collaborative conversations and learning experiences between students, so that children could learn from and with their peers. If a child had a question, Sara did not answer the question immediately. She instead wrote the question on the board to return to later the same day or added it to their growing list of what they needed to know for further exploration. In doing this, Sara was able to highlight for students how often *they* were answering each other's questions. This ultimately helped develop their confidence and led them to trust in their curiosity and their skills as the project and year progressed.

This was the first stage in *research*. A problem was identified, questions were asked, resources were suggested, and student interests were discerned. While older students and younger students may take these early research steps in different directions, we hope it's clear that this sort of learner-centered approach can be done with young children, especially when the teacher is prepared to facilitate the learning process.

How Will Children Have Opportunities to Draw on What They Already Know in Order to Support Their Learning and Understandings?

From the beginning, Sara had thought through some of the ideas the students might suggest but was pleasantly surprised by some of their ideas as well. She had thought, for example, that they might suggest a dress-up area and a space for books, but she did not anticipate the puppet theater or music area. It was very important to Sara that the class be able to incorporate as many student ideas as possible. At the completion of the project, Laura, the Instructional Aid in Sara's classroom, reflected on a particular moment when children were offering up their different ideas. She shared how she didn't think the class would actually be able to do all the things they had come up with. In the end, Laura said, "I learned that with flexibility and openness to children's ideas, everything was feasible. We *could* make it all work." They focused in on one idea at a time and looked at the project in "chunks" rather than trying to tackle all of the elements at once. The children's ideas were incorporated by drawing upon the resources they had on hand in addition to reaching out to the community for support.

Here, "research" is a moment where the driving question and the students' lived experience come together. A four-year-old in September may not be able to read a book about outdoor spaces, but can use his/her own experience and creativity to propose early suggestions, all of which will further the inquiry as the project progresses. First and second graders can also draw on their lived experiences, from both in and out of school, to successfully enter into the research process. Sometimes, teachers can use the students' background knowledge and experiences to make connections between projects and sometimes we find ideas in the misconceptions and assumptions the students bring to a project. It is important to acknowledge your students' thinking, even when there is a misunderstanding. Starting with what the students know to be true or what they understand about a topic are effective strategies for strengthening student learning.

How Will Student Questions Guide the Inquiry Process?

One of the goals during a PBL unit is for teachers to valldate children's questions as they come up rather than jumping in to give children an immediate "right" answer or giving a cursory response like, "Good question. We will get to that later," only to never get to it. In PBL, "the rigorous process of learning to develop and ask questions offers students the invaluable opportunity to become independent thinkers and self-directed learners" (Rothstein & Santana, 2011 p. 3). Curiosity, which reveals itself in early childhood, can empower young children and inspire deeper learning. In his keynote address at PBL World 2019, Pedro Noguera, distinguished professor, acclaimed scholar, and renowned author of several best-selling books related to education, social justice, and public policy, pointed out,

> "Why?" is the most common question you've ever heard from any 3-year-old. It turns out that 'Why' is a higher order question… Kids are naturally curious and curiosity can be a driver of achievement. When we tap into their curiosity and children are encouraged to seek answers to their questions, they can become independently motivated learners. When we get our kids to utilize those higher order thinking skills that go beyond memorization, they can apply what they've learned to solve real problems. When this occurs, learning becomes more powerful because it becomes a habit of the mind that is integral to who they are and how they see the world.

Teachers can scaffold and guide young children's questioning skills in a variety of ways. One way is to thoughtfully plan questions in advance and intentionally build in time for students to pause, think, and respond. Asking open-ended questions that require students to think is different than ending a lesson with "Okay, any questions?" We want to convey to students that questioning is a learning strategy, not an afterthought. In the beginning of the year, many children may need guidance to differentiate between a "comment" and a "question," so this process may need to be teacher-led and supported. Teachers can also inspire and acquire questions from younger children when they "observe children's interest and comments… and reframe some of the children's thoughts into questions" (Helm, 2015, p. 75). Some children made *comments* about the instruments, for example, "The drum is loud" or "It was made of strings." Sara intentionally reframed the child's comment by saying, "Are you wondering why the drum is loud?" or "Are you curious about what made the instrument loud?" Look for opportunities like these to change statements into questions, thereby allowing students' own interests to guide instruction.

Sara often helped children form questions as a part of the *Outdoor Classroom* project. After the children had time to explore various musical instruments, Sara asked them, "*What questions do you have?*" rather than saying, "Any questions?" Notice a subtle but important difference. Sara's approach points to the assumption that children *will* have questions and that this is an essential and valuable part of the lesson and experience, not an afterthought. This differs vastly from presenting a handout of ten prepared questions about musical instruments and just having the students answer the questions. Embracing this difference is a crucial step in appreciating the *values* that come from constructivism and Project Based Learning.

Teachers are often reluctant to allow students to ask their own questions because they are worried that the questions will be unrelated to the project or "not good enough." But it is okay if students ask questions that initially seem simple or unrelated. This gives us a peek into their thoughts and ideas about the project, which often uncovers an opportunity for additional learning experiences during the project. In our experience, these questions are often the "how much" and "how many" questions that are fantastic things to wonder about, but not essential need-to-knows in terms of answering the driving question. These questions may just need to be answered for or with the students, so the children can free up their mental capacity to identify questions they need to know. However, the "how much" and "how many" questions may also be great launching points for asking follow-up questions that take the inquiry deeper.

Sara's trip to the Guitar Center provided the space for children to ask questions, many of which were quite simple, but led to others that were more complex. After asking the owner of the Guitar Center questions about how much various guitars cost, the children were able to go deeper into the inquiry process because they started considering why certain guitars cost more to make. After finding out that the type of material they were made of impacted the price, the students were inspired to think more about their own musical instrument designs and how they could use different materials. Inevitably, the types of questions the children ask and the thought processes needed to answer the questions evolve over the course of the year as a result of scaffolding, mental modeling by the teacher, the use of protocols like the question formulation technique (Rothstein & Santana, 2014), and the development of critical thinking skills and dispositions.

Take a moment to look at the sets of student questions in Table 4.1, both generated by the same group of students. Notice how the depth and complexity of the questions evolve from November to May. Also notice how the questions from November are close-ended and related to very specific aspects of the project and use of materials as opposed to the questions from May that are open-ended and inspire deeper inquiry.

Table 4.1 Two Sets of Questions: November and May

November	May
What do we need to know about creating puppets and doing puppet shows?	How can we take care of plants and bugs (or animals?)
What will we make it out of?	How can we plant something?
How do we make some of the sounds?	Where could we do it?
How do we make hair?	How much water and dirt do you need to plant stuff?
How can we make our own puppets?	
What materials will we use to make puppets?	How do we feed an animal?
	How do plants and animals stay clean?
How will we do voices?	What do we need to plant a seed?
Will it be hard?	How do we keep bugs alive?
How will we make our own voices loud?	Where do we need to plant a seed?
	How do plants grow?
How will we get the puppets?	How do plants survive?
How do we make skin?	How do bugs survive?
What stories should we use?	What do grubs eat?
	How would we take care of a pet?
	When will we see roots?
	Why are plants different colors?
	What do living things need to survive?
	What is alive and what is not alive?
	How do we know that something is alive?

Reflect and Connect

As you consider the role that inquiry plays in Project Based Learning, think about the following:

- How do you currently honor student questions?
- Do children have the chance to follow through on their questions in your classroom through investigation and exploration?
    - If yes, are their questions used authentically within a project or as additional research opportunities for independent study?
    - If no, what opportunities could you create within a project that could utilize the students' questions for sustained inquiry?

Questions bring students into the inquiry process and the need to find answers that sustain the research. While engaged in a PBL unit, our role as teachers is to support and guide learners toward discovering answers to questions for themselves and with peers. All children, even our youngest learners, are able to think critically about the world around them. They have thoughts and ideas and sometimes ask questions to which they may already know the answers and can certainly theorize possible explanations to their questions. It is our responsibility to communicate that we believe in children's abilities so that they continue to ask questions and trust themselves to discover answers independently from us. When a child asks a question, consider responding first with, "What do you think?", "How do you know?", "Why do you believe?". These responses honor the question and empower children to look inside themselves, think critically, use their existing knowledge, and trust themselves. And if the answer is still "I don't know," a further reply could be, "How do you think we could find the answer?" This small shift supports the role of the teacher as a guide and the child as the owner of his learning.

The What

Determining the Content for Engaging Students in Sustained Inquiry

In Project Based Learning, curriculum is viewed as a road map for a year-long journey rather than as a linear or hierarchical plan to get from Point A to Point B. It is important to identify topics within the year's curriculum that work best for a project while considering what our students want to learn about. We recognize that some topics in curriculum are not well suited for an in-depth investigation through PBL. Therefore, it is helpful to look at content standards and learning goals first. Then ask yourself, "What will my students care about?" and "What do *I* care about?" We believe the answers to these questions will help you select content for a PBL unit.

Sara experienced this same thought process when she designed the *Outdoor Classroom* project. Rather than deciding on all of the content she would teach ahead of time and building a project with a clear endpoint in mind, Sara selected some standards, but as we learned in the previous

Questions to Consider as You Plan

- What content gives the most meat?
- How is this content authentically used in the adult world?
- Where can I go deeper and make connections to adult work?
- What aspect of this content and context will be most relevant to my students?
- Where are opportunities for cross-curricular connections?
- What types of experiences will allow students to apply their knowledge in new situations?
- How might I integrate subjects so that children can make connections between them and see how content is related?
- What ways can I build students' capacity to learn?

chapter, she added others along the way. In the fall, Sara drew from both the end-of-year preschool learning standards and beginning-of-year kindergarten standards. Sara knew she had to teach children to take greater initiative in their learning (California Department of Education, 2008) and wanted to introduce children to the engineering and design standards for kindergarten (NGSS Lead States, 2013). She also knew that she wanted to integrate geometry into her project (National Governors Association Center for Best Practices, Council of Chief State School Officers, 2010), but was not sure exactly in what capacity. Sara knew they would design an outdoor classroom because the empty, uninviting space was an authentic challenge that her students would be heavily invested in. She used the three layers of integration throughout the project, allowing students' questions to guide the inquiry while still meeting the predetermined standards. Sara did not plan the details for how the students would present and celebrate that public product at the culmination of the unit, instead, she left that decision up to her students.

Using students' questions to guide the inquiry meant Sara had to take a flexible approach to planning. This approach works well when teaching young children because it holds the grade level curriculum and standards at the center, while maximizing and emphasizing student ownership and investment in the work. Additionally, it is a helpful approach because it offers early childhood teachers more flexibility with timing to account for the unpredictability of working with younger children. For instance, Sara knew that the public product would involve some type of celebration and sharing of the new space, but she did not set the date until about two weeks before the sharing took place. She wanted to make sure that all of the content had been completed and her students were ready to present and share, so she left it flexible within a set two-week window.

How Will I Gauge Student Interest in the Project Along the Way and Make Changes if Necessary?

The form of inquiry demanded by PBL is based, ultimately, on student interest. While the teacher may develop the driving question and prepare for both intentional and parallel integration, the goal is to allow students interests, and their resultant questions, to guide learning. There are many ways to gauge student interest throughout a PBL unit including basic, outward enthusiasm for learning and the project. Do the children enter the classroom each day with excitement to find out what they will be investigating? Do they have stories to tell about going to the library and borrowing books on the subject of your current project? Do they bring in items for the discovery table like caterpillars in jars, birds' nests, and coins from other countries? Do you see students playing or talking about the project during unstructured times? If your students aren't genuinely excited about the project, consider revising or refining the driving question and including more opportunities for investigation with hands-on, minds-on experiences.

Another way to gauge student interest and determine a project's effectiveness is by observing student engagement levels. As a teacher, it is essential to reflect on your practice and your plans to see where you could lose your students. Here are some things to consider if you are questioning interest and engagement.

- Are the students able to engage in sustained inquiry with minimal support for learning tasks or do you have to work hard to maintain the children's attention?
- Are the students continually seeking your assistance?
- Is the task too challenging for them to do independently or is it too easy and lacking rigor?

- Is the project developmentally appropriate?
- Are the intricacies and nuances of how everything connects too abstract?
- Have the lessons become a string of activities instead of opportunities to inquire?

Often, we think of "classroom management" as the rules and expectations we set for student behavior. Have you ever noticed how little you need to "manage" when your students are excited and interested in the work they are doing? That is because the most effective type of classroom management is planning consistently engaging and relevant learning experiences for your students. So when you start to see the opposite – challenging behavior issues, constant side conversations, social conflicts, and children dependent on your help – it is usually a cue that engagement is waning and you may need to make changes. Consider where students are seated, amount of group/partner work, instructional methodologies, time of day, length of lessons, among others.

> "Rather than promoting a climate of controlling student behavior, classroom management in inquiry classrooms should be aimed at creating conditions that support students' reasoning around conceptual issues and complex problem-solving. Students assume more responsibility as they collaborate and communicate around authentic tasks and investigations, and participate in a community of scientific practice."
>
> (Harris & Rooks, 2010, p. 230)

If you find that students seem disengaged or unmotivated to discover and inquire, it most likely means that your project plans need some changes. Consider modifying the length of time for tasks, adjusting the rigor, and implementing or removing scaffolds. If the lack of engagement becomes a pattern over many lessons, then perhaps the project as a whole is not quite right. Don't be afraid to scrap a project mid-way through if children don't seem consistently interested. Or if you begin the project only to find there really isn't enough "meat" to sustain inquiry, see if there are ways to add or deepen the inquiry. Look for extensions, or possible connected systems or related topics that you may have overlooked during initial planning.

 The How

Sustained Inquiry Methods

How exactly do teachers facilitate inquiry-based learning with so much content to cover? How do we effectively act as guides who help children to discover content on their own? It can be difficult to see that our role as teachers is more than to simply deliver information and cover content. But if we look to a learner-centered approach for *how* we are guiding children through sustained inquiry, it is possible to rediscover strategies and find new ways to facilitate inquiry-based learning in our classrooms. **Inquiry-based discussions, fieldwork, and visits from experts** are all important structures teachers can utilize to engage young children in the research portion of inquiry through collaborative conversations, questions, observations, and investigations.

How Can I Facilitate Inquiry-Based Discussions to Enhance My Students' Social Conversation Skills?

Inquiry-Based Discussions

Inquiry-based discussions are an essential component of developing young learners' research skills. From the project launch to the presentation of the public product, conversations can focus on planning, collective problem-solving, idea generation, feedback, and more (Krechevsky, Mardell, Rivard, & Wilson, 2013). Participating in a discussion increases student engagement and enhances learning by challenging students to think, formulate ideas and opinions, and respond. Inquiry-based discussions can take different forms, depending upon the intended outcomes. Here are three types of inquiry-based discussions.

Artifact Exploration

Plan a discussion that revolves around an idea, image, or artifact. Teachers initiate these discussions by having partner teams look at different artifacts or items related to the project and share their observations and thoughts. The artifacts serve as a scaffold and provide a natural entry point into the conversation for all students. As a way of recording their thinking, children may draw their ideas on cards or sticky notes for the teacher to post. For example, students may discuss and record what they think the artifacts are, how they work, how they are related, or how they might be useful to us in our school or homes. Looking at artifacts may also generate more questions for the students to research. Teachers can start with simple open-ended questions like "What do you notice?" as they pass around the item for students to investigate.

Fishbowl

Use a "fishbowl" format as a means to focus the discussion giving children opportunities to talk in a smaller group, and help sharpen other students' listening skills. Begin by setting 4–6 chairs on the inside of a circle. Introduce the discussion topic or question to students and ask for volunteers to sit in the center while the children sitting around the circle listen. For example, "How do you want to share our learning with our families?" With as little teacher intervention as possible, the inner circle discusses the prompt. If a child on the outside of the circle wishes to contribute, she simply walks in, taps a child on the shoulder, and they switch places. Alternatively, a child in the center of the circle can leave the chair if he is done talking. Teachers are free to create other norms or parameters for a fishbowl discussion and can take notes as children share ideas. Following the discussion, children in the outer circle can share what they heard.

Essential Questions

Begin a discussion by asking a question that is essential to moving students' learning forward. These questions are not always student-generated, but they are necessary to answering the overarching driving question. As an example, read through the discussion in Table 4.2 that took place in the beginning weeks of Sara's third project of the same school year. The driving question of the new project was, "How can we take care of animals and plants in our outdoor classroom?" The children were beginning to engage in research about plants and animals. They had already begun planting seeds and keeping observation journals about their individual plants, but Sara wanted to shift the focus of their thinking to how they might learn more about animals.

Table 4.2 Class Dialogue and Sara's Thoughts

Class Dialogue	Sara's Facilitation Thoughts
Sara: We've been talking about our big question, or our driving question, which is *"How can we take care of plants and animals in our outdoor classroom?"* We've started to learn more about plants from the seed experiments we've been doing. Now I'm wondering – what about animals? How do you think we can learn more about taking care of animals?	Sara had an idea of where she wanted her class to get to in terms of answering this question. She wanted them to suggest asking experts, as well as to make some suggestions of ways to learn, like getting a pet to observe and taking care of an animal firsthand.

When only a few hands went up, Sara probed further.

Class Dialogue	Sara's Facilitation Thoughts
Sara: Have any of you taken care of animals?	This question tied directly to students' current experiences and knowledge. Sara's goal here was to draw on what students confidently knew so they could connect to what they needed to learn.
Narin: I made a home for bugs we found at recess.	
Sara: Oh, so do you think we should learn more about what kinds of homes animals live in? And would that help us to take care of them?	Sara specifically reworded the student's comment into a question, scaffolding others into the conversation and encouraging discussion.
Narin: Yeah	
Sasha: We should talk about the food that animals eat.	
Emil: People are animals.	
Sara: People are animals?	Sara jumped on the chance here to draw out student knowledge and connect it to the focus content standard of what people and animals need to survive.
Emil: Yes, like they eat food, and animals eat food.	
Sara: What other things are the same about people and animals?	

(continued)

Table 4.2 Class Dialogue and Sara's Thoughts (Continued)

Class Dialogue	Sara's Facilitation Thoughts
Joshua: They drink! **Alan:** And they sleep!	**At this point, Sara began making a T-chart with columns labeled "people" and "animals" so students could compare them. She wanted to specifically honor students' thinking by documenting their ideas to refer to later.**
Joshua: Also, plants drink. And their soil is their food. But Ms. Sara, one thing – one question – one question I have is, how does water swirl up to make the plant?	**Sara recognized the student was trying to make a connection between what they were learning about plants with this discussion about animals.**
Sara: Let's add your question to our list of things we really want to know. How else can we learn about how to take care of animals?	**Sara intentionally chose not to answer the question. Instead, she added it to the list of existing questions for students to follow up on and research later. Her goal was to empower students to find answers in a way that was accessible to them.**
Callie: A dog is an animal. **Sara:** That's true. How can we learn more about dogs?	**Sara looked to incorporate the student's comment into the discussion prompt in order to help scaffold student questioning by adapting the statement into a question.**
Alan: I have a dog! I know everything about dogs! **Sara:** Should we ask you?	**Sara took this opportunity to draw on the student's expertise and knowledge. She used this to help guide students closer toward speaking with "experts" as a way to learn more.**

(continued)

Table 4.2 Class Dialogue and Sara's Thoughts (Continued)

Class Dialogue	Sara's Facilitation Thoughts
Sara: So, one way we can learn more animals is to ask an expert, like Alan. Let's look at our chart. So far, here are some ways we can learn more about taking care of animals: we can research and learn about different kinds of animal homes, we can talk about the food that animals eat so they can survive, and we can ask an expert. We also know that animals and people have some similarities in terms of what they need to survive. And Joshua also said that plants need to drink in order to grow and survive. We already planted our seeds and have been watering them, and observing them grow, so that might also give us some answers. So what should we do next?	**Sara paused to summarize and consolidate research ideas and students' answers to questions. She also made sure to highlight the connection between plants and animals since this was another learning goal for the project.**
Risa: I know a lot about lizards because I have a lizard. Maybe we should have a class pet like a lizard.	**If the idea of having a pet had not explicitly come from a child, Sara would have said something like "it sounds like a lot of you who are animal experts have pets at home. I wonder how we could become more of an animal "expert." Most likely, that would have led to a child saying, "we should have a class pet!" If it didn't, Sara would have probed further, saying something to the effect of "I wonder what would happen if we got a class pet?"**
Alan: Or a dog?	
Sara: Well, I'm not sure we can have a dog in our class…	
Joshua: Because a dog is too active?	
Sara: Maybe. But we can talk about other kinds of pets we might be able to get to help us learn how to take care of animals.	**Sara knew part of the project plan was to get a class pet, so she led students to this next step. It didn't matter that she wasn't sure what kind of pet they would get; she knew she wanted the idea to come from her students hence her concluding statement here.**

This discussion took place first thing in the morning, right after Morning Meeting. Per her routine, Sara had written the question on the whiteboard for children to read and discuss, *"How do you think we can learn more about taking care of animals?"* Notice how Sara guided the conversation and responded in different moments based on what children said. She often followed student questions with new questions, rather than answering them directly and immediately.

Notice how Sara used questioning to carefully facilitate an inquiry-based discussion all while having a learning goal in mind. She wanted children to suggest the need for experts, she wanted to draw on their own experiences, and she wanted to lead them toward using hands-on experiences to learn more. She intentionally took multiple responses and ideas before interjecting, giving several students time to think and comment. When teachers hold the learning goal firm, they can strategically and skillfully lead discussions in specific ways that honor children's ideas.

Consider the power of leading children to make these types of discoveries and suggestions for their learning rather than just being told, "Let's learn about animals by talking to some experts." It would certainly be faster just to *tell* children how they will engage in a learning process, but the benefit of setting the conditions for children to develop an awareness and understanding of *how* to learn is key. When children construct their understandings, and hear their peers do the same, they realize they have power over their learning. They are not dependent on an adult "showing them" how to learn something or imparting knowledge. Rather, children realize their ideas matter, that they can go in search of knowledge and thus are on their way to becoming more independent learners.

Before facilitating inquiry-based discussions with your own students, spend some time considering what you *anticipate* children might say. Try to come up with questions that will draw on their knowledge and experiences. At the same time, remain open to ideas you *hadn't* thought about. For example, when a child commented that he "made homes for bugs during recess," Sara turned the statement into a question. She then decided that one learning experience would be to observe animal homes and then create their own homes for particular animals based on what children imagined the animals' needs might be. Discussions like these, where the children's ideas are communicated and charted, directly impacted Sara's project plans.

Tips for Facilitating a Discussion

1. Use Protocols or "thinking routines" (see appendix B for specific resources).

2. Extend children's thinking through questioning: e.g., How do you know? What makes you think that? Why?

3. Ask other students to answer or add to other students' questions "Does anyone want to add to that?" or "Does anyone think they might know the answer?"

4. Listen to quiet words ("self-talk") children say under their breath or side conversations between students. Draw out the comment or ask follow-up to that student.

5. Model thinking aloud and wondering.

6. Reference conversations you overhear during social times such as lunch, snack, and recess when you are back in the classroom. Use these to launch deeper discussions.

7. Enter into a discussion with multiple ideas for how the conversation may go so you are prepared to facilitate and guide the children. Anticipate what students might say. Develop a framework in your mind (or even on paper) that takes the form: "I know I want to get them to understand _____, so I should consider asking/listening for/saying _____." This mindset may help prevent conversations from going down the proverbial rabbit hole.

8. Chart what students say, so they can see their own words and so you can refer back to the conversation multiple times. This will help children build confidence in their own ideas.

Social Conversations

Teachers can also extend the research in a project by drawing upon children's social conversations. During snack one day, Sara listened to children as they discussed their puppet theater and what kinds of stories they could act out. One child mentioned a recent visit to see a puppet show with his family and that he saw a production based on a book they read in school. One child exclaimed, "Hey, we should do that! We could write stories and then act those out." During writing time that day, Sara shared the idea she had overheard. She suggested that any stories the children

Figure 4.2 Children's original stories posted on the puppet theater for inspiration

wrote be placed in the puppet theater for everyone. Her hope was that the children might use their stories to get ideas during choice time and in turn act out original stories with their puppets (Figure 4.2).

Observing children during unstructured time gives teachers a window into the students' interests and what they are learning, providing fodder for classroom discussions, project extensions and research opportunities, and future projects. Unstructured social times such as lunch, snack, and recess enable a teacher to be a fly on the wall and take note of what genuinely sparks children's interests. During recess one day, Sara noticed children using large blocks to build and act out a library. They asked her if they could borrow some books to "play library" on the yard. She agreed and then proceeded to watch them role-play being librarians, clerks, and patrons. Sara could have just chalked this up as their play. She may have even missed these interactions if she hadn't taken the time to observe children's play at recess. These play time observations led to a full project where her students created a library for other kindergarteners on a campus that didn't previously have one.

What Resources Can I Draw Upon in My Community in Terms of Fieldwork, Experts, or Other Instructional Methods?

Fieldwork and Expert Visits

Fieldwork and expert visits are two more ways teachers can facilitate the process of research by taking something that might seem abstract in a classroom setting and making it practical and tangible. This can be accomplished by visiting professionals at their places of business or expertise or inviting them into the classroom to share through a practical, hands-on experience. The goal here is to engage children in learning that is connected to an authentic context and to "watch and learn from experts performing successfully" (Sadler & Whimbey, 1979). It is inevitable that students who come into contact with people, places, and things related to their project will generate the kinds of questions and curiosity that drives a project forward in unpredictable, educational, and exciting ways. It's in these moments – either with a visitor or as visitors – that research occurs. It is through these investigative opportunities that students are gathering information for their project and finding answers for their questions.

It is important to distinguish *fieldwork* from the more commonly known *field trip* (Katz, Chard, & Kogan, 2014). A field trip is a site visit that may or may not be related to a project or unit of study. Sometimes, field trips are arranged by teachers or suggested by parents because the adults want children to experience a special exhibit or show. While these may have an educational value, and are probably also entertaining, field trips are usually one-off experiences unrelated to a project or even what students are learning in class. The traditional trips to the zoo or the theater are common examples. Traditionally, field trips may serve as culminating events, rites of passage for a grade level, or an end of the year celebrations; by definition, however, a field trip is not typically something associated with Project Based Learning.

In contrast, *fieldwork* is pursued in direct relation to a project. Students enter into a *field of study* to observe, inquire, investigate, and learn from firsthand experiences. When students engage in fieldwork, they are engaging with the tools, environment, and other resources used every day by the professionals. There are instances where fieldwork is less participatory; OSHA restriction or designated age-limits may relegate students to looking without touching. But these are still valuable opportunities to meet with experts in the settings where they work so students begin to understand that their own project unit is directly connected to the larger community. Learners thus construct and apply new knowledge based on observations of *how* that new knowledge is actually used in the world outside of the classroom. This leads to children developing a deeper understanding of skills and concepts that are more broadly applied. When beginning a project, think about the content or skills you are teaching and then ask yourself, "Who uses this content in the adult world and how?" This question will lead you to planning relevant fieldwork and authentic encounters with visiting experts.

There is one instance in which a field *trip* may intersect with Project Based Learning. A field trip – often more generally referred to as simply a "trip," could spark an idea for a project by either the students or the teacher. A trip to the theater might prompt the students to inquire or wonder how a production is created or how the lighting system works in the auditorium. An attuned teacher will notice the genuine curiosity expressed by the students and develop a driving question for a class project. A teacher might also plan a trip as an entry event in order to launch the inquiry process.

When Sara began to plan the *Outdoor Classroom* project, she thought about who in the adult world designs and builds spaces. The list she brainstormed included interior designers, construction workers, architects, and more. While these were all possible options, she felt an interior designer seemed most aligned to the tasks the children were going to need to do and provided the best approach for answering the driving question *"How can we **create** an outdoor classroom?"* Because her class was designing and reworking a preexisting space, rather than building or constructing something from scratch, an expert visit from an interior designer made the most sense. At that point, she reached out to students' parents and other teachers at the school to see if they knew any interior designers who might be willing to visit.

Sara went through the same process as the project unfolded and the children added musical instruments and puppets to the investigation. For the instruments, there were many directions she could go: concerts, music teachers, performances, instrument factories, composers, conductors, and professional musicians. She emailed the parents in her class to see if they knew any musicians. One of her parents was able to ask a composer to come in to speak with her class. She also tapped into the school community by asking the school music teacher to lend expertise and resources. And when one of her students asked if they could go to a music store, Sara jumped on that idea. Experiencing the music store firsthand would be purposeful at this point in the project and Sara knew she could intentionally target certain aspects of the store during the visit based on the direction the project was going and the children's need-to-know list.

In terms of the learning around puppets and puppet theater, Sara considered visiting a studio like Jim Henson's (which happened to be nearby) or going to see a puppet show and meeting the actors and puppeteers. However, because there was little time left in the project at that point and she had already taken students to the Guitar Center, this additional trip didn't feel feasible. Instead, she asked around and found a parent at the school who was a puppeteer who volunteered to come speak to the class.

It is important to note, once again, that Sara did not plan any of these experiences at the outset of the project, but instead left the space in the calendar for possibilities. The puppet theater and music area were, as discussed, suggestions made by the children themselves. She waited to plan field experiences and visitors until these suggestions were made. While there are definitely projects for which you can anticipate potential fieldwork and plan them at the outset, it is always important to be open to the students' ideas that emerge from their questions and new learning.

In order to reap the benefits of fieldwork and expert visits, teachers need to take an active role in arranging for student learning if children are going to get the most out of the encounters (Table 4.3). This is crucial. Expert visitors may not have experience working with a class of young students, so it is important to prep them by sharing details like how long the class' attention span might last before needing to engage in a hands-on activity, whether or not you have prepared questions for the expert, and if there will be a need for technology.

Table 4.3 Considerations for Fieldwork and Expert Visits With Young Children

If You Want...	Then...
to have a clear plan and understanding of what children will be doing...	visit the field site or talk to the visitor ahead of time. Talk to the manager or docent to clarify the plan, walk through the site to help you get ideas for where to focus the visit.
children to be engaged and focused...	talk to the visitor or manager at the field site ahead of time. Describe your class' language and typical needs in terms of balancing direct teaching with hands-on experiences. Learn as much as you can about what the expert has planned. Suggest sharing any tangible objects or adult world tools.
children to collaborate effectively during an experience or fieldwork...	make small groups that are chaperoned or supported by an adult if possible. Consider the personalities and needs of your learners. Consider how you might group students. For instance, you might choose to have all students with higher academic needs together and support them by differentiating tasks. Or you might choose to mix abilities present in the groups. Either way, be prepared to scaffold for student success.
parent volunteers or other teachers to support the learning process...	talk to volunteers *prior* to the experience. Clarify their roles or what you are hoping children learn from an experience. Communicate adult roles clearly (i.e., parents are supporting *all* children, not just helping or spending time with their own child). Share questions with volunteers they might ask to help guide the learning on a trip.
children to be intellectually and emotionally prepared for fieldwork or a visitor...	facilitate a discussion around what children "think they might see" or questions they have for a visitor. During a visit, you can remind children of their questions and give them a chance to ask them, or you can ask for them if they feel shy. Talk to students about expectations for the field site (i.e., if it is a quiet space, or the importance of staying with the group since it might be crowded).
children to document their learning...	give them clipboards with pencils to jot down observations and share what they noticed and/or learned after the trip or visitor.
children to reflect on the experience upon their return or after the visit...	immediately following the visit or experience: chart students' observations (What did you see?), create a class book, or write a thank-you note to the visitor sharing what children learned.

Aim high when you plan for fieldwork or a visitor; clarify for yourself the ideal experience. You can always amend the plan if things don't end up working as anticipated or aren't possible for any variety of reasons. For example, when emailing parents about building the puppet theater, Sara said, "My *hope* is for children to design and build the puppet theater themselves. Does anyone have expertise in this area or know someone who does?" She told the interior designer, "My *ideal* is for the children to come up with all the areas they want, create a design, and make it happen. Can you help with that?"

Prior to the classroom visit, Sara spoke to the designer, describing both the project and what she hoped children would take away from the expert's visit. Sara also learned what the designer's process looked like in advance of the visit. Sara also asks visiting experts what tangible objects or tools they can bring with them and includes this in reminder emails. Once they had discussed everything, she co-planned an activity with the designer. They decided students would create Idea Boards for the space during the visit, followed by the interior designer giving feedback on their designs.

When you are clear about your vision, experts will draw on their knowledge and usually work to support you and your students as best they can. They may need guidance in how to talk with young children or how to structure their visit to ensure maximum engagement. The time and energy you invest in this process at the outset is worth it; these research opportunities are invaluable both for the project at hand, and to open children's eyes and minds to the larger world.

Expert visits, fieldwork, and inquiry-based conversations play key roles in students' successfully engaging in sustained inquiry. How you arrange for student learning and the opportunities you structure for students to ask, research, and answer their questions will directly impact how deeply the students engage and how they connect their learning to new contexts and situations.

What Hands-on Classroom Experiences Can I Include in the Project?

Young children will further research new ideas and apply newly learned concepts when they have ample opportunities for open-ended play and uninterrupted, unstructured conversations with their peers. This is yet another important aspect of sustained inquiry. In the context of a PBL unit, teachers should plan for these experiences by integrating structures like choice time and, as mentioned above, by taking the time to listen to children's conversations during social times like recess, snack, and lunch. When teachers make time for children to investigate and process learning alongside their peers, they encourage students to learn and explore new concepts and ideas on their own terms in relevant, meaningful ways. For our young learners, especially, these opportunities provide low-stakes ways to engage in sustained inquiry.

Choice Time

There is extensive research that supports the importance of play in children developing theories and understandings about the world (Dickey, Castle, & Pryor, 2016; Mraz, Porcelli, & Tyler, 2016; Rushton, Juola-Rushton, & Larkin, 2010). "Play allows children to use their creativity while developing their imagination, dexterity, and physical, cognitive, and emotional strength" (Ginsburg, 2007, p. 183). Through play, children learn to take risks, develop their own personalities, express themselves, and practice social negotiation with peers (Ashiabi, 2007; Dickey, et al., 2016; Elkind, 2008; Ramani & Brownell, 2013). With new demands on academics in terms of instructional minutes, some early childhood teachers feel they cannot regularly include these open-ended learning times in their day. We believe, however, that including choice time (or something similar) enables children to investigate materials, share theories, make predictions and connections, and act out scenarios that parallel the adult world. Choice time is an effective research opportunity for young students because the skills and content that students practice carry over into the discussions and can drive the learning forward.

In the *Outdoor Classroom* project, Sara's work times were directly related to the research the students were conducting for that portion of the overall unit. When the students were learning about music, Sara placed musical instruments she had borrowed from the music teacher in a bin during choice time. She invited children to play with these instruments but gave them no direct instruction. Instead, she observed how they interacted with each other and the instruments. She noticed that children were playing with the instruments in small groups, creating rhythms and singing specific songs. They sometimes asked Sara to play music on her computer to accompany them. She even witnessed children taking on different adult roles; one child picked up a stick and pretended it was conductor's baton and acted as a conductor in an orchestra, while other students were the musicians. When the children were researching the design process, the choice time options included exploring with rulers, measuring tape and other design tools, and using magazine photos and images to create Idea Boards. Throughout each phase of the project, Sara structured each version of choice time to encourage children to freely select what they wanted to play with and investigate.

 ## The When and Where

Incorporating Sustained Inquiry Into the Instructional Day

In Chapter 3, we explored several ways that you can integrate content into your regular schedule. In a literal sense, research can happen whenever students are engaged in inquiry-oriented learning experiences and investigations. We don't announce that it is "inquiry time" or designate a particular hour in the school day for "research." Rather, we look for ways to authentically create opportunities to inquire and wonder within different parts of the day. Depending upon where the class is in the project, learning experiences may be heavier on inquiring and generating questions and at other times, on exploration and investigation. Scientific inquiry is similarly recursive, not step-by-step, and research happens frequently throughout the learning process (Llewellyn, 2013). Since research happens whenever the learners are engaged in the inquiry cycle, it stands to reason that research happens wherever the students are learning. This could be in the classroom, in an outdoor space, at the music store, in the school garden, on the playground, at the library, etc.

 ## Effective Integration

Facilitating developmentally appropriate research experiences for our young learners is key to successful Project Based Learning. Using an inquiry approach to learning invites the students into the learning process, developing essential skills in a variety of ways. When students have input into what they are learning, where, when, and how they are learning, they begin to identify themselves as learners. The quote below punctuates how the essential elements of sustained inquiry are aligned with both the constructivist principles and many of the learner-centered premises:

> *Inquiry approaches to learning require students to take an **active role** in knowledge construction to solve a problem or probe a question. Inquiry may take place in a single day's lesson or a long-term project, centered around a question or problem that requires conjecture, investigation, and analysis, using tools like research or modeling. The key is that – rather than just receiving and memorizing pieces of information – inquiry provokes **active learning** and **student agency** through questioning, consideration of possibilities and alternatives, and applications of knowledge.*
>
> (Darling-Hammond, Flook, Cook-Harvey, Barron, & Osher, 2019, p. 20)

Overcoming the Misconception

Young children are natural researchers because they inherently inquire about everything. As they interact with the world around them, they wonder, investigate, theorize, and seek answers to their questions. When they are interested and curious, they seek to understand. In fact, children's level of engagement and interest are heightened when there is a challenging problem or question to tackle and when they must work to find the solution or the answer.

We can see that children at this young age can undisputedly participate in the research that Project Based Learning requires. The research most likely looks different than what we traditionally imagine, but it is research just the same. Expanding our view of research to include a careful or diligent search and a studious **inquiry** or examination, especially **investigation** or **experimentation** aimed at the discovery and interpretation of facts, allows for rich academic, social, and emotional learning experiences with positive long-term outcomes.

References

Ashiabi, G. S. (2007). Play in the preschool classroom: Its socioemotional significance and the teacher's role in play. *Early Childhood Education Journal*, *35*(2), 199–207. doi:10.1007/s10643-007-0165-8.

Banchi, H., & Bell, R. (2008). The many levels of inquiry. *Science and Children*, *46*(2), 26–29.

California Department of Education. (2008). *California preschool learning foundations* (Vol. 1). Sacramento, CA: Author. Retrieved from: https://www.cde.ca.gov/sp/cd/re/documents/preschoollf.pdf

Chouinard, M., Harris, P. L., & Maratsos, M. (2007). Children's questions: A mechanism for cognitive development. *Monographs of the Society for Research in Child Development*, *72*(1), 1–129.

Darling-Hammond, L., Flook, L., Cook-Harvey, C., Barron, B., & Osher, D. (2019). Implications for educational practice of the science of learning and development. *Applied Developmental Science*, 1–44. doi:10.1080/10888691.2018.1537791.

Dickey, K., Castle, K., & Pryor, K. (2016). Reclaiming play in schools. *Childhood Education*, *92*(2), 111–117.

Elkind, D. (2008). The power of play: Learning what comes naturally. *American Journal of Play*, *1*(1), 1–6.

Ginsburg, K. R. (2007). The importance of play in promoting healthy child development and maintaining strong parent-child bonds. *Pediatrics*, *119*(1), 182–191. doi:10.1542/peds.2006-2697.

Harris, C., & Rooks, D. (2010). Managing inquiry-based science: Challenges in enacting complex science instruction in elementary and middle school classrooms. *Journal of Science Teacher Education*, *21*(2), 227–240. doi:10.1007/s10972-009-9172-5.

Helm, J. (2015). *Becoming young thinkers: Deep project work in the classroom*. New York, NY: Teachers College Press.

Helm, J., & Katz, L. (2016). *Young investigators: The project approach in the early years* (3rd ed.). New York, NY: Teachers College Press.

Holland, B. (2017). Inquiry and the research process: Tips for ensuring that your students' research fosters genuine inquiry Retrieved from: https://www.edutopia.org/article/inquiry-and-research-process

Katz, L., Chard, S., & Kogan, Y. (2014). *Engaging children's minds: The project approach* (3rd ed.). Santa Barbara, CA: Praeger.

Kloppenborg, T. J., & Baucus, M. S. (2004). Project management in local nonprofit organizations: Engaging students in problem-based learning. *Journal of Management Education, 28*(5), 610–629. doi:10.1177/1052562904266008.

Krechevsky, M., Mardell, B., Rivard, M., & Wilson, D. (2013). *Visible learners: Promoting Reggio-inspired approaches in all schools*. San Francisco, CA: Jossey-Bass.

Larmer, J., Mergendoller, J., & Boss, S. (2015). *Setting the standard for project-based learning*. Alexandria, VA: ASCD.

Lev, S. (2018, July 6). "Lowering the Driving (Question) Age" [Blog Post]. Retrieved from: https://www.pblworks.org/blog/lowering-driving-question-age

Llewellyn, D. (2013). *Inquire within: Implementing inquiry- and argument-based science standards in grades 3-8* (3rd ed.). Thousand Oaks, CA: Corwin Press.

McDonald, J., Mohr, N., Dichter, A., & McDonald, E. (2003). *The power of protocols: An educator's guide to better practice*. New York, NY: Teachers College Press.

Mraz, K., Porcelli, A., & Tyler, C. (2016). *Purposeful play: A teacher's guide to igniting deep & joyful learning across the day*. Portsmouth, NH: Heinemann.

Musa, F., Mufti, N., Latiff, R. A., & Amin, M. M. (2011). Project-based learning: Promoting meaningful language learning for workplace skills. *Procedia Social and Behavioral Sciences, 18*, 187–195. doi:10.1016/j.sbspro.2011.05.027.

National Council for the Social Studies (NCSS). (2013). *The college, career, and civic life (C3) framework for social studies state standards: Guidance for enhancing the rigor of K-12 civics, economics, geography, and history*. Silver Spring, MD: Author.

National Governors Association Center for Best Practices and Council of Chief State School Officers. (2010). *Common core state standards for mathematics*. Washington, DC: Author.

NGSS Lead States (2013). *Next generation science standards: For states, by states, Appendix C*. Washington, DC: The National Academies Press.

Noguera, P. (2019). Keynote address, PBL World, Napa, CA, June 19, 2019.

Ramani, G. B., & Brownell, C. A. (2013). Preschoolers' cooperative problem solving: Integrating play and problem solving. *Journal of Early Childhood Research, 12*(1), 92–108. doi:10.1177/1476718X13498337.

research (2019). In Merriam-Webster.com. Retrieved June 6, 2019, from: https://www.merriam-webster.com/dictionary/research

Rothstein, D., & Santana, L. (2011). *Make just one change: Teach students to ask their own questions*. Cambridge, MA: Harvard Education Press.

Rushton, S., Juola-Rushton, A., & Larkin, E. (2010). Neuroscience, play and early childhood education: Connections, implications and assessment. *Early Childhood Education Journal, 37*(5), 351–361. doi:10.1007/s10643-009-0359-3.

Sadler Jr., W. A., & Whimbey, A. (1979, April). Developing a cognitive skills approach to teaching. *Paper presented at the conference of the American Association of Higher Education*, Washington, DC.

Walker, A., & Leary, H. (2009). A problem based learning meta-analysis: Differences across problem types, implementation types, disciplines, and assessment levels. *Interdisciplinary Journal of Problem-Based Learning, 3*(1), 6–28.

Purposeful Literacy in Early Childhood PBL

My students can't read and write yet. How can they do projects?

Many teachers believe that their students must be fluent readers and writers to fully participate in Project Based Learning (PBL) because they believe children will need to access information from informational texts, write down notes, and make formal presentations. Furthermore, some teachers believe that PBL does not effectively teach literacy, so the idea of integrating literacy into projects as a way of teaching these key skills seems inadequate. Early childhood teachers are often more comfortable with traditional approaches to literacy instruction which typically involve teaching skills and strategies in isolation. But this belief contains misunderstandings both about literacy and about PBL. Just as Chapter 4 broadened our understanding of research, below you will discover a broader approach to literacy; an approach that gives our youngest learners an opportunity to purposefully engage in reading, writing, speaking and listening through authentic, age-appropriate opportunities in the context of Project Based Learning.

To a classroom teacher, the concept of literacy is often limited to teaching children to read and write. But the meaning of literacy, or becoming literate, is much broader. Becoming literate includes reading and writing, along with the subskills of listening and speaking, in addition to the **ability to use these skills to think critically, problem-solve, analyze, infer, and visualize** (National Governors Association Center for Best Practices, Council of Chief State School Officers, 2010). Teaching for acquisition, meaning, and transfer of all the skills and subskills related to each of these essential literacy components is nearly impossible if instruction is restricted to just a literacy block. Learning may lack depth when

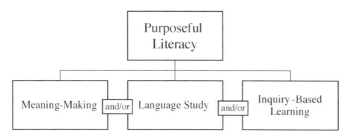

Figure 5.1 Purposeful literacy (Harste, 2003)

things like decoding strategies, phonics skills, and sight words are taught in isolation. Also, the start-stop nature of teaching within a confined block of time can feel disjointed to both students and teachers, preventing them from experiencing and developing language as it was intended. Adopting a broader view of literacy allows us to intentionally integrate literacy instruction into our projects so that young children develop relevant key foundational skills and knowledge in a meaningful way.

If we want students to communicate effectively, to become lifelong readers, and to value writing across the curriculum, then we must give them purposeful literacy instruction. But "purposeful" does not require it to be "isolated." According to Harste (2003), "A good language arts program for the 21st century continues to be comprised of three components – meaning-making, language study, and inquiry-based learning" (p. 8). The three components of purposeful literacy, as depicted in Figure 5.1, form the foundation of our approach to literacy integration in an early childhood PBL classroom.

- **Meaning-making** includes those instructional strategies that allow students to process and understand content through various types of communication or social experiences by way of reading, writing, or visual texts (visual literacy). Visual literacy means the "ability to interpret, recognize, appreciate, and understand information presented through visible actions, objects and symbols, natural or man-made" (Institute of Museum and Library Services, 2019).

- **Language study** means not only learning about phonics, spelling, and grammar, but learning to think critically to understand the purpose for language, how words work, and the reciprocal relationship between listening, speaking, writing, and reading. Students acquire language through experiences that incorporate language, high-quality literature, and daily interactions with peers. Language-based activities that connect to everyday texts help children understand where literacy occurs in learning and in their daily life.

- **Inquiry-based learning** means students engage in learning through a cycle of inquiry that includes questioning, researching, and responding. Every stage of the inquiry process, as described in Chapter 3, includes opportunities for students to use literacy. Pointing out to students how the reading and writing they are doing during literacy time is similarly used during project work and enables children to apply and connect their learning to broader contexts.

Project Based Learning sets the stage for teaching children how to think, read, write, listen, and speak within these purposeful contexts because "projects are rich with potential literacy experiences leading to accomplishments because reading and writing enhance the investigation process and are used in clearly purposeful ways" (Helm & Katz, 2011, p. 104). Consider how deeply learners can engage with literacy when it is integrated across curricular areas and when it connects to the world beyond the classroom rather than being confined to a single "literacy block." Viewing literacy as the sum of these three essential components (to make meaning of language, understand the varied purposes for language in everyday life, and to explore inquiry) empowers growing readers and writers to make meaning of the world around them in a social context by using "reading, writing and other sign systems as tools and toys for learning" (Harste, 2003, p. 11). If we want students to learn literacy skills and learn to apply them effectively, then we need to embed meaningful literacy experiences throughout the day.

In this chapter, we introduce several structures that support literacy integration within a project. You are most likely familiar with these structures, as they are common and effective practices in many early childhood classrooms. Our goal is to highlight how these structures can be used purposefully within the context of your Project Based Learning unit. Some of these elements are specifically suited for emergent readers and writers and are more often utilized in preschool and kindergarten. But we encourage first- and second-grade teachers to reflect on how all of these structures might be adapted or modified to meet the needs of your students.

Note that these structures do not require children to be fluent readers and writers; rather, these structures scaffold children's skills and abilities in literacy by complementing and reinforcing (instead of replacing) stand-alone phonics, reading, and writing programs. While we recognize that there are times when teachers need to explicitly teach essential reading and writing skills outside the context of a project, Project Based Learning absolutely allows for that. (This is not unrelated to the parallel integration discussed in Chapter 3.) We encourage you to find ways to intentionally connect the learning that takes place during your literacy block to the relevant learning goals that are a part of the PBL unit. This will help your students apply their developing literacy skills to broader contexts.

Reflect and Connect

- How could current literacy structures and strategies naturally be folded into project work?
- How do your current literacy practices encourage students to find purpose to literacy and connect learning across content areas?

The *Outdoor Classroom* Project: Purposeful Literacy Structures

Let's revisit Sara's *Outdoor Classroom* project to illustrate how PBL creates the conditions for purposeful literacy integration. At the start of the project, all of Sara's students were four years old or had only just turned five. None of her children were reading independently yet, although a few students were able to identify some letters and a handful were able to identify a few consonant sounds. Sara also had multiple languages represented, and along with that, a range of fluency with the English language. She knew that some of her students' English proficiency would be a challenge for which she would need to intentionally plan and scaffold throughout the project.

As we learned in Chapter 1, Sara spent the first six weeks of school building her classroom community and setting up a learner-centered environment that would honor the many skills her students *did* have, which included literacy skills. For instance, many children could recognize and write their names, and represent ideas in pictures. They enjoyed sharing ideas during their Morning Meetings and read-alouds. They negotiated and cooperated during their play times, often communicating their needs by asking questions or gesturing. They acted out elaborate stories when building Legos and blocks, as well as during dramatic play. Sara knew that any project she implemented should not only leverage these important emergent literacy skills, but also build on them.

Acknowledging her children's strengths and identifying which areas needed growth was at the forefront of Sara's mind as she began to design the *Outdoor Classroom* project. While the project was predominantly focused on social studies and science, Sara knew that literacy would be an important part of the overall PBL unit. Many literacy goals and skills emerged as the project moved along; so Sara sought authentic purposes for their integration along the way. And while she knew it was not necessary to formally assess each of these skills within the context of the project, there were certainly informal observations that impacted her literacy instruction outside of the project context. Most importantly, her students learned literacy content in meaningful and purposeful ways.

Throughout the course of the project, Sara incorporated a variety of structures and instructional strategies that supported the various facets of her children's developing literacy. Project Based Learning is a powerful vehicle in which early childhood teachers can give students ownership over their learning of essential literacy concepts; not just of phonics, grammar, and spelling, but of communicating with peers and learning how to interpret, understand, and make meaning of the world. In the coming pages, we will unpack each of these structures, so that you have a menu of choices when it comes to integrating literacy into a project.

Class Discussions

As we mentioned in Chapter 3, discussions are an excellent way to draw students into the learning process. From a literacy perspective, facilitating a discussion promotes student involvement and increases verbal interactions (Costa, 2001; Kloppenborg & Baucus, 2004; Thacker, 1990). Discussions offer opportunities for students to engage in authentic conversations and are often the space to help students develop questions, clarify ideas, prepare for a guest speaker, or reflect after fieldwork or a learning experience.

This helps develop children's vocabulary, grammar, turn-taking, and listening skills. Because the conversations revolve around the needs of the project, children are usually deeply engaged and invested. They learn that their ideas really matter and will impact the course of the project.

When planning for discussions with your class, it is important to consider utilizing a variety of seating configurations. Discussions are often most effective when children are seated in a circle so that everyone can see each other, and they can practice looking at the speaker. Frey, Fisher, and Smith (2019) call these "communication circles." Circles allow everyone in the class to see one another. Students talk to one another (rather than the facilitator) and you might even experiment with *not* calling on children, rather allowing them to have discussions and work out who speaks when. Communication circles can be *sequential* (each member of the group passes a talking piece or moves one direction around to allow anyone who wants to speak) or *non-sequential* where students recognize the next person to speak (perhaps by a signal of a raised hand or thumb). When students are seated near one another on the carpet, you might use assigned "thinking buddies" to easily identify for young children who their partner will be for turn-and-talks or small group conversations. This not only facilitates the process, but also encourages children who may not want to share ideas in front of the whole class. Some conversations may involve the teacher charting student ideas to reinforce the connection between speaking, writing, and reading. In this case, children might sit on the floor in rows so that they can follow along with the chart or sit at their desks if they can see you record easier.

In each of these configurations, the goal for you as a teacher is to ensure that students are engaging in *effective communication*. Elements of this invaluable life skill include focusing attention, active listening, remaining on topic, and indicating that you have something to contribute, as well as the very basic skill of choosing a seat that allows one to best hear and focus on the speaker. In order to scaffold these skills, Sara used the Interactive Modeling strategy she learned in her Responsive Classroom training to illustrate how group discussions should look and feel. You might also use strategies like talking chips, talking sticks, or talking pieces, so children can practice waiting their turn to speak and actively listening to others (Hollie, 2017). Keep in mind that young children need plenty of opportunities to practice these skills; so don't be discouraged if reminders of effective communication are required often, especially in the beginning of the year. The many benefits of these types of discussions will make all the time and energy worth it.

Sara's project began with a discussion about the unused outdoor space and what children thought they might want to do with it. As the project progressed, the class held frequent whole group, small group, and partnered talks during project work time. As a class, they discussed their experiences with different instruments and talked about wanting to learn about making puppets. They had small group discussions to share design ideas for the instruments they were planning and again for feedback on their creations. In partners, children told one another about their Idea Boards for how they thought the outdoor space should be used. These discussions fostered a sense of community since children had so many opportunities to talk to and learn from one another. After the students conducted fieldwork at the music store, Sara and Laura, her instructional aide, took time to engage the students in a rich discussion. Sara launched the conversation with an open-ended question. Her goal was to leverage their shared experience, giving children the chance to practice their speaking and listening skills while at the same time encouraging them to make meaningful connections with the project content.

Sara: *What was your favorite part of the trip?*
Alan: *The practice room.*
Narin: *The drums.*
Giselle: *Ukulele and guitar.*
Anna: *The bus.*
Sam: *It's not a bus!*
Anna: *It IS a bus.*
Sam: *It was a van-bus.*
Aiden: *The piano.*
Marco: *I liked when the teacher, he teach us the instruments.*
Sara: *You mean Gary? The person who … or the woman?*
Marco: *The woman.*
Ashley: *Riding with… The musical and riding with my friends.*
Jaelin: *My favorite one was when I was sitting with my daddy and Alina.*
Rachel: *Shaking.*
Sara: *My favorite part was probably when there were lots of people in that big room with the band and there were some people on drums and some people on piano and some people playing ukulele.*
Sam: *Me too! Me too!*
Sara: *And it almost looked like our class was playing in a band. (Turns to another student) What was your favorite part – What did you like on the trip?*

Jayden: *My favorite part was Cora. Cora and outside play.*

Jasmine: *My favorite part was… we were… we were on the bus.*

Evan: *We went into practice rooms.*

Sid: *I don't have a favorite part.*

Sara: *Did you like the trip?*

Sid: *Yes.*

Laura: *My favorite part was also when you guys were all in the practice rooms and you were all playing music together.*

Laura (to another student): *Taj, did you like our field trip? Did you like the drums? (No response) Did you play drums? (No response) Caleb, what did you like on our trip? On our music trip?*

Caleb: *Bradley (the name of another student – meaning, he liked playing with Bradley.)*

Molly: *My favorite part was the scavenger hunt.*

Sara: *Joshua, what was your favorite part?*

Joshua: *Uh… mic.*

Sara: *Mic? Oh… the microphone! You were singing.*

Notice how Sara used simple prompts to provide the structure for the children to reflect on their experiences, make meaning of what took place, and construct a deeper understanding of content. Another way to have the students reflect on their learning is during Closing Circles (Northeast Foundation for Children, 2012). Closing Circles often provide a regular time for children to share new learnings or favorite parts of the day. A quick reflection such as a "thumbs up," "thumbs to the side," "thumbs down" can help children to do a short self-reflection of their understanding or experience. Think Pair Share (Kagan & Kagan, 2009) can also help children to reflect with a partner by having students engaged in a conversation for a predetermined amount of time. Regular discussions throughout the course of a project provide ample opportunities for dialogue and reflection, strengthening both expressive and receptive language skills.

Print-Rich Environment

As we saw in Chapter 2, a learner-centered classroom is a print-rich environment, where everything that is hanging on the walls, adhered to the tables, and labeled around the room is directly in support of learning.

Teachers who are implementing Project Based Learning document their projects in visible ways to tell the story of the project, while making strong literacy connections for the students. The use of environmental print helps students develop and integrate new literacy skills on a daily basis (Duke & Bennett-Armistead, 2003). Anchor charts, displays of children's own work, and project documents are all part of purposeful literacy instruction. Consider the following examples of how each of these structures elevates a print-rich environment for students.

Project Walls

Project Walls serve as a designated space to display student learning for the PBL unit such as the project calendar, need-to-know questions, images, and student work. The Project Wall enables children to interact with the project regularly and helps them make connections to their learning. The images and student work displayed on the Project Wall help children recall important events and discussions by way of familiar language, as well as communicate the process of the project with parents, experts, or other visitors.

Anchor Charts

Anchor charts serve as a tool to capture the learning that takes place on a daily basis. They also help students share the learning with the community. The charts that are created represent a focus for learning, may be interactive, and certainly should be displayed in a way that encourages the children to reread and reference the charts as needed throughout the project. Anchor charts are living documents that teachers return to frequently throughout a project, especially to add questions to the need-to-know list or record ideas and answers that have been discovered. Sara, for example, created anchor charts around project plans and next steps from the *Outdoor Classroom* project. She charted: "What do you notice about the instruments?" and "How should we thank our visitor?" Her students also used their anchor charts to indicate their plans for choice time and as reminders for class-room expectations and agreements. These charts provided a window into the meaning-making, language, and inquiry questions which guided the learning for her students.

In the *Outdoor Classroom* project, Sara recorded the majority of the whole group classroom discussions on paper so that children would develop familiarity with letters, sounds, words, and other written conventions of print. Her anchor charts usually included pictures and labels so that children could associate a picture with the written text (Clay, 2013). Often, Sara would write words on a chart and children would exclaim, "Hey, there's a C! That letter is in my name!" or "You wrote that word twice!" Children regularly used the pictures to read the anchor charts later on. For example, when participating in "Read the Room" during literacy centers, students walked around the room with a pointer, reading familiar anchor charts, posters, or student work. Children would also read numbers on a calendar or friends' names posted around the room, on cubbies, or other environmental print. And because project-related anchor charts were so relevant and familiar in terms of content, children often "read" them, even if their reading was not so much true decoding as remembering and recognizing key concepts and ideas.

One effective strategy to use when creating anchor charts of student conversations is to write each child's name next to his or her comment. This serves a few different purposes. First, children love to see their own names in print because it makes them feel valued. A child's name on a chart can also serve as an incentive to participate and share ideas by engaging those who participated and encouraging those who are still preparing their thoughts. Writing down names is also a quick way for the teacher to informally assess who has participated in the discussion and who has not. Finally, children's names are often among the only words young children recognize, so seeing their names and their friends' names on a chart gives them a sense of confidence in their developing reading abilities.

Interactive Writing

Interactive writing is another powerful structure that allows young children to practice identifying and forming letters and words in an authentic context. In an interactive writing lesson, the teacher invites one or two children to contribute to the group text that she is composing in front of the children while the other students practice writing certain letters or words on their individual white boards. Teachers can easily differentiate or modify this structure depending on student needs, encouraging everyone to participate in a way that advances their literacy learning while collaboratively investigating the project topic.

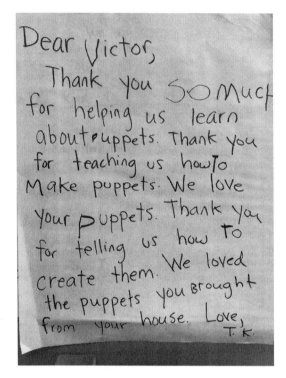

Figure 5.2 Interactive writing sample – a thank-you letter to the puppeteer who visited

Sara used Interactive writing when children composed a thank-you letter to Victor, the puppeteer who visited the class. As a part of their stand-alone phonics and reading curriculum, children had been learning initial consonants and sounds that were associated with their first names (Calkins, 2018). When it came time to write words that started with those letters, Sara invited several children to the board to write them. To differentiate for a student who was already reading and knew all his letters and sounds, Sara invited him to come up and write the words "so much," (see Figure 5.2) since she knew it would challenge him.

Expert Visits and Fieldwork

Each of these experiences supported children's literacy development – their vocabulary, comprehension, and collaborative conversation skills – by providing multiple opportunities to engage with adults in authentic conversations in different contexts and for different purposes. Students had time to ask

Figure 5.3 A puppeteer comes for a visit

questions, practice language use and conventions, make connections to prior learning, and synthesize new information. Students who were English language learners benefited tremendously from using authentic tools and by engaging in hands-on activities (realia) that reinforced their collaborative, interpretive, and productive language skills. Speaking and listening skills such as engaging in a collaborative conversation, asking questions, describing and recalling information from an oral presentation, and expressing thoughts can all clearly be developed through authentic conversations related to a project topic (National Governors Association Center for Best Practices, Council of Chief State School Officers, 2010).

Interviews

In the *Outdoor Classroom* project, the children had multiple opportunities to participate in conversations with adults who worked in fields relevant to the project. A puppeteer brought in the puppets he performs with and taught children how to create puppets and perform puppet shows (Figure 5.3). An interior designer visited during the first week of the project to talk to the class about her work. Children listened attentively as she shared her design process and showed them the tools she uses, including tape measures, paint chips, and "Idea Boards." The school co-principals visited so that the class could pitch their classroom design for approval. Later, a cellist/composer visited to teach the students what makes instruments "work" and to tell them about her job in the music industry. The school music teacher told the students a little bit about each instrument he was loaning them for the next few weeks. When the children visited a music store so they could learn about instruments, they interviewed the store's manager as well as one of the store's music teachers. While these activities aren't usually thought of this way, they are, in fact, all directly related to literacy.

Class Books

Creating short class books immediately following fieldwork or an expert visit helps students to make meaning of the experience by narrating events in sequence through drawing, writing, or dictation. Generating the text for the pages often sparks new wonders and questions, which advances the project through inquiry. Writing and illustrating a class book or dictating sentences for picture captions are both authentic uses of literacy and project integration. Children should be encouraged to reference the anchor charts, alphabet chart, word wall, and Project Wall when communicating their thinking through writing. Creating a class book could also serve as a tangible mode of reflection which could be a part of the final project portfolio and used when students celebrate their learning.

Sara initiated a class book about the outdoor classroom by asking her students to put the photos she had taken during their trip to the music store in chronological order. Then the class reflected on the shared experience in a whole group setting. Following that activity, Sara asked each child to dictate a line of text that would match one or two of the photos. Sara recorded the children's words verbatim, so that they could see the connection between listening, speaking, reading, and writing. Reflecting on the experience to the music store first, both through a discussion and by looking at the pictures, greatly enhanced the quality of ideas the students were able to include in the book. You might also choose to complete these types of reflections over the course of two or three days to allow for more time for quality responses (and to avoid student fatigue).

Their class book for the *Outdoor Classroom* project quickly became a beloved item for the class and children returned to it day after day. In time, some children had memorized the text, others could at least identify many words, and still others could read it independently. The book was a tangible reminder of all they learned on their field experience and the students loved seeing their friends in the pictures. Even after the project was over, the children repeatedly read this book, which strengthened their concepts of print, alphabetics, word recognition, vocabulary, and grammar.

Read-Alouds

Read-alouds are an integral component of any rich literacy program. Depending on the needs of the PBL unit, both nonfiction and fiction books draw children into the world of the project, helping them to make meaning of new (and perhaps abstract) concepts that may be present in the project. When children were learning about musical instruments, Sara read picture books such as *Zin! Zin! Zin! the Violin* (Moss, 1995) and *This Jazz Man* (Ehrhardt, 2015). To learn about different materials used to construct instruments, Sara introduced nonfiction books such as *Musical Instruments* (Doney, 1995). These book choices introduced children to the notion that reading can serve many purposes; not just as entertaining stories but as "teaching books" to help them gain knowledge that will teach them about the world around them.

Read-alouds help students develop questioning skills, learn to read for information, and make connections between the text and children's lived experiences. During read-alouds, teachers can ask questions and encourage the students to respond based on what they heard in the text and what they are learning. Reading nonfiction texts aloud can be an especially powerful tool in helping our seven- and eight-year-old learners understand how to make connections to or pull out important information to share. Language skills can develop when teachers conduct interactive read-alouds focused on comprehension, literary elements, and concepts of print. Big books that are connected to the project topics can be used to model numerous literacy skills for beginning readers. Teachers can support their students' fluency development when they model how to read with prosody and expression. Additionally, read-alouds are essential components of inquiry because learners continue to ask, revisit, and refine their questions about the project and its content as they engage with texts.

Read-alouds can also help by introducing or reinforcing ideas and concepts present in the project. When Sara knew the children would be designing puppets for the puppet theater, she intentionally chose books each day for read-alouds that exemplified strong, interesting characters. She chose books with characters she knew her children already loved, such as *Amazing Grace* (Hoffman, 2007), *Stand Tall, Molly Lou Melon* (Lovell, 2003), *Peter's Chair* (Keats, 1997), and Mo Willems' Elephant and Piggie books in hope of inspiring original puppet designs. Sara modeled her own thinking with her class as she read. She thought aloud about what the characters were like – how might she describe them? What were their traits? She also asked her students to describe the characters: How did they act? How might their voices sound? How did they change throughout the story? Linking these books and these discussions to the puppets they would construct brought yet another authentic purpose to light – *characters in books connect to the characters in storytelling, writing, and puppetry* – in the context of the PBL unit.

Choice Time

Choice time, also called Choice Time Workshop by Mraz, Porcelli, and Tyler (2016), is a classroom structure that invites children to play and engage with learning in a variety of modalities, often leading to symbolic thinking and storytelling. When we offer young children opportunities to explore materials such as blocks, dress-up clothes, or writing tools within a project context, they frequently surprise us by directing their own learning toward deeper connections with desired concepts and skills. As we shared in Chapter 4, the open-ended nature of choice time provides the space and time for children to explore a myriad of concepts in community including developing and sharing stories, participating in discussions, and diving into imagined worlds. Children enjoy having the time of complete ownership over their learning of important literacy concepts all within the context of the project.

Choice time should not necessarily always take place after all of the "academic" learning is complete. Rather, choice time can take place during children's most focused learning so that we reap its many benefits, like promoting the development of language and interaction, and pro-viding opportunities to practice emerging skills (Dinnerstein, 2016). Choice time presents a rich structure that teachers can use to facilitate the learning of concepts specifically relevant to a PBL unit by harnessing children's participation in play and various experiences that are connected to students' learning and their lives.

Teachers may structure choice time in a variety of ways, and there are many resources that guide teachers in establishing choice time routines (Dinnerstein, 2016; Mraz, et al., 2016). We advocate for creating areas of the classroom or "centers" that invite play and exploration of unstructured materials. Centers could also include specific items related to the PBL unit. We also find it helpful to frame choice time in the same way that the workshop model for instruction frames a lesson, with a teacher-led mini-lesson or focus point and closing with a meeting that allows students to share their reflections of learning (Calkins, 1994; Graves, 1994; Mraz et al., 2016). Remember to allow for as much self-direction as possible. Our role is to create a rich environment for literacy learning, not to tell children what to do or how to do it.

In her classroom, Sara regularly includes choice time in her daily schedule, offering students four or five center choices. Some of her choice time centers include blocks, paint, natural materials (pinecones, stones), clay, fabric, and a variety of writing tools (pastels, crayons, markers, sharpies, and different sizes of paper). For the *Outdoor Classroom* project, Sara specifically included dramatic play, block building, puppetry, and music, so the students could frequently engage and play with the materials they were learning about. Children also took advantage of choice time to use their new puppet theater. One child had an idea to hang up the written and illustrated stories from Story Workshop (opalschool.org) *on* the puppet theater. This way, during choice time, children could use the stories to get ideas for puppet shows using the puppets they created. Choice time also allowed children to create original puppet shows using musical instruments as background music. They were often so proud of their compositions that they would invite others to pull up some chairs and watch the shows.

Imaginative Play

Imaginative play is another essential structure of any early childhood literacy program that can be utilized within a PBL unit. When children build in the block area, dress up in the dramatic play area, or play with puppets, they enact both fantasy and real worlds in dramatized stories. Children's stories include characters, settings, plots, conflicts, and resolutions. Through play, children get to use and develop abstract thinking and vocabulary. They employ context-specific language, practicing communication, turn-taking, and collaboration skills, all of which are critical components of emergent literacy and developing new knowledge and skills within the context of the project. "When children create imaginary situations in pretend play, they invent and inhabit 'alternative' or 'possible worlds.' This is similar to what they do when they listen to storybooks, and to what they do when they read or write stories themselves" (McLane & McNamee, 1991, p. 3). Play experiences are especially important for students who are learning English as a second language because the materials and props can support their story ideation and enactment. The project-related materials that we offer to students in the imaginative play areas, and the ideas we casually mention before choice time, can informally guide students to engage with the content in a way that makes sense to them.

After a visit from the composer, children pretended to be conductors and members of an orchestra. They dressed up in costumes and took on the roles of performer, musician, conductor, and audience member. Children enacted working in a music store like the one they had visited. Through this play, children used communication skills and new vocabulary. For example, children enacted buying and selling instruments (using language like "How much does this cost? Is this made of real wood? Do you *strum* this instrument?") Children pretended to hold a concert and invited others to come watch, selling tickets, and showing audience members to their seats.

Another way students can engage in imaginative play is through "Communication Centers" that invite children to draw, write, and express ideas in different forms. These centers include materials like paint, paper, magazines, scissors, and various types of writing tools that inspire children to explore letters, words, and other means of visual literacy. Children might choose to send written notes to each other, make labels for their block buildings, or create signs to post on the walls. Regardless of how students choose to interact with imaginative play, a wide range of literacy skills are being developed that can be integrated into projects.

Written Expression

PBL units provide powerful opportunities for children to engage in a variety of written language forms. For young children, the first step to formal "writing" is representing their ideas through pictures and drawings.

Children demonstrate various representational capabilities including picture writing, "scribble" writing, and the inclusion of random letters (Routman, 1994). As they practice composing with pictures, young children develop greater competency with the craft of writing and writing conventions (Serravallo, 2017). Furthermore, as children begin to develop stronger phonemic awareness and are exposed to a print-rich environment, they begin to incorporate letter-like shapes and letters to their writing, later transitioning to invented spelling. All of these experiences contribute to young children's developing expressive, written language. Throughout a PBL unit, students will work along this entire continuum, from drawings to words, all in an inquiry-based, purposeful context.

Illustrations

Beginning at a young age, children are usually able to express their ideas through illustrations. Even simple lines and squiggles help children communicate their thoughts. In Project Based Learning, teachers can leverage children's interest in drawing as a way to engage them in project work, especially when they are asked to record their thinking in response to an open-ended question, guest speaker, or other project-related prompt, for example, *What do you want to ask the visitor? How do you do your job? What do we need for our outdoor classroom?* Teachers can scaffold children's drawing with prompts like: *What are the different shapes that make up what you want to draw? Can you think of the first part of the picture, and then the next part? Are the lines straight or curvy? Can you make a movie in your mind to help you picture what you want to draw?* (Serravallo, 2017). With this type of support, most emergent writers can use illustrations to explain their thinking, articulate their questions, and give feedback to their peers. Even if a child is not yet able to draw independently, teachers can encourage written expression by listening to a child's ideas, and then offering to draw a picture to represent the thoughts. It Is essential that regardless of what a child puts on a paper, we positively reinforce their attempts because drawing is a pathway to more formal writing (Horn & Giacobbe, 2007). We encourage you to include opportunities for illustration in your PBL units as a way to ignite children's interest in expressive language and written communication.

The *Outdoor Classroom* project provided many opportunities for the students to express their ideas through illustrations. For example, after the

Table 5.1 Student Writing Samples

| This student used a variety of line types to express his ideas. | "Art area with paint." | "Drawers, toys, and blocks on a shelf." |

class brainstormed their initial list of suggestions for the space, each child was prompted to draw a picture of the area they most desired in the outdoor classroom. After everyone was finished drawing, students returned to the class meeting space and shared their pictures. Every child was able to participate in the conversation, with some using their pictures as a scaffold to their verbal expression of ideas. As you look at the student work samples found in Table 5.1, notice differences in the ways that children expressed their ideas with.

Invented or "Brave" Spelling

As children engage with the print around them, participate in spelling and word-work mini-lessons, and practice writing down their ideas, they naturally begin to include approximations of conventional spelling in their own writing. This is a structure called "Invented Spelling" (Bear, Invernizzi, Templeton, & Johnston, 2016; Gentry & Gillet, 1993; Lutz, 1986; Paul, 1976). Teachers should encourage every attempt at writing, individualizing their support as children transition from squiggles to letter approximations, to invented spelling and finally conventional spelling. In these moments of transition, we ask children to be *brave spellers* and put down everything they know about letters, sounds, and words on paper. "Outdoor" may, for example, be rendered "awtr," and this is completely acceptable because invented spelling encourages students to take risks while discovering their voice matters as a writer. If children are continuously asking adults "How do you spell…?" they will struggle to trust in their own abilities and will fixate on "getting it right" rather than on communicating effectively and expressing themselves.

Additionally, in Project Based Learning, teachers can create structures to support independent spelling skills, for example, by placing relevant words to the PBL unit on the class Word Wall or giving children personal dictionaries that contain a section for essential project-related vocabulary. When conferring with young writers, teachers can take note of common writing confusions or spelling mistakes and use the context of the project to teach writing lessons that address these needs. Sometimes direct literacy instruction (specifically spelling and word-work) may not occur during Project Based Learning, but the lesson ideas gathered during project writing can inform instruction for other parts of the day. The goal is to strike a balance. Find the sweet spot between teaching emergent writers essential skills while also encouraging them to freely communicate their ideas.

Labeling

Labeling illustrations is another simple structure that supports children's emergent literacy and is easily incorporated into a PBL unit. In the *Outdoor Classroom* project, when children designed their musical instruments, Sara asked them about the instruments and then she labeled the different parts of their illustrations using the exact words children said. A few weeks later when children designed their own puppets, some children were able to do part of the labeling themselves, like adding beginning consonants to the names of their puppets or for characteristics, such as adding the letter "P" for "Piggie." Thank-you notes, journals, and illustrated reflections also support expressive written language and can be labeled. These provide children with a medium to express their thoughts, communicate ideas, and share new understandings. After the children engaged in the interactive writing lesson where they co-created the class thank-you note, each child drew his or her own thank-you note (using pictures or words). Then the individual notes were collected and given to the puppeteer.

Consider the range of literacy skills and strategies the children were learning and using through drawing and labeling in Sara's classroom (Table 5.2). What are the benefits to having children generate their own ideas as opposed to simply a teacher-generated thank-you note where children might copy words from the board or trace letters in a pre-written note? What is the potential impact on students when they are given opportunities to create their own thank-you notes and letters?

Table 5.2 Student Writing Samples

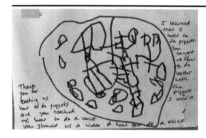

"Thank you for teaching us how to do puppets and you taught me how to do a voice. You showed us a video of how you do a voice. I learned that I love to do puppets. You taught us how to do better with the puppets. I loved it."

The student who completed the sketch above spoke only Korean. He pointed around his picture and showed Sara all of the parts of the classroom when the puppeteer (Victor) and his daughter (Audrey) visited. Notice the students in the picture have speech bubbles over their heads that say "Wow" and "Cool." This student had seen these speech bubbles frequently in Elephant and Piggie books by Mo Willems and emulated it in his own work!

Project Based Learning provides many opportunities for children to engage with purposeful literacy. Through a variety of classroom structures, emergent readers and writers participate in meaning-making, language study, and inquiry-based learning in the context of authentic projects. Ideally, the structures mentioned in this chapter will be used to embed literacy instruction within a project context to foster growth in emergent readers and writers, as well as supporting children's speaking and listening skills. We encourage you to consider every aspect of literacy learning as a potential instructional opportunity within a project. Routinely engaging in purposeful literacy helps students grow and develop, giving you multiple opportunities to leverage the students' learning for future projects. We recognize that some literacy skills may need additional direct instruction, and that is certainly possible while implementing PBL. At the same time, the literacy-rich learning opportunities that happen in Project Based Learning invite students to express their ideas, listen to others, ask questions, and engage with texts, providing developmentally appropriate instruction on those key skills that are unique to our youngest learners.

Overcoming the Misconception

Young children are emergent readers and writers, learning about the many features of the print world around them. Whatever structures you currently use or pull from this chapter to implement, a literacy-rich environment should also invite students to express their ideas, listen to others, ask questions, and engage deeply with texts. Children should know that their voices are important and that there are many relevant purposes for literacy not only in reading and writing, but also in communicating thoughts, questions, and ideas. When children realize that they can bring their voices to these contexts, they have meaningful reasons to engage fully in their literacy development. We often hear that we, as teachers, must "give students a voice." But this is inaccurate. We don't give students a voice. Every child has a voice. It is our job to create learning environments where children are encouraged and supported to make their voices heard. Project Based Learning allows every voice to be heard by providing young children with relevant and authentic opportunities to practice and learn key literacy skills and concepts as they grow and develop. We urge you to use these structures to help your students make connections across content areas, making the "why" meaningful and authentic.

References

Bear, D., Invernizzi, M., Templeton, S., & Johnston, M. (2016). *Words their way: Word study for phonics, vocabulary, and spelling instruction* (6th ed.). Boston, MA: Pearson.

California Department of Education (2014). *California English language development standards: Kindergarten through Grade 12*. Sacramento, CA: California Department of Education. Retrieved from: https://www.cde.ca.gov/sp/el/er/documents/eldstndspublication14.pdf.

Calkins, L. (1994). *The art of teaching writing*. Portsmouth, NH: Heinemann.

Calkins, L. (2018). *Units of study in phonics, Grade K*. Portsmouth, NH: Heinemann.

Clay, M. (2013). *An observation survey of early literacy achievement* (3rd ed.). Portsmouth, NH: Heinemann.

Costa, A. (2001). *Developing minds: A resource book for teaching thinking* (3rd ed.). Alexandria, VA: ASCD.

Dinnerstein, R. (2016). *Choice Time: How to deepen learning through inquiry and play, Prek-2*. Portsmouth, NH: Heinemann.

Doney, M. (1995). *Musical instruments*. New York, NY: Franklin Watts.

Duke, N., & Bennett-Armistead, V. S. (2003). *Reading and writing informational text in the primary grades: Research-based practices*. New York, NY: Scholastic.

Ehrhardt, K. (2015). *This jazz man*. Boston, MA: Houghton Mifflin.

Frey, N., Fisher, D., & Smith, D. (2019). *All learning is social and emotional: Helping students develop essential skills for the classroom and beyond*. Alexandria, VA: ASCD.

Gentry, J., & Gillet, J. (1993). *Teaching kids to spell*. Portsmouth, NH: Heinemann.

Graves, D. (1994). *A fresh look at writing*. Portsmouth, NH: Heinemann.

Harste, J. (2003). What do we mean by literacy now? *Voices From the Middle, 10*(3), 8–12.

Helm, H., & Katz, L. (2011) *Young investigators: The project approach in the early years* (2nd ed.). New York, NY: Teachers College Columbia University.

Hoffman, M. (2007). *Amazing grace*. London, England: Frances Lincoln Children's Books.

Hollie, S. (2017). *Culturally and linguistically responsive teaching and learning: Classroom practices for student success* (2nd ed.). Huntington Beach, CA: Shell Education.

Horn, M., & Giacobbe, M. E. (2007). *Talking, drawing, writing: Lessons for our youngest writers*. Portsmouth, NH: Stenhouse Publishers.

Institute of Museum and Library Services (2019). *Museums, libraries, and 21st century skills*. Washington, DC: Institute of Museum and Library Services, 24. Retrieved from: https://www.imls.gov/issues/national-initiatives/museums-libraries-and-21st-century-skills/definitions

Kagan, S., & Kagan, M. (2009). *Kagan cooperative learning*. San Clemente, CA: Kagan Publishing.

Keats, E. (1997). *Peter's chair*. New York, NY: Turtleback Books.

Kloppenborg, T. J., & Baucus, M. S. (2004). Project management in local nonprofit organizations: Engaging students in problem-based learning. *Journal of Management Education, 28*(5), 610–629. doi:10.1177/1052562904266008.

Lovell, P. (2003). *Stand tall, Molly Lou Melon*. New York, NY: Penguin Putnam Inc.

Lutz, E. (1986). ERIC/RCS Report: Invented spelling and spelling development. *Language Arts, 63*(7), 742–744.

McLane, J. B., & McNamee, G. D. (1991). The beginnings of literacy. *Zero to Three Journal, 12*(1), 1–8.

Moss, L. (1995). *Zin! zin! zin! the violin*. London, England: Simon and Schuster.

Mraz, K., Porcelli, A., & Tyler, C. (2016). *Purposeful play: A teacher's guide to igniting deep & joyful learning across the day*. Portsmouth, NH: Heinemann.

National Governors Association Center for Best Practices, Council of Chief State School Officers (2010). *Common core state standards English language arts*. Washington, DC: Author.

Northeast Foundation for Children (2012). Closing circles. Retrieved from: https://www.responsiveclassroom.org/sites/default/files/Closing Circles_intro.pdf

Paul, R. (1976). Invented spelling in kindergarten. *Young Children, 31*(3), 195–200.

Routman, R. (1994). *Invitations: Changing as teachers and learners K-12*. Portsmouth, NH: Heinemann.

Serravallo, J. (2017). *The writing strategies book: Your everything guide to developing skilled writers with 300 strategies*. Portsmouth, NH: Heinemann.

Thacker, J. L. (1990). Critical and creative thinking. *ERS Spectrum, 8*(4), 28–31.

6

Embedding Social and Emotional Learning Into Project Based Learning
Developing Independence and Collaboration

My kids are too needy and can't work together.

Many early childhood teachers doubt that their students are able to participate successfully in Project Based Learning (PBL) because they are at the early stages of their social and emotional development and lack key skills related to being able to work independently and collaborate with others. Young children enter school as mostly dependent learners (Hammond, 2014), and they appear to require teacher guidance in nearly every aspect of this new structure called "school." Even first and second graders rely on strategies that support their attempts to navigate the learning process, especially when adjusting to a new teacher, classroom, and peer group. Teachers have shared thoughts with us like:

"Although all learning experiences benefit from a supportive social and emotional learning process, the interactive and in-depth nature of PBL heightens the importance of attending to the social and emotional demands."

(Baines, DeBarger, De Vivo, & Warner, 2017, p. 8)

My students are just starting out at school. They can't work independently, and they can't collaborate. Children need so much support regulating their attention and emotions, especially when they encounter new experiences and challenges. The thought of getting them to work together successfully seems like a huge lift. How can young children possibly engage in any project? But young children's initial dependence and developing collaborative skills should not be an obstacle to having them participate in Project Based Learning; these challenges are, in fact, the very reasons to have them participate. PBL gives students authentic opportunities to practice essential social and emotional skills that lead to collaboration and independence because PBL naturally embeds those skills into relevant learning environments by way of authentic problems and contexts.

Social and Emotional Learning Frameworks

Over the last few decades, educators have begun to recognize that school needs to be more than just a place to learn academic content. It must also be a place where children learn key *social and emotional skills,* which include competencies that enable children to work alone and with others – in short, skills that lead to greater independence and more effective collaboration. Jones & Kahn (2017) believe "social and emotional development is multi-faceted and is integral to academics – to how school happens and to how learning takes place" (p. 5). They argue that schools have a significant role in helping children develop these key skills alongside academics and that everyone from teachers, family members, and the greater community has a role to play in supporting children's growth and development on multiple levels (Jones & Kahn, 2017).

Including social and emotional learning (SEL) in a classroom environment has consistently been a part of education whether addressed formally through programs and curricula or indirectly through the values and beliefs determined by teachers and the broader school community. Social and emotional learning skills have regularly

> ## Social and Emotional Learning Defined
>
> "The process through which individuals learn and apply a set of social, emotional, behavioral, and character skills required to succeed in schooling, the workplace, relationships, and citizenship."
>
> (Jones et al., 2017 p. 12)

been integrated into preschool programs for years and are rapidly gaining traction in elementary classrooms. Perhaps you already have a model, framework, or curriculum in place for helping your students develop SEL skills alongside academics. Some schools have decided to utilize a stand-alone SEL curricula, explicitly teaching these skills in isolated lessons, often with accompanying SEL standards that teachers must assess (Berman, Chaffee, & Sarmiento, 2018; Jones & Bouffard 2012; Jones et al., 2017). Certain schools have decided to support students' social and emotional development through character education or conflict-resolution programming, anti-bullying education, service learning, and behavior management strategies (Character Education Resource Center, 2013). Some schools are also beginning to connect SEL to race, equity, and identity work as they recognize the importance of approaching SEL in a larger sociopolitical context (Simmons, 2019). Although these approaches differ from one another in purpose and specific focus, they all address students' social and emotional learning in schools.

Three primary frameworks are currently shaping and influencing school communities' decision-making around how and what to incorporate when it comes to social and emotional learning. These include the work of the Collaborative for Academic, Social and Emotional Learning (CASEL) (2012), Jones and Bouffard (2012), and Frey, Fisher, and Smith (2019). Each of these frameworks helps to identify specific skills that comprise SEL and inform how we think about classroom instruction.

CASEL built their framework on the five core competencies of **self-awareness, social awareness, self-management, relationship skills,** and **responsible decision-making** (https://casel.org/core-competencies/). CASEL has been in existence since 1994, researching, revising, implementing and developing resources to support SEL education. CASEL situates the learning of skills and dispositions related to each competency within teachers and instructional strategies, school-wide practices and policies, and home and community partnerships. CASEL's competency wheel and research base are consistently being used across the country to inform the development of state standards, district implementation plans, and curricular material adoptions. Definitions for each of the five competencies can be found on the CASEL website.

A second framework, developed by Jones and Bouffard (2012), identified 12 concrete SEL skills that are important for developing the whole child. They organized these skills into the three domains of **cognitive regulation, emotional processes,** and **social/interpersonal skills**. In 2017, Jones et al. released a seminal report entitled *Navigating SEL From the Inside Out: Looking Inside & Across 25 Leading SEL Programs*, where they identified two additional skills that repeatedly emerged as important for instruction in social and emotional learning programs. The two skills were "**mindset,**" which refers to "children's attitudes and beliefs about themselves, others and their own circumstances" and "**character,**" which describes a set of "culturally determined skills, values and habits," which guide children's understandings and actions and leads to "perform to one's highest potential" (Jones et al., 2017, pp. 17–18).

Most recent to this publication, Frey et al. (2019) propose an SEL framework that draws on prior research including CASEL and Jones and Bouffard (2012). This third model organizes 33 social and emotional learning skills under broad categories (see Table 6.1). Examples of the skills in this five-part model include self-efficacy, growth mindset, identifying emotions, recognizing and resolving problems, sharing, teamwork, and respect for others (Frey et al., 2019). In their book *All Learning Is Social and Emotional: Helping Students Develop Essential Skills for the Classroom and Beyond*, the authors articulate the scope of each skill and offer teachers numerous strategies for integrating SEL instruction into the academic day. Frey et al. (2019) encourage teachers "to take advantage of the many opportunities academic learning presents for an integrated SEL approach" (p. 14).

Table 6.1 Overview of SEL Frameworks

CASEL (2012)	Jones & Bouffard (2012)	Frey, Fisher, & Smith (2019)
Key Skills and Dispositions	**Key Skills and Dispositions**	**Key Skills and Dispositions**
Self-awareness	Cognitive skills	33 competencies under the following 5 categories:
Social awareness	Emotional skills	
Self-management	Interpersonal skills	Identity and agency
Relationship skills	Jones et al. (2017)	Emotional regulation
Responsible decision- making	added skills:	Cognitive regulation
	mindset	Social kills
	character	Public spirit

SEL in the Context of PBL

> SEL has tremendous potential to create the conditions for youth agency and civic engagement and, ultimately, social change.
>
> (Simmons, 2019, p. 2)

Project Based Learning is an ideal approach for embedding and teaching social and emotional skills that result in students' independence and collaboration because of the opportunities to integrate these skills into authentic contexts (Baines, DeBarger, De Vivo, & Warner, 2017). Children are beginning to assert their independence, make decisions for themselves, and want to initiate learning activities. It is essential that we allocate class time to give students multiple opportunities to develop their awareness of specific SEL skills, as well as monitor growth in those areas. In the same way that children can only learn to make good decisions by actually making decisions (Kohn, 2010), children learn how to work and think independently when they are actually working and thinking independently. Similarly, children learn to collaborate if they are given plenty of opportunities to be collaborators. As with content integration, embedding SEL instruction into Project Based Learning is more sustainable and feasible because the students see the *purpose* behind the learning (Jones & Bouffard, 2012).

Given that many early childhood teachers assume that a lack of independence and collaboration skills prohibit young children from successfully participating in PBL, it is important that we understand what it means to be an **independent learner**, and what it means to **collaborate effectively**. These two competencies help us frame and understand social and emotional learning in the context of a project. While at first glance, independence and collaboration seem to be at opposite ends of the spectrum, they actually overlap. For example, a child's ability to self-regulate emotions or cope with stress profoundly impacts his/her ability to effectively collaborate with teammates. When working within a group, a child may need to demonstrate independence by setting clear, manageable goals for herself and her team. As children learn new academic content or confront challenging problems, they might need to identify and manage emotions. Students practice self-awareness skills such as identifying feelings during meetings or goal setting during project work time. Children learn to navigate social conflicts with their peers when they *practice* having compassion for others and *experience* what it means to understand another's perspective.

It is important that we unpack each competency separately to ensure we have a common understanding of both independence and collaboration, consider where the two overlap/connect, and highlight how independence and collaboration may be embedded in a PBL unit. In this chapter, we will give in-depth examples of how social and emotional learning competencies can be embedded in all phases of early childhood Project Based Learning. We will also share examples of how Sara planned for the integration of SEL into the *Outdoor Classroom* project and will meet three of her students. Through these stories and examples, you will see how children are able to develop their social and emotional skills in the context of a project.

Reflect and Connect

As you consider how independence and collaboration can be embedded in Project Based Learning, pause and reflect on:

- *What role(s) do independence and collaboration currently play in your classroom?*
- *What do you find challenging about helping children to develop social and emotional skills that lead to independence and collaboration?*

 ## What Does It Mean to Be an Independent Learner?

One of our key jobs in the early school years is to help students become independent learners.

(Hammond, 2014, p. 13)

Constructivist principle #4, *having ownership over one's learning*, places an emphasis on students becoming independent learners. In order to understand how Project Based Learning sets the conditions for this, we must first unpack what *independence* looks like in the context of a learner-centered classroom in terms of SEL skills. According to Hammond (2014), in order for learners to be independent, there must be ongoing opportunities for students to utilize specific strategies that empower them to take on new challenges, attempt new things without scaffolds, and draw on skills to navigate their own productive struggle. Independent learners must also have agency and a strong sense of identity (Frey et al., 2019). Our own experiences have brought us to enumerate four key tenets included within this sense of independence: **self-regulation, self-efficacy, perseverance**, and **self-management**. Although young children are just beginning their school experiences, there is much that they *can* do and *can* learn to do independently, and these key social and emotional skills together support a young child's growing independence.

Self-Regulation

The first tenet of an independent learner is **self-regulation**. Children begin to develop their self-regulation skills as early as two years old, when they recognize they can take control over their behaviors (Kopp, 1982). As they grow and develop, children learn to regulate their emotions in accordance with social standards. Entering school for the first time or adjusting to a new peer group in the older grades creates a new dynamic. Although children have started to develop their strategies and tools for self-regulation, they often need additional support structures for the new contexts. In addition to social and emotional self-regulation, young children are encountering cognitive situations that also require self-regulation skills. For example, students are learning to focus their attention, ignore distractions, and follow multiple-step directions (drawing upon their working memory).

Self-Efficacy

The second key tenet to the idea of independence is that children must have **self-efficacy**, a belief in their own abilities, from the very beginning of school. They should find the confidence to know that they need not passively rely on others to give them information, but that they can be more active learners who ask questions, use strategies and approaches to find answers, problem-solve, and confidently share their ideas. In short, children must have plenty of opportunities to carry the cognitive load (Hammond, 2014). They need opportunities to engage in productive struggle that leads to learning, with their teacher as a guide. Arranging learning experiences that allow for students to engage in productive struggle requires the teacher to consider whether the students will need scaffolds before an activity, during work time, or during discussions (Barlow et al., 2018). It also means that teachers must know when to remove scaffolds. For teachers of young children, this can feel counter-intuitive. We are so used to "doing for" young children, but in reality, the best thing we can do for our youngest learners is to provide them with chances to move from dependence to independence by giving them opportunities to develop self-efficacy, so that they can "do for" themselves. Children can develop their confidence through competence when engaged in developmentally appropriate learning experiences where they learn to create order, engage their intelligence, and learn to concentrate for an extended period of time (Dorer, 2018). We want all students to understand they have the tools to make their own choices and to develop the confidence in believing their choice is right (Maddux & Kleiman, 2016).

Perseverance

The third tenet of independence is **perseverance**, where students persist with a task even though it is new, challenging, or perhaps, simply uninteresting to them. In order to develop perseverance, young children need to understand that setbacks, mistakes, and risk-taking are a part of the learning process. Collet (2017) highlights the importance of creating a culture where problems are seen as opportunities for growth, where children can develop resilience and move beyond what they might at first see as "failure." Teachers can support children by offering them specific ways in which to navigate disappointment and frustration so that they are not deterred when they don't achieve (perceived) success immediately. Children need plenty of opportunities to solve their own problems and navigate learning over an extended period of time to build their stamina.

Self-Management

Self-management is the fourth tenet of independence, encompassing three interrelated elements: managing time and tasks, taking ownership and responsibility for work and actions, and setting attainable goals. To learn to self-manage, children must be given chances to experience both time and task management, which can often feel challenging with young learners. While young children may need significant scaffolding to develop cognitive tools to help them independently manage their time and tasks, the goal is to gradually release responsibility to students as they are ready. When children make a plan for work time, we can teach them about self-management by ensuring that their original plan seems doable within the allocated amount of time or by giving reminders throughout work time to help students monitor their progress. Children also need opportunities to make responsible decisions, and once again, this process is successful when scaffolded. Chunking the learning process helps students see that the work can be done, and that it doesn't have to be done all at once. Building in reflection opportunities also helps students value goal-setting and self-assessment. Setting and revisiting short-term goals with a variety of tools, such as rubrics and journals, enable children to practice decision-making, and self-managing time-bound tasks.

Independence in PBL

In PBL, children "develop responsible decision-making skills through community-based projects" (Simmons, 2019, p. 2). Therefore, the very nature of Project Based Learning empowers children to become independent learners. With the teacher in the role of facilitator, students drive the project forward with their questions, discovering answers and presenting their products publicly. These opportunities empower children to develop the key social and emotional learning skills that contribute to a child's growing independence as a learner. Let's unpack these ideas further by zooming in on each the four phases that take place along a typical project path (Boss, Larmer, & Mergendoller, 2012) and highlight the opportunities for *independence* in early childhood classroom.

1. **Launch project (Entry Event)**
   Key social and emotional learning skills and dispositions: self-efficacy, self-awareness, self-regulation

After students understand the driving question, they begin to generate questions that guide the learning process. Questioning and seeking answers to those questions is an essential part of young children's shift toward greater independence as they become aware of what they want to know. Young children frequently demonstrate curiosity and wonder, and if we take the time to observe, we can see where that curiosity lies, even when a child is not able to articulate a specific question. Teachers can coach students toward asking meaningful questions by supporting them in knowing the correct context in which to ask questions, teaching the different question words, and helping students recognize the differences between questions and comments.

2. **Build knowledge, understanding, and skills to answer the driving question**
   Key social and emotional learning skills and dispositions: problem-solving, perseverance, self-management

   Once key questions have been identified, students are given opportunities to use a variety of resources to seek answers to their questions. Identifying answers, solution strategies, or alternative problem-solving approaches give students a sense of accomplishment. With independence comes self-efficacy, pride in oneself, and a greater sense of security. These skills often inspire confidence, which allows students to do work without needing constant approval, checking in every few minutes to ask, "Is this right?" As the project proceeds, there are plenty of opportunities for independent thinking and learning. The "buzz" and steady hum of students engaged in project work reflect their independence, as they work together, problem-solve, and apply new learning. Children are able to engage with their peers and contribute their ideas to benefit the group.

3. **Develop and critique products and answers to the driving question**
   Key social and emotional learning skills and dispositions: self-awareness, growth mindset, emotional regulation, coping with stress

   As children develop their projects, they must be given opportunities to reflect on their work and look toward making changes.

This often requires not only a growth mindset as they must make adjustments and revisions, but also the ability to manage emotions and impulses, and cope with stress. These skills require students to utilize self-regulation and perseverance as they seek help when they need it, and, with support, intentionally set new and meaningful learning goals, monitoring the process of *how* they are learning alongside *what* they are learning. Even if students initially do not meet their goals, they are learning new things within a space that allows them to take risks. This risk-taking often happens when young children feel supported enough to begin to assert their independence and initiate activities on their own. Children also practice independence when they give and receive feedback to one another and participate in discussions where they need to make revisions to their work.

4. **Present products and answers to the driving question**

   Key social and emotional learning skills and dispositions: self-regulation, perseverance, self-efficacy

   The presentation of students' work and new learning comes naturally when students feel empowered throughout the project process. Children confidently communicate what they learned and how they learned it. They are often eager to present their work and ideas to others and enjoy deciding how to share their learning with people outside of their classroom. Public products often take place in the context of a larger community and enable even young children to demonstrate leadership or civic responsibility. In sharing the public product, all children are able to leverage their strengths and utilize scaffolds and supports when needed, demonstrating self-confidence and resilience in the face of challenge. It is important to consider the needs of all learners when discussing with students various ideas for how to share their work. There may need to be specific scaffolds to set up and considerations to explore in order to help all learners feel successful and independent with this phase of the project. Keep in mind that all public products are not necessarily "public presentations," and what and how a student is able to independently share publicly will vary. We will explore public products in depth in Chapter 8.

What Does It Mean to Collaborate?

> *Being a skillful collaborator…involves cognitive, emotional, and social aspects, **used together**. You need to be able to see the world through other people's eyes, which involves the highly cognitive ability to build accurate mental models of their knowledge structures and to keep them updated during a conversation.*
> (Claxton, Costa, & Kallick, 2016, p. 63)

Both parts of the second constructivist principle – *engaging in social negotiation* and a *shared responsibility as part of learning* – point to the importance of teaching students to collaborate. As Claxton et al. (2016) note, effective collaborators can navigate the cognitive, emotional, and social aspects of learning and working with peers. From a cognitive lens, collaboration might include attention to detail, goal-setting, and planning for a group or partnership. Emotionally, collaboration draws upon a child's self-awareness, self-regulation (impulse control, ability to handle stress), perseverance, and self-efficacy. Socially, collaboration involves prosocial skills like sharing, turn-taking, empathy, communication, and developing and sustaining relationships.

Working collaboratively should not be confused with working *cooperatively*. "Cooperation means working together to accomplish shared goals. Within cooperative activities individuals seek outcomes that are beneficial to themselves and beneficial to all other group members" (Johnson, Johnson, & Holubec, 1994, p. 1). Conversely, when students are *collaborating*, there is a common goal or situation that requires the knowledge, creativity, and ideas of everyone in the group to be successful. "One way to do this is through rigorous projects that require students to identify a problem and agree – through research, discussion, debate, and time to develop their ideas – on a solution which they must then propose together" (Burns, 2016, para. 5). True collaboration "respects and highlights individual group members' abilities and contributions. There is a sharing of authority and acceptance of responsibility among group members for the group actions" (Panitz, 1999, p. 4). In collaborative situations, students should be held accountable for contributing their own ideas, while genuinely listening to others, to the end of co-constructing a product drawing from the know-ledge they collectively pooled together (Love, Dietrich, Fitzgerald, & Gordon, 2014).

As Steineke (2017) notes, successful collaboration requires students to develop both interpersonal and intrapersonal skills. This means that students must learn how to manage their own thoughts, feelings, and emotions (intrapersonal skills) while navigating the social situation of being part of a team or group (interpersonal). Since collaboration has many moving components, it is important to teach students the skills they will need to work successfully as part of a team (Burns, 2016). The complexity of the problem to be solved, or question to be answered, should inform how many students are in a group (Steineke, 2017). A task should be com-plex enough that multiple students are needed to contribute input and problem-solve solution strategies. Too many students in the group results in off-task behaviors and too few students make it challenging to have a meaningful dialogue. In a collaborative situation, students should seek to make connections and develop new understandings through cognitively rich conversations and problem-solving. Learning how to take the perspec-tive of others through collaboration can positively impact future of a child's social and emotional development.

Collaboration in PBL

We know that Project Based Learning offers young children consistent opportunities to initiate and drive their own learning. PBL also asks students to collaborate with peers during project work by communicating respectfully and cooperating. Through collaborative experiences, children learn to take another person's perspective or consider alternative points of view while learning to demonstrate attentiveness and compassion. Through Project Based Learning children also develop their leadership skills, which means sometimes students lead and other times they step back and let others lead. Developing these skills and a variety of inter-personal competencies can happen throughout all four project phases, as shown below. Again, we highlighted some of the social and emotional competencies related to *collaboration* that we feel align best with each phase of Project Based Learning.

1. **Launch Project/Entry Event**

   Key social and emotional learning skills and dispositions: communication, turn-taking, respect for others

   When launching a project, children usually participate in an engaging entry event that inspires questions. As a group, children collaborate to create a list of essential questions to guide the project. They must communicate effectively with one another to determine which questions are most essential and discuss which questions take priority. In disagreeing, children must demonstrate respect for others. Children also sometimes collaborate to determine next steps of the inquiry. With young children, this process is usually facilitated by a teacher. Protocols and structures such as the Question Formulation Technique and the Reading and Analyzing Nonfiction (RAN) chart (introduced in Chapter 1) enable learners to generate questions in small groups, prioritize questions, and then determine which questions to share with the whole group. Additionally, creating team contracts, using task logs, or common planning documents support students in building relationships with their team and in handling problems as they arise. We encourage you to look at the sample contracts and logs on pblworks.org for inspiration or direct application in your classroom.

2. **Build knowledge, understanding, and skills to answer the driving question**

   Key social and emotional learning skills and dispositions: problem-solving, sharing, teamwork, relationship building

   Ideally, there are many opportunities for children to collaborate in the context of the building-knowledge phase, but these opportunities must be intentionally planned and scaffolded in order to achieve maximum potency within the project tasks. Students must be taught how to effectively work in project teams with their peers. Sometimes students work with the same teammates throughout the whole project and other times the teams change by day, lesson, or phase of the project. Students engaged in a PBL unit often collaborate with experts in a project-specific field of study, other adults in the learning community, or a variety of other guests. It is through the project that the children learn to recognize and resolve problems, both in their work and in their relationships. When children are expected to share in the work-load and use teamwork in learning situations, they strengthen their relationships with peers, often learning how to repair social conflicts when they arise. Working with peers to navigate new learning provides the context to learn to empathize with others and appreciate different perspectives.

3. **Develop and critique products and answers to the driving question**

   Key social and emotional learning skills and dispositions: empathy, pro-social skills, leadership

   When children collaborate to create a public product, they learn to share ideas and responsibilities and begin to see their part in a larger whole. They know that others are relying on them, so they feel empowered to uphold team contracts and meet group expectations. Collaboratively creating a public product leverages children's natural skills and abilities within an environment that supports trying new things. Children are able to recognize and draw upon their strengths, while at the same time stretch themselves to improve by observing and working alongside other children. In addition, seeing themselves as "experts" creates a positive work environment, and inspires a respect for others and the work that is being created. Equitably taking on various project responsibilities prepares each student to share and then reflect on the process and content throughout the project.

   Throughout these collaborative experiences, students are also critiquing and revising. Teaching children how to provide effective feedback to their peers is an essential component of the learning process in PBL. Young children can use protocols (see Chapter 7), sentence stems, or other feedback tools when critiquing work. Once students receive their feedback, it is important for them to work together to process the suggestions. Critique conversations also help students to gain a sense of respect for others' ideas and practice empathy. Together, teams set goals based on the feedback they receive from their teacher, peers, and field experts and decide what revisions and changes should be made to team products. With our youngest learners, it is especially important to intentionally include lessons on the different social skills that are needed to engage in collaborative conversations. For example, children benefit from role-playing how to focus during discussions. They might learn how to "mirror feelings," by using a Responsive Classroom technique where after a child speaks, the group looks at that child's face and one child volunteers "It looks like you are feeling _____." Working collaboratively in the context of a project helps students develop essential leadership skills like learning to communicate effectively, negotiate conflict, and demonstrate respect for their peers.

4. **Present products and answers to the driving question**

   Key social and emotional learning skills and dispositions: leadership, service learning, communication

   Teams also use collaboration when deciding how to share their learning at a culminating celebration or presentation. They must come to agreements about how to listen when others are talking, how to answer audience questions, and how best to share the learning they did during the project. All of these experiences encourage students to communicate and adjust their register and style depending upon the audience.

You may find it helpful to use rubrics as a tool to teach children how to self-assess their collaboration skills and reflect on ways to improve. Rather than using a checklist of every social and emotional learning competency or a generic rubric, it is important to create tools that tightly align with the skills you are teaching, and expecting your students to demonstrate during this project. Developing a three-row rubric that places individual components of collaboration on separate lines may be all you need for a project. Another approach is to include the essential elements of collaboration within a larger project rubric. Since different phases of the project require different skills, you might build your rubric with the class, adding to the rubric as the project unfolds. This allows you to establish the rubric language while you teach and model the expectations. Showing the students a rubric, checklist, or evaluation tool for collaboration in advance helps students understand what they are learning by outlining a clear criteria for success.

Embedding SEL Into PBL

Project Based Learning presents an ideal approach for embedding and teaching social and emotional skills that result in students' independence and collaboration. As we have seen, there are plenty of opportunities to integrate these skills throughout your projects. And like the integration of academic skills and content, we encourage you to design and implement projects that grow children's skills in both independence and collaboration. It is helpful to select some specific social and emotional learning skills prior to beginning the project and let others naturally emerge. This allows you to address challenges in the moment and further support children's social and emotional development.

The ideas found in Table 6.2 offer some examples of how Sara intentionally embedded social and emotional learning in the *Outdoor Classroom* project, specifically in terms of *independence* and *collaboration*. It may be helpful to refer back to the three frameworks introduced at the beginning of this chapter as they were our reference points in defining which SEL skills were addressed.

As you read through Table 6.2, reflect on how the learning experiences during this PBL unit authentically supported students' as they developed their SEL skills. In what ways does SEL instruction appear to naturally align with intended learning outcomes? If you wish, take some time to jot down a few thoughts on how you might plan for SEL opportunities within your own projects.

The intersection between the project content, processes, and SEL skills is a delicate balance to anticipate, so it might be helpful to note two or three potential SEL skills during the planning process so that you have options once the project launches. As you approach your project design and implementation, consider that PBL is an effective way to support *all* young children's social and emotional development. Teachers should not assume that young children will know how to navigate all the intricacies of the individual social and emotional skills and dispositions without support, guidance, and instruction (Millis, 2014). The role of the teacher is to create the conditions for _____[insert SEL skill to be learned], thoughtfully consider group members and sizes when appropriate, scaffold group expectations for interactions, and monitor work time (Dillenbourg, 1999). As you plan your project, it will be tempting to try and focus on multiple

Table 6.2 Embedding SEL in the *Outdoor Classroom* Project

PBL Experience	SEL Skills
Students design original musical instruments.	• Planning • Growth mindset • Decision-making • Stress management

- Initial instrument designs and drafts
  - Project plan – build in explicit lessons about revision
  - Gave a "heads up" and making a plan for when it can be worked on again
  - Role-play how to ask for more time or making a plan for finishing something later
  - Taught "Growth mindset" concept
  - Utilize read-alouds as discussion starters
- Final 3D model
  - Modeling decision process with materials ("Think-aloud")
  - Put the project products and materials in a "safe place" students can visit.
  - Take photos of the project in process to ensure that if something happened, representations could be recreated.

PBL Experience	SEL Skills
Students embark on a field experience at the Guitar Center.	• Teamwork • Relationship building • Respect for others • Communication

- Scavenger Hunt
  - Work with a partner to share ideas/give feedback
  - Role-plays of disagreeing with ideas, not people
  - Role-plays on how to take turns with materials (clipboard, pencil, scribing, etc.)
  - Practiced using "I messages" to support teamwork and relationship building

PBL Experience	SEL Skills
Students plan the layout of the outdoor classroom.	• Self-management • Organizational skills • Attention • Problem-solving

- Individual classroom layout plans and idea boards
  - Modeled brainstorming and making choices
  - Modeled how to organize layouts and ideas for space
- Whole group layout
  - Led a think-aloud as class evaluated each individual idea board
  - Used sentence stems (e.g., I disagree because…) to support reaching consensus

SEL skills, and certainly multiple skills will be addressed. But we encourage you to home in on the skills that it will take for students to engage successfully with the project and sort them into three categories:

1. skills my students excel at already
2. skills I can leverage with minimal instruction
3. skills my students will need more opportunities to learn, practice, and utilize

Using skills at which students already excel and considering which skills you can leverage will help you purposefully identify a new SEL skill to introduce during your project. In the following pages, we go inside the classroom and meet three of Sara's students. It is through their stories that you get a window into the lived experience of a young child and understand the struggles and successes that come when social and emotional needs and skills are elevated and supported within a project.

The *Outdoor Classroom* Project

Embedding Social and Emotional Learning Into Project Based Learning

As Sara began planning the *Outdoor Classroom* project, she was fully aware of the challenges that many of her students demonstrated. Rather than letting these challenges dictate or limit her project, she saw them as opportunities for *all* of her students' social and emotional growth. She believed that embedding social and emotional learning into Project Based Learning made space for the greatest learning potential in her TK classroom.

From the first day of school, Sara intentionally created a learner-centered environment that she hoped empowered children to feel a sense of safety and belonging. She wanted to develop a classroom culture where children did not need to check their emotional selves at the door. Rather, she worked to cultivate children's emotional knowledge and awareness so that they could develop a positive sense of self and strong relationships. Sara made her students' social and emotional development a priority and integrated opportunities for learning throughout the day, through both intentional lessons, and by responding in the moment. For example, Sara held regular teacher-guided discussions during Morning Meetings and Closing Circles (Januszka & Vincent, 2012) as a way to build a sense of community and belonging. She supported her students' conflict-resolution language by teaching them to use "I-Messages" with their peers. For example, Sara coached children to use the sentence stem, "I felt _____ when you_____" and to give the other person a chance to respond – whether it be with an apology or "Next time I will_____." By teaching students to manage their emotions and resolve conflicts, these stand-alone lessons promoted greater independence.

In the following stories, we meet three children from Sara's class. As you read, think about the social and emotional skills each child is developing, and how the project supported each child's growth. Specifically, consider the skills that led students to become more independent and more collaborative.

Milo

Milo entered Sara's TK classroom having never attended preschool or daycare. A curious and playful boy, Milo loved drawing and writing letters. He was mesmerized by the alphabet chart, carefully drawing each letter during independent, quiet times. Milo was an engaged learner and often shared thoughtful observations and connections. In terms of his emotional knowledge, he seemed developmentally young. He often struggled to identify, express, and regulate his feelings, which frequently manifested as tantrums when he was frustrated or anxious. He struggled to transition from one part of the day to the next. For example, if literacy ended and it was time to finish drawing a picture and line up for recess, Milo would often cry, throw his body into a heap on the rug, and scream, "WHAT? WHY?? I'm not FINISHED!" He needed support to identify and manage his emotions. As Sara got to know Milo, she began to anticipate his needs. Before children transitioned from one time of day to another, Sara would quietly go up to Milo, give him a sand timer, and tell him he had five minutes left. Sara taught him to ask, "Can I have more time please?" giving Milo an alternative strategy to communicate his needs. He role-played using this language so that in those moments, Sara could remind him about using that strategy *before* it was time to transition.

Milo also often demonstrated a very fixed mindset about his work. If he made even a tiny mistake, he would crumple up his paper dramatically and throw it in the trash. "I can't DO THIS!" he would scream. Milo did not yet have language for his emotions. He would often physicalize his feelings through clenched fists and tears. Milo depended on an adult to help him know what to do when these big feelings took over and was unable to continue working if he didn't get that help. Many children have similar frustrations about making mistakes. Sara often took this opportunity for whole class lessons and discussions about mindset, drawing on children's ideas. Children shared their individual strategies for what to do when they make a mistake, like cross it out, turn it into something else, and turn over your paper and start again, and Sara charted their suggestions. The next time Milo expressed this kind of frustration, she showed him the chart and asked him which strategy he would like to choose.

A teacher might look at Milo and think, "He isn't independent enough to work on a project over several days. He won't be able to handle stopping for the moment and resuming work later. He'll get too frustrated when things don't go his way if they don't turn out how he is envisioning them. I don't have time to help Milo every time he has a temper tantrum when he makes a mistake. I can't do a project with him." And what happens if you have other students who are similar to Milo? Or children who seem to present other social and emotional challenges? These situations can make Project Based Learning seem daunting.

What if, however, rather than thinking "Kids like Milo can't do this," we think "Project Based Learning is an ideal way to *support* children like Milo in developing his social and emotional skills"? What if, as we plan our projects, we anticipate student needs and build in learning experiences so children have opportunities to practice SEL skills, get feedback, and have more time to practice until they have gained tools to develop these dispositions, in the same way we do academic content?

The musical instrument design process in the *Outdoor Classroom* project was a key example of how PBL can help young learners develop independence. Through several authentic learning experiences, including the instrument design, Milo was empowered to express and manage his emotions in challenging contexts. Over the course of several days during the project, he had to imagine his instrument, decide how it worked, draw it, receive feedback on it, and then revise it. Milo needed a great deal of support being "okay" with leaving an unfinished product, or knowing that it was not going to be perfect on the first try. Sara offered him support by taking photographs of his "work-in-progress," and introducing him to materials ahead of time so he could experiment with the material before making his actual instrument. He needed to work with various materials like cardboard, wire, and plastic to make his designs a reality, and grew frustrated when the materials didn't do what he wanted them to do. Sara was able to coach Milo to identify his feelings within the context of their project work, which encouraged him to use the SEL skills they were learning. She supported Milo as he learned to harness a growth mindset regarding revision and making improvements to his work.

For a child like Milo, engaging in this project meant gaining the necessary tools to weather the frustration when asked to work on a project over several days, or when receiving feedback to the end of revising his work, or navigating a new material that didn't always bend to his will. It meant learning that mistakes were not a sign of failure but were challenges that actually helped his "brain to grow" and learn new skills (Deak, 2010). In the end, Milo cared about his original instrument and wanted to see it come to life, so he seemed more willing to push through challenges that arose. As a result, he learned to become more independent along the way.

Evan

Evan was the youngest boy in the class and didn't turn five until the end of November. He had trouble managing his anger during social conflicts, and would often grab, hit, or scream at children when he was frustrated. Following these social conflicts, Sara and her teaching assistant, Laura, would talk to Evan about his actions. They would go over alternative choices he could have made and role-play scenarios. In each moment, Evan would seem to understand he had hurt another child and would appear to comprehend the need for different actions in the future. But over and over again, he would "forget" and was unable to engage in effective strategies to resolve conflicts with his peers. Many children began choosing not to play with him, which made Evan sad and socially isolated.

Sara had two, stand-alone, 20-minute SEL blocks each week where the class would engage in discussions, role-plays, and activities to explicitly teach a variety of skills that supported students' social and emotional development. For example, children learned that when they feel angry or frustrated, rather than hitting or biting someone, they can use a "Cool Tool" (UCLA Lab School, 2002) such as "Exit Feet" (walking away to get help from a teacher) and "Stop Sign" (saying in an assertive voice, "please stop"). Children also practiced "I-Messages" by first identifying feelings and then considering what situations make them feel a certain way, such as feeling angry when others call them names or feeling sad when parents say goodbye at school. Then they role-played using their "I-Messages" in imagined social conflicts. Despite all this intentionality, Evan continued to need support in becoming a caring member of the classroom community. So, Sara made sure to take Evan's needs into account when she designed and planned the *Outdoor Classroom* project. She looked for ways to integrate learning experiences that would foster interpersonal skills such as understanding social cues, utilizing problem-solving strategies during social conflicts, and social skills such as listening/communication, cooperation, and what it means to be a good friend. These experiences supported Evan along with all her other students in learning how to navigate the new landscape of community, relationships, and collaboration in TK.

Throughout the *Outdoor Classroom* project, Sara knew she wanted her students to engage in whole group, small group, and partner activities. This meant Sara needed to intentionally find and provide opportunities for students to practice effective communication. Sara asked students to practice listening from the heart, which meant listening with their whole bodies: ears, eyes, voices quiet, still bodies, and an open heart. The class reviewed these "listening rules" daily and also before engaging in the various discussion scenarios (Committee for Children, 2011; Provisor, 2009). Sara made sure to reinforce positive behaviors and then reminded or redirected students when necessary. She also asked her class to participate in "turn and talk" conversations where they needed to take turns listening to each other and then sharing what the *other* person had said. Sara asked the children to describe their ideas to a partner and then share out what their *partner* said during their initial brainstorm of what ideas they had for the outdoor classroom. Using collaborative structures such as these taught Sara's students to interact with others appropriately and to respect the ideas of their peers (Panitz, 1999).

Sara also planned for her students to collaborate in a variety of contexts for the duration of the *Outdoor Classroom* project. She wanted them to make decisions about the proposed layout of the classroom, share a variety of materials, and plan a family celebration. During fieldwork to the Guitar Center, small groups were going to need to complete a scavenger hunt together. After the children made their musical instruments and puppets, Sara knew the children were going to need to give and receive feedback from one another.

Sara knew she needed to build in multiple opportunities for students to practice communicating with respect, hearing another's perspective, and building positive relationships in order for her students to collaborate successfully. In one instance, before the class went to make a joint final decision floor plan of the outdoor classroom, Sara asked children to think through and role-play what might happen if someone had an idea they disagreed with. How might they disagree respectfully? What are some words they might say when they don't like or don't agree with what someone else says or thinks? Children also had to navigate sharing materials when they placed printed pictures on their Idea Boards. Before moving into the Idea Board activity, Sara modeled what children might say if two students reached for the same picture at the same time. Could two people have the same idea? How might they handle that? What did it mean to be flexible? These questions guided her PBL lessons. Because Sara anticipated conflicts taking place, she was able to give her students effective language and strategies they could use to solve conflicts independently.

These types of practices offered all the children, especially Evan, tools that could transfer outside of the classroom. Sara closely observed interactions and coached into challenges, which helped lead Evan to gain independence and interact positively with his peers. After practicing interpersonal skills within the context of the project, Evan was eventually able to use his newly acquired language with disagreements on the playground or at lunch, as well as challenges in the classroom. He was also able to develop positive relationships by working with partners and in small groups. Soon, other children began to see him as someone they could work with, and eventually, they began playing with him too. The safety of the structured classroom environment that Sara created by teaching lessons about respect and caring, and by facilitating meaningful opportunities to interact with others within the context of a project positively contributed to Evan's overall development.

Christina

Christina began TK having been in and out of preschool for a few years. Her mother often traveled, and Christina stayed with her grandmother, so expectations often shifted depending on whom Christina was living with. Her mother described Christina as needing significant one-on-one attention and not really being able to play by herself. When she started school, Christina struggled to adjust to the new classroom routines constantly asking why it was time to do each part of the day. *Why was it time to clean up? Why did they need to go to art or music class?* "I just want to play!" Christina would say. When the whole class met to do something together, Christina would often get distracted with objects and materials around the classroom. When faced with a task that required concentration, Christina would often blurt out "I'm bored!" or "I want to go home!" or "I'm hungry!" Even sitting and listening to a read-aloud was a challenge as Christina had a pattern of asking to go to the bathroom just as children were settling into hear a book or when Sara was about to start a mini-lesson. It seemed that Christina was struggling to adjust to her new school environment and was having difficulty managing the many tasks in school that required focus and concentration.

Sara decided to break the *Outdoor Classroom* project into manageable chunks in order to help Christina and others independently navigate the project. The goal was to help students master the small parts that led up to the completion of the whole project: the classroom design and floor plan, the puppet theater, the music area, a mural, and the plan for the celebration. Organizing the work in this way helped Christina not to try to think too far ahead, but instead to see one piece at a time and then eventually step back and look at the whole. Engaging with the project in this manner also helped Christina to isolate one element at a time. She was able to make small, conscious choices, managing her time and tasks with support from a teacher.

The first task in the project was to brainstorm a list of possible outdoor classroom areas. Although Christina was not able to make any suggestions, she listened to others offer up ideas. The next chunk in this experience was to select images for an Idea Board. With a pile of pictures in front of her (different snack table styles, puppet theaters, musical instrument walls), Christina selected what she liked and glued them on her Idea Board. Next, she needed to "map" the area and think through what area would go where. Making these types of plans and decisions was new for Christina, but she was able to do it with some guidance and seemed proud to share her initial outdoor classroom plan.

The project continued and there were more opportunities for Christina to make decisions and plans. She could tackle single steps like thinking about what kind of character she wanted her puppet to be, what shapes she wanted to include for her puppet theater, or how she would label the blocks on the block shelf. All of these experiences helped Christina to grow into a more independent learner as she was able to draw upon strategies to help her manage time and tasks.

We've listed a few of the key social and emotional skills that Sara's students were developing through the context of the project (Table 6.3). Maybe you've identified a few others as well.

Hopefully, you've begun to notice that there is quite a bit of overlap among social and emotional learning competencies, yet they all point back to independence and collaboration. It will be important to determine the learning competencies within independence and collaboration that you want to include in your project so you can identify the related subskills. *If you would like, take another walk through the SEL competencies. Highlight one or two you think your students would benefit from learning, practicing, and applying.*

Overcoming the Misconception

Social and emotional development is a process that follows us from early childhood into adulthood. Early learners are at the beginning stages of their social and emotional development, but their limited social skills should not be seen as a hindrance to participating in PBL. If we want children to develop and hone essential social and emotional skills that lead to greater

Table 6.3 Three Students at a Glance

Milo	Evan	Christina
Emotional regulation	Empathy	Cognitive regulation
perseverance	communication	attention
stress management	interpersonal skills	decision making
self-awareness	relationship building	planning
growth mindset	communication	problem-solving

independence and collaboration, then we must include intentional opportunities for them to practice these skills throughout the school day. PBL is one of the most effective ways to do this because a project allows students to navigate those skills in authentic settings. The learning experiences created through PBL make social and emotional learning more relevant and accessible to children, thereby giving them essential skills in their work and relationships both inside and outside of school.

References

Baines, A., DeBarger, A. H., De Vivo, K., & Warner, N. (2017). *Why is social and emotional learning essential to project-based learning?* (LER Position Paper 2). San Rafael, CA: George Lucas Educational Foundation.

Barlow, A. T., Gerstenschlager, N. E., Strayer, J. F., Lischka, A. E., Stephens, D. C., Hartland, K. S., & Willingham, J. C. (2018). Scaffolding for access to productive struggle. *Mathematics Teaching in the Middle School, 23*(4), 202–207.

Berman, S., Chaffee, S., & Sarmiento, J. (2018). *The practice base for how we learn: Supporting students' social, emotional, and academic development.* Washington, DC: Aspen Institute, National Commission on Social, Emotional, and Academic Development.

Boss, S., Larmer, J., & Mergendoller, J. R. (2012). *PBL for 21st century success: Teaching critical thinking, collaboration, communication, and creativity.* Novato, CA: Buck Institute for Education.

Burns, M. (2016). 5 strategies to deepen student collaboration: Use these five best practices to help your students build a valuable 21st-century skill. Retrieved from: https://www.edutopia.org/article/5-strategies-deepen-student-collaboration-mary-burns

Character Education Resource Center. (2013). The character umbrella. University of San Diego, San Diego, CA. Retrieved from: https://sites.sandiego.edu/character/blog/2014/11/07/the-character-umbrella/

Claxton, G., Costa, A., & Kallick, B. (2016). Hard thinking about soft skills. *Educational Leadership, 73*(6), 60–64.

Collaborative for Academic, Social, and Emotional Learning (CASEL). (2012). 2013 CASEL guide: Effective social and emotional learning programs, preschool and elementary school edition. Author.

Collaborative for Academic, Social, and Emotional Learning (CASEL). (2017). CASEL SEL wheel. Retrieved from: https://casel.org/what-is-sel/

Collet, V. (2017). I can do that! Creating classrooms that foster resilience. *Young Children, 72*(1), 23–32.

Committee for Children. (2011). *Second Step: Skills for social and academic success.*[Kit]. Seattle, WA: Committee for Children.

Deak, J. (2010). *Your fantastic elastic brain: Stretch it, shape it.* Naperville, IL: Little Pickle Press.

Dillenbourg, P. (1999). *Collaborative learning: Cognitive and computational approaches* (pp. 1–19). Oxford: Elsevier.

Dorer, M. (2018). Independence: A montessori journey. *Montessori Life, 30*, 40–45.

Frey, N., Fisher, D., & Smith, D. (2019). *All learning is social and emotional: Helping students develop essential skills for the classroom and beyond.* Alexandria, VA: ASCD.

Hammond, Z. (2014). *Culturally responsive teaching and the brain: Promoting authentic engagement and rigor among culturally and linguistically diverse students.* Thousand Oaks, CA: Corwin.

Januszka, D., & Vincent, K. (2012). *Closing circles: 50 activities for ending the day in a positive way.* Turners Falls, MA: Northeast Foundation for Children, Inc.

Johnson, D. W., Johnson, R. T., & Holubec, E. J. (1994). *The new circles of learning: Cooperation in the classroom and school.* Alexandria, VA: ASCD.

Jones, S., & Bouffard, S. (2012). Social and emotional learning in schools: From programs to strategies. *Social Policy Report, 26*(4), 1–33. doi:10.1002/j.2379-3988.2012.tb00073.x.

Jones, S., & Kahn, J. (2017). The evidence base for how we learn: Supporting students' social, emotional, and academic development. *The WERA Educational Journal, 10*(1), 5–20.

Jones, S., Brush, K., Bailey, R., Brion-Meisels, G., McIntyre, J., Kahn, J., … Stickle, L. (2017). *Navigating SEL from the inside out: Looking inside & across 25 leading SEL programs: A practical resource for schools and OST providers (Elementary School Focus).* New York, NY: The Wallace Foundation.

Kagan, S. (2013). *Cooperative learning structures*. San Clemente, CA: Kagan Publishing. Kagan Online Magazine, Issue #53. www.KaganOnline.com

Kohn, A. (2010). EJ in focus: How to create nonreaders: Reflections on motivation, learning, and sharing power. *The English Journal, 100*(1), 16–22.

Kopp, C. B. (1982). Antecedents of self-regulation: A developmental perspective. *Developmental psychology, 18*(2), 199–214.

Love, A. G., Dietrich, A., Fitzgerald, J., & Gordon, D. (2014). Integrating collaborative learning inside and outside of the classroom. *Journal on Excellence in College Teaching, 25*(3-4), 177–196.

Maddux, J., & Kleiman, E. (2016). Self-efficacy: The power of believing you can. In C. R. Snyder, S. J. Lopez, L. M. Edwards, & S. C. Marques (Eds.), *The Oxford handbook of positive psychology* (3rd ed.). doi:1093/oxfordhb/9780195187243.013.0031

Millis, B. J. (2014). Using cooperative structures to promote deep learning. *Journal on Excellence in College Teaching, 25*(3-4), 139–148.

Panitz, T. (1999). Collaborative versus cooperative learning: A comparison of the two concepts which will help us understand the underlying nature of interactive learning. Retrieved from: https://pdfs.semanticscholar.org/82fe/2f093ed061f192e7e5fa44db8588d0f48a9a.pdf?_ga=2.137606706.387320780.1561926027-1211785422.1561926027

Provisor, J. (2009). *The Ojai foundation's council in schools program. An introduction to council for educators: Training manual*. Retrieved from: http://dragonscouncils.weebly.com/uploads/1/7/8/7/17878891/training_manual_council_rev_9-24-09_w-o_pixcopy.pdf

Simmons, D. (2019). Why we can't afford whitewashed social emotional learning. *ASCD Education Update, 61*(4), 2–3.

Steineke, N. (2017). Five keys to helping students collaborate successfully. Corwin-Connect. Retrieved from: https://corwin-connect.com/2017/11/five-keys-helping-students-collaborate-successfully/

UCLA Lab School (2002). *Cool tools curriculum guide*. Los Angeles, CA: Author.

Reflection, Feedback, and Revision

Taking an Active Role in the Learning Process

My students are too young to reflect on their learning. And I'm not sure that they have the patience to revise their work. They think they are done after the first try.

Many early childhood teachers carry assumptions about young children's capabilities in three essential areas of the learning process: reflection, feedback, and revision. They think children lack the ability to think about their own thinking (metacognition) and therefore cannot reflect upon or revise their work. Some teachers also believe children don't have the patience to sit and reflect or offer feedback to peers. Others assume that even if children *are* willing to try to make revisions, the feedback will crush their spirit or squelch their creativity. A second issue is that those who have attempted to include reflection, feedback, and revision opportunities into the curriculum often use these at the "completion" of learning, only as a type of wrap-up. Teachers want to weave these practices into the learning process but are unsure how to do this with young children, or within the context of a project. Throughout the course of a project, there are a variety of opportunities to use developmentally appropriate ways to engage children in reflection, feedback, and revision. It is essential that we make time for these three practices so children are empowered to develop new skills and abilities that lead to greater independence and ownership of their learning.

The three constructivist principles of *knowledge construction, shared responsibility,* and *shared ownership of learning* remind us that learning must be viewed as a process – specifically, a process where students engage in an experience, reflect on the experience, identify what was learned from the experience, and try out what was learned (Kolb, 2015). Each of Kolb's phases of the experiential learning model (experience, reflect, think, do) offers teachers multiple entry points for engaging students in the construction of knowledge and taking ownership over their own learning. When teachers layer in opportunities for students to reflect on their thinking and actions, give and receive feedback, and revise their work, students are drawn into the learning process. Intentionally planning for reflection, feedback, and revision when implementing Project Based Learning (PBL) with young children is important because these elements are important to the overall learning process.

Initially, it may seem like you are giving up content instruction time, but in fact, as Hammond (2014) suggests, we consider time for reflection, feedback, and revision, *to be* instructional time. They are essential tools that develop independence and shared responsibility in learning. She writes, "Make time for reflection and data analysis often. Protect this time as sacred. Don't let it get whittled away by less important busy work that often takes up time in the classroom" (p. 101). We must respect the amount of time it takes for learning to occur. Viewing learning as a long-term goal, a process that ebbs and flows through various cycles, helps young children appreciate the time it takes to engage in reflective opportunities and creates a culture that values multiple attempts at learning. To help students make this shift from a "one and done"' mindset and encourage them to thoughtfully engage in metacognitive experiences. Thinking about their own learning motivates students to learn and the students' ability to transfer strategies from context to context improves (Hall & Simeral, 2015; Larkin, 2010). Learning how to make a plan and follow through encourages students to engage in the learning process while teaching them to self-regulate, gain independence, experience decision-making and problem-solving, and enhance their oral language development (Hohmann, Weikart, & Epstein, 1995). Classroom teachers must be fully committed to supporting the development of these skills in their children because learning is about knowledge **construction**, not solely knowledge acquisition (Applefield, Huber, & Moallem, 2000).

Reflect and Connect

Consider your current reflection, feedback, and revision practices.

- *How often are students encouraged to think about how they are learning or what they need in order to be successful?*
- *How do your children share in the process of learning?*

Project Based Learning naturally offers multiple opportunities for this knowledge construction to take place because the emphasis is on learning as a process, one in which young children play an important role. When the three interconnected skills – reflection, feedback, and revision – are used throughout a project, they help students develop important conceptual understanding of the content while simultaneously developing the skills and dispositions to work collaboratively, to engage in inquiry, conduct research, test ideas and theories, draw conclusions, revise work, and create products. Figure 7.1 visually depicts the relationship between these essential elements of the learning process. The three constructivist principles of knowledge construction, shared responsibility, and shared ownership of learning grow out of the three key PBL practices of reflection, feedback, and revision. These principles allow children to develop skills, strategies, and dispositions that transfer to broader contexts both in and out of the classroom.

How, then, can teachers intentionally arrange experiences for students to take an active role in this learning process? Intentional instruction, guided opportunities, scaffolded learning experiences, and mental modeling can help young children learn the metacognitive skills that allow them to think about their learning (Driscoll, 2005). There are numerous ways to engage students in the processes of reflection, giving and receiving feedback, and revision. Often these practices are reserved for the teacher, but we believe young children can learn to:

- use reflective practices to think about their own thinking and learning.
- critique and make changes to their own actions and behaviors, to their own work, as well as the work of their peers.
- take part in setting relevant learning goals, monitoring, and observing their own progress.

Figure 7.1 Helping learners grow through reflection, feedback and revision

In this chapter, we examine a variety of instructional strategies that lead students to realize that they can take greater ownership and shared responsibility for their learning. Through the story of Sara's *Outdoor Classroom* project, we discover the interconnectedness of these three processes and how intentionally including reflection, feedback, and revision into a PBL unit builds content knowledge, develops many social and emotional competencies, and improves students' metacognition.

Reflection in Early Childhood PBL

When we engage children in reflection, we encourage them to go beyond merely reporting what they've done. We also help them become aware of what they learned in the process, what was interesting, how they feel about it, and what they can do to build on or extend the experience. Reflection consolidates knowledge so it can be generalized to other situations, thereby leading to further prediction and evaluation. Thus planning and reflection, when they bracket active learning, are part of an ongoing cycle of deeper thought and thoughtful application.

(Epstein, 2003, p. 2)

In constructivist learning environments, where students are continuously engaged in complex experiences, it is important that teachers intentionally arrange opportunities for students to pause and reflect on the various experiences. Experiences without reflection stop short of awakening students to the deeper meanings and connections to what and how they are learning. It is in those moments of thoughtful reflection in the classroom that children learn to:

- develop our awareness about a topic
- analyze
- seek solutions to problems
- make meaning
- think flexibly
- determine next steps
- analyze situations
- consider multiple perspectives
- evaluate
- transform and advance thinking

It is through reflection that students wrestle with their thoughts, deepening their understanding, knowledge, and skills in such a way that they can transfer this learning to new contexts (Kolb, 2015). Opportunities for reflection lead to learning when students understand a situation, consider their assumptions, and detect uncertainty with their thoughts (Carr, 2011; Zelazo, 2015). Knowing how to talk about reflection and using the language of reflective practices helps students name their thoughts and better understand others' perspectives. The authenticity of Project Based Learning, along with numerous opportunities for students to make their own decisions, provides an excellent context for teaching young children about reflection.

A teacher's role is to guide students through reflective practices using a scaffolded approach, which helps students develop tools for reflection in developmentally appropriate ways. Teachers can support children's metacognitive skills by carefully considering the types of questions they are asking children. By choosing open-ended, probing questions as compared to closed ended, clarifying questions, children gain practice reflecting upon their thoughts, feelings, and ideas. How do you know if the type of question you are asking will inspire reflection? A good rule of thumb is that If you already know the answer to the question you are asking, it is most likely *not* a reflective question. Questions with teacher-known answers serve a very different purpose, one that is tied to recall or checking for fact retention. Our goal is to primarily use open-ended questions that encourage students to think because *reflection* is "remembering with analysis" (Epstein, 2003, p. 2).

Look at these examples. Notice the difference between the two sets of questions. The questions in bold require students to think, notice, connect, and analyze, as compared with the other questions which can be answered with one- or two-word, "right or wrong" responses.

> **What feelings do you have when you play this instrument?**
>
> Is this instrument loud or soft?
>
> **Does this instrument remind you of anything?**
>
> What is this instrument made of?
>
> **What do you think makes this instrument sound this way?**
>
> What is the name of this instrument?

For students to learn through reflective practices, they need to understand what they are reflecting about and how engaging in reflection fits within the larger learning process. Therefore, teachers should consider the purpose for including reflection in the learning process by asking themselves if the students are to reflect on the content, process, product, personal goals, team goals, and/or intended outcomes. Taking time to reflect, with a purpose and goal, is an excellent way for students to think about what they are learning. Reflection also leads to critical thinking and encourages students to understand how their thoughts fit in with those around them and broader contexts (Peltier, Hay, & Drago, 2005). Reflection, like any skill, becomes more efficient with use. Reflecting at different points in the learning process, using varied methods, and increasing the frequency positively contribute to developing and enhancing reflection efficiency. To support the intentional inclusion of reflective opportunities in your projects, we identified key reflective practices and routines that facilitate learning in PBL as well as tips for implementation (see Table 7.1).

Table 7.1 Opportunities for Using Reflective Practices in PBL

Practices & Routines	Tips for Implementation
Before engaging in fieldwork Return to the Need to Know list and identify questions that might be answered through the upcoming fieldwork. Collaboratively generate more questions, if needed.	Chart the questions in front of the class or mentally model how you are generating questions from the Need to Know list for this visit. Role-play asking the questions ahead of the visit. Then bring the chart with you as a reference and ask the children if they remember their questions – if not, review them and see if they want to use the chart for support.
During fieldwork or other learning experiences Provide a "Reflection Sheet" for children to draw observations or write/dictate questions they have to an adult. Have children take photos (using iPads, Chromebooks, or polaroid cameras). Print the photos and have children dictate captions to the photos and create a book or chart.	Create a list of things or objects to look for (using pictures or symbols) like a scavenger hunt. To prevent this from being the focal point for the whole trip or too restrictive, designate a portion of the reflection sheet for "additional observations and questions." Children who are comfortable writing words should be encouraged to do so independently.

(continued)

Practices & Routines	Tips for Implementation
After an expert visit to the class Reflect on the visit by asking children to draw a picture, write words, or label what they learned, saw, or felt.	Before having children reflect independently, facilitate a class reflection of the visit and chart potential ideas with actual photos of the trip or quick sketches. Then support children as they choose one aspect to reflect on independently.
After a field experience or classroom learning experience Engage students in a thinking routine like "See, Think, Wonder" using photographs from the field experience (visiblethinkingpz.org). Use the ideas that students are wondering about to intentionally plan upcoming lessons.	Break the reflection experience up into three different periods in a day or over two-three days. For example, during a Morning Meeting create a "What did we *see* on the trip?" chart. The next day add to the chart, "What do we *think* about what we saw?" The next day, or later in the day, add "What do we still *wonder?*"
Frequently during a project Children keep daily or weekly journals to draw thoughts or feelings about a project.	Journals can be premade with specific sections (e.g., a space for the date, a space for a picture, a space for labels or writing) depending on the goals for the reflection.
At various points in a project Partner Talk – guided by a teacher, have children talk with a friend in response to a question or prompt – for example, "What was the most challenging part of making your instrument?"	Support children with special needs or who are English language learners. You might partner two children who speak the same language and suggest they reflect together in their home language; bring in a teacher who speaks that language for this activity, or front-load/pre-teach the conversation prompts or skills prior to doing it as a class.
During group conversations Ask open-ended questions for students to discuss in whole group, small groups, or partners. Use a thinking prompt for individual reflection. Interpret and expand upon what children do and say during group conversations and learning experiences (Epstein, 2003). Chart children's words and ideas during conversations. Refer to these ideas over the course of a project.	For example, "What was challenging about X and how did you overcome that challenge?" "Does your 3-D model of your instrument look the same or different than the first design you drew? What is different and why did you change it?" or simply "Can you tell me about your instrument design? What shapes did you use?" Use a reflective question about the learning process of how a learner is supporting another learner in the classroom so students learn to think about the learning of others (McDowell, 2017). Also, consider using sentence starters or discussion frames to help the conversation get started or stay focused.

(continued)

Table 7.1 Opportunities for Using Reflective Practices in PBL (Continued)

Practices & Routines	Tips for Implementation
Throughout the day Identify non-project times during the school day for students to reflect on their thinking, understanding, actions, and learning processes. Use formative assessment strategies like thumbs up/thumbs side/thumbs down from time to time for children to reflect on their understanding or actions. For example, "How did we do as a class following our agreement for working together as a team?" Engage students in reflective practices related to key skills and dispositions that you are fostering in your classroom.	Invite reflection during Morning Meetings ("What was your favorite part of the weekend?") or Closing Circles ("What part of the day challenged you?") or after recess or lunch ("What worked well when we lined up and transitioned outside?). Depending on what you observe when students respond, talk to children about what they could do to make improvements for next time or pose a follow-up question to take the reflection another step deeper. For example, if you are learning about growth mindsets, engage students in conversations where they reflect on an area of their life where they already exhibit a growth mindset. Preview tasks with students so they are prepared for challenges. This sets students up for success and helps them realize they have the tools to solve their own problems and reflect on the challenges and solutions.
During unstructured choice time As children are engaged in choice time or other unstructured work periods, make observations and say out loud what you see children doing or playing. Add descriptive words to describe their actions (particularly with more non-verbal children). After choice time, engage students in a reflection meeting, intentionally looking for ways to broaden the comments the children express. Stretch their thinking to include reflection and analysis after the initial telling or recall.	Rather than trying to record every word the children share, identify the "big ideas" to record. For example, during an *Outdoor Classroom* project "Work Time," children were building with blocks. When it was time to clean up, Sara observed children putting blocks on different shelves, trying to organize them, but unsuccessfully. During the class' reflection meeting, she asked, "How could we keep our blocks organized?" She hoped they would notice the 3-D shapes and suggest creating specific shelf spots for each shaped block. Children did more than that - they also suggested creating *names* for the blocks (based on their unique 3-D characteristics). In subsequent work periods they labeled the shelves with the names the class developed and agreed on.

Feedback in Early Childhood PBL

> *One of the fastest ways to improve student performance and build independence is to provide the learner with useable, actionable feedback.*
>
> (Hammond, 2014, p. 101)

In a traditional class, feedback is given by the teacher after the completion of a project to indicate a level of success, often in the form of a letter grade. However, in Project Based Learning, the purpose is to use feedback, along with reflection and revision, to deepen the learning and move student work forward. Students can take an active role in the learning process and experience a shared responsibility for learning through feedback. Feedback plays an integral part of the learning process because it enables children to take specific, actionable steps to make improvements (Wiggins, 1993). PBL is an ideal way to learn about feedback because students are continuously designing and creating public products that can be improved upon through feedback.

Teachers of early learners might think that their students are incapable of giving effective feedback because they do not have the critical thinking skills to analyze and suggest changes to the work of others. Others worry that young children can't use the feedback they receive because they are too "fragile" to revise their work. However, we suggest that young children can *give* and *receive* feedback if they are taught the procedures through explicit modeling and instruction and are given ample opportunities to practice. If we want our young children to review their work and make changes, they must have opportunities to give, receive, and analyze feedback.

Feedback is most productive in a classroom environment both physically and systematically tailored for it. Developing class norms for the critique process or revisiting the co-created classroom norms from the beginning of the year right before using feedback tools helps create and sustain a safe environment where children are comfortable with the feedback process. You may also find it helpful to create an area of the room where students meet to give/receive feedback. Charts with picture clues or other visuals are good scaffolds for younger children, as well as for English language learners. Practicing asking questions that lead students to analyze their work can also be a beneficial approach to modeling how to engage in a feedback session. Arranging for students to use peer conferencing or Socratic seminars empower and motivate children because they feel like a valued member of the learning community who has something to offer to others.

The creation of a feedback-ready classroom, and the ongoing use of feedback protocols allow children to see themselves as not just learners, but as teachers; this builds their self-esteem, confidence, and self-efficacy while developing agency and enhancing content knowledge. If a young child knows she will be responsible for supporting a peer with her project and providing feedback about the content of the work, then she must deeply understand the learning goals. The rationale for learning becomes meaningful and relevant to everyone, as opposed to just the teacher who wrote the target and posted the daily learning objectives on the board. When children participate in a collaborative feedback process, they are often more motivated and engaged because they understand they are learning alongside their peers. Teaching students to give effective feedback, therefore, improves their ability to focus their attention, honor and hold multiple perspectives, and demonstrate respect for their peers as well as for the learning process.

To teach students to give and receive feedback, it can be helpful to use protocols that place parameters on elements and help students know where to focus their attention, thus learning to keep a conversation on track. Organizations like the National School Reform Faculty, School Reform Initiative, EL Education, and Making Thinking Visible are excellent places to find inspiration for feedback protocols and strategies for supporting children with giving feedback. Two developmentally appropriate protocols are "Two Stars and a Wish" or "I like ____ I wonder____," both of which can be conducted orally (for emergent readers and writers) or written down using a feedback

> Protocols provide equity of voice by giving parameters to a conversation. Protocols usually dictate at what point participants speak and listen, and for how long. They make clear the crucial differences between talking and listening, between describing and judging, or between proposing and giving feedback. In the process, they call attention to the role and value of these in learning and make the steps of our learning visible and replicable.
>
> (McDonald, Mohr, Dichter, and McDonald, 2003, p. 5)

protocol recording sheet. The "Gallery Walk" protocol encourages students to give effective feedback anonymously, without requiring them to interact directly with one another, thus putting some less confident students at ease. Notice how these protocols use sentence starters that reflect the language of feedback. Over time, students will begin to adopt this language as their own. It is helpful for young children to use the same feedback protocol over multiple instances so that children are familiar with the process and can therefore focus on the specific feedback they are giving or receiving.

Another tip for implementing feedback protocols with young children is to thoughtfully consider who is in the best position to give the feedback. In peer-to-peer feedback situations, this might mean strategically assigning feedback partners, so children work with the same person throughout the project, learning how to adjust their comments as the project progresses. In these scenarios, you may want to use different protocols, but maintain the same partnerships. When different perspectives are needed, the teacher may arrange feedback partners from buddy classrooms, outside experts, or other teachers. In these scenarios, we encourage the use of the same protocols for all outside perspectives so that children are familiar with them.

Learning how to receive feedback is also important. Receiving feedback encourages the development of self-regulation skills because students learn to monitor their *internal* feedback, the thoughts they develop when they think about their learning with respect to the task, expectations, and their performance (Butler & Winne, 1995). Internal feedback helps students discover discrepancies between what they are thinking and what they are learning as well as awareness of the cognitive processes that happen when they are engaged in a task (Butler & Winne, 1995). Learning how to receive feedback from an *external* source helps students learn to monitor their progress in regards to classroom expectations and personalized learning goals. They begin to engage in conversations about learning and discern what feedback is helpful to give and what feedback is helpful for their own revisions. Internal and external feedback moves learning forward at an accelerated pace because the students are not waiting for grades or "good job" comments on their work *after* it is completed. Rather, they are continually engaging in the feedback cycle *throughout* the learning process, using feedback to make decisions about what to do next. We are confident that incorporating the principles found in Table 7.2 into your PBL units can help boost your students' independence in giving and receiving feedback.

Table 7.2 Key Features to Consider When Giving Feedback in Early Childhood Classrooms

Timely and ongoing	Feedback is given while the student is thinking about the work and when there is still time for reflecting on the feedback and making changes or improvements. Timely feedback communicates to the child that learning is important and that we share in the responsibility to make work high quality. Ongoing feedback also communicates that learning is a process and feedback is not something that happens in the end, it is simply an ongoing *part* of the learning context. *For young children, this is particularly important because they will most likely forget what they were working on if too much time passes. Providing children time to respond to the feedback during the work period, or immediately after, increases the effectiveness of the feedback and ensures relevancy to a child.*
Descriptive of work	When providing feedback, the teacher or peer should identify multiple strengths of the work and provide at least one actionable suggestion for consideration. Rather than critiquing the *person* doing the work, the feedback is focused on the *work itself*, the process, or product that is being presented for revision. Teachers and students may find it helpful to isolate one learning target as the focus of the feedback. This helps ensure the dialogue is related to the success criteria previously taught and publicly identified through rubrics and checklists. *Rubrics should be in child-friendly language, that is, language that a 3–8 year-old would actually use. Avoid language that is quoted directly from standards (i.e. "I will be able to count forward beginning from a given number within the known sequence instead of having to begin at 1"). Avoid saying things like "good job" or "it's beautiful." Instead, consider saying something like, "I noticed you connected our big question to what you saw during our field experience." or "I wonder what might happen if we change this sentence into a question?" This provides feedback that is tangible, user-friendly, and non-evaluative. It also gives children specific language they can incorporate into future goals or work.*

(continued)

Table 7.2 Key Features to Consider When Giving Feedback in Early Childhood Classrooms (Continued)

Positive	A positive tone conveys to the student that the teacher thinks of him/her as an important, valued member of the classroom who can share in the responsibility for learning. You've likely already established positive relationships with your students where reflecting, receiving/giving feedback, and revising are part of the climate and culture of your classroom. Positively addressing feedback opportunities communicates how learning is a journey forward, and on this journey we must be honest about both building on our strengths and improving on our weaknesses. *While saying "Good Job!" is positive, young children will begin to rely on your positive affirmation rather than learning from the specific feedback. You can still convey positive feelings (for example with a big smile, or an expressive, happy sounding voice) but the language you use should be specific to your observations rather than a judgement about the work or their performance. A helpful tip is to remember to engage, not praise (Wilson, 2012). Children want to know that you see them and notice their effort. Positive feedback communicates this idea, not through your "approval" of their work, but from the reinforcement and naming of positive observations.*
Clear and specific	Feedback should be sufficiently specific so the student understands what to do next, but leaves the student with some thinking to do. This is different from surface level suggestions where students are left with corrections edits to make. Consider using particular rows of the rubric and portions of the checklists to keep the feedback specific and aligned to the learning goals and outcomes. Avoid overloading the students with too much feedback so they have time to process and apply. *For young children, offer only one or two pieces of feedback and check for understanding to make sure your feedback is clear. Model the changes you suggest if that is applicable (to your own work sample, not theirs). For example, if you suggest a child's 3-D model more accurately match the drawing, have your own sample to show the suggestion. Use language like "watch how I _____" or "look at how I _____" to help children hone in on the specific feedback you are giving. You might also use questioning, for example, "How do you think we can make this building more stable?" Leave the child and return to see what kind of changes were made based on your specific question. Then provide feedback that highlights the growth that was made or how students are progressing toward their goals.*

(continued)

Table 7.2 Key Features to Consider When Giving Feedback in Early Childhood Classrooms (Continued)

Differentiated	Feedback should meet the needs of each individual student with respect to their current work. For some students, a reminder is all that's needed to take the next step, while others may need prompts or examples. Avoid using generic or blanket feedback statements for the whole class. Instead, use observations and conferences to identify misconceptions and determine who needs individual feedback and/or large or small group follow-up lessons.
	As with all ages and grade levels, it is essential to differentiate instruction according to the specific needs of your students. Within one early childhood classroom you most likely have a wide range of skills and abilities. Be aware of these needs and your expectations for growth. Stay cognizant that your feedback is developmentally appropriate to each learner. As you provide feedback to one student, most likely other children around that student will hear your feedback and take it in, even if it is targeted for someone else. Students will improve their own work by simply listening in while you confer and support others around them.

Students must learn that not all feedback is created equal and not all feedback is helpful for moving work forward. This parallels the the adult world of work. In our work as teachers, we frequently decide what to do with the feedback we receive from students, parents, colleagues, and administrators. We get to decide what is valuable and thus can effectuate change and conversely, what simply isn't helpful. Students can learn to discern helpful feedback by engaging in whole group feedback sessions facilitated by a teacher. Teachers can also lead critique sessions (using work samples collected from students outside of the current classroom) to highlight how to give and receive feedback. We encourage you to break the feedback process into multiple steps or mini-lessons. For example, lessons on giving feedback, receiving feedback, and discerning quality feedback should happen over multiple days for maximum effectiveness.

It is also important to honor the age of the students and vary the expectations depending on the grade level and the time of year that children are engaging in the process. It might be enough for kindergarteners to give one piece of specific, rubric-based feedback to a peer in October or November and then two-three pieces by February. First graders might be able to provide feedback aligned to the mini-lessons at the beginning of the year. Second graders might be capable of giving kind, specific, and helpful feedback on a more frequent basis with scaffolding and support. Regardless of age, explicit instruction on how to give, receive, and use feedback is important. If you want to learn more about giving good feedback, we encourage you to read the second edition of *How to Give Effective Feedback to Your Students* by Brookhart (2017).

In PBL, children share the responsibility for learning when they engage in reflection, continuing as they learn to seek input and accept feedback, and finally when they implement suggestions in the form of revisions (Sackstein & Berkowicz, 2017). Pausing to reflect on learning, and giving and receiving feedback about the learning, can be very powerful for young learners who are developing the stamina and skills to persevere and make changes to their work. These skills, perseverance and self-efficacy, are two additional tenets of children becoming independent learners. Teachers should model for students how to monitor progress toward a goal and draw on the student's strengths, assets, interests, and challenges when giving feedback and identifying new goals (Hattie, 2012). Monitoring goals and evaluating learning through feedback is an important component of the learning process (Boud & Molloy, 2013; Wiggins, 2012). Ideally, the feedback students are learning to give, receive, and analyze is in a narrative form and a by-product of engaging in discourse and dialogue.

Revision in Early Childhood PBL

Most children do four to five drafts before marking the rubric and formally assessing their own work. Each draft will take thirty to forty minutes. At this point in the process, children decide if they have accomplished "best work" or if they wish to try again. A surprising number will want to try again. They are hooked. This process has led them far beyond what they ever thought possible.

(Berger, 2014, p. 150)

In traditional classrooms, revision is typically taught during writing time, and most often occurs toward the very end of the writing process. Often, students are introduced and guided through the writing steps and allowed to fully complete a draft before the notion of revision is introduced. Alternatively, students are often told to return to a previous piece of work to be used as source material for a "lesson in revision." The type of "revision" usually taught and carried out is closer to *editing*, which is a valuable, though distinct and different skill which often places an emphasis on handwriting, grammar, punctuation, and capitalization mistakes. In the end, students come away with the belief that revision is a series of quick fixes that are completed between drafting and publishing. This is not what we are labeling as "revision."

In fact, revision is a skill that applies well beyond writing, and should be an ongoing part of the learning process. It is not just editing, it is reconsidering and making changes to the very concept and structure of the material, as well as – in the case of writing – the more superficial considerations of word choice and grammar. And this is not to be compartmentalized into the final stages; revision is an ongoing process that happens repeatedly and frequently throughout all phases of the creative process. We concur that writing time is an excellent part of the day in which to introduce young children to revision practices. But our goal is for students to transfer and apply the revision strategies and process to other areas and especially during projects.

While reflection empowers children to know themselves as learners and feedback helps them to build a growth mindset and honor other people's perspectives, learning how to revise helps students develop an awareness that they play an essential role in their own learning and can make positive, impactful changes to their work. Revision allows young children to envision and re-envision their work, rather than just seeing revision as a means of editing for errors (Hicks, 2017). This process of revising and resubmitting projects for further feedback leads to a greater sense of pride and satisfaction when children realize they created several drafts and overcame challenges and frustrations to develop a product just as they wanted. In PBL, revising can be a powerful teaching tool because it is challenging for young children to fully visualize how a project will come together during the initial creation and construction process (Kuby, Rucker, & Kirchhofer, 2015). Revising gives children the space to look at their work again, making changes and adjustments based on feedback and reflection.

The benefits of the revision process are worth the time and energy it takes to establish a culture for reflection and for implementing feedback routines. When students undertake revision, they develop persistence, their engagement increases, and they continue to deepen their understanding that learning is a shared responsibility (Hicks, 2017). Not only does engaging in the process of revising improve the quality of a current piece of work, future work is also enhanced when learners apply their newly acquired knowledge and skills to the *next* project (Berger, 2014). "Rough draft thinking," where students share ideas that are newly emerging, leads to the development of intellectual courage, normalizes imperfection, and encourages risk taking by learners (Jansen, Cooper, Vascellaro, & Wandless, 2017). Sharing ideas in their infancy stage also gives students a chance to change their thinking, communicating that we make more than one draft. Learning to revise by sharing ideas early on also conveys to students that we value thinking and the learning process over correct or "right" answers.

To learn how to make effective and meaningful revisions, teachers should (1) make time for revision, (2) offer conferring opportunities (teacher-student, student-student), (3) use examples of quality work, and (4) intentionally provide instruction on revision-based strategies (Saddler, Saddler, Befoorhooz, & Cuccio-Slichko, 2014). Making time for revisions is as simple as identifying one or two points within a project where students would benefit from engaging in intentional instruction about how to revise, as well as time for making the revisions. This could be planned as a whole class lesson, small group work, or as individual conferences. Using concrete revision examples within these conferences is an excellent scaffold. You can find a place within the students' project where you can model for them how to revise and then call for similar revisions in the future. Allowing students to generate their own examples, either within their own project or for a peer, is also beneficial. Asking students to revise, without scaffolding, support, or time, discourages learners. It is essential that we leave young students with ideas for how to revise and empower them to make their own revision decisions.

The focus of revision lessons, whether in writing or in project work, should vary. Just as teachers are likely to only have children revise after they complete a draft of a piece of work, it is quite common that the focus of the reflection is on the product. Rather than reinforcing this view of revision, we believe children should learn to revise:

- the content in a product
- their thinking about the content
- project processes

Revising for content within a project is often related to accuracy. After students learn new ideas and information, they should have time to revise their work to reflect new learning. Revising thinking takes time and intentionality, but young children can learn how to merge new ideas and various perspectives with their thoughts. Products are often revised at incremental stages, usually after new content is learned or new processes are introduced. Allowing children to adopt their own revision strategies for classroom and project processes might be followed by mini-lessons or discussions encouraging students to reflect on how the processes are working and then revising using student-generated suggestions. Table 7.3 provides you strategies and possible topics for revising in the areas of content, processes, and products.

Teaching students about the processes of reflection, feedback, and revision will positively impact the academic knowledge, success skills, and dispositions of our youngest learners. Engaging young children in reflection, feedback, and revision increases their ownership in the learning process and independence over their learning. These three processes also bring an awareness to the shared responsibility for learning and an awareness of how knowledge is constructed. As early childhood teachers, we must embrace the opportunity to invite students into the learning process and intentionally create opportunities for deeper learning, which includes clearly understanding learning goals, making plans and adjustments, and then looking back on their growth and progress. Through their classroom experiences, children will develop perseverance, determination, reflective thinking, self-efficacy, and self-regulation (Frey, Fisher, & Smith, 2019; Helm & Katz, 2011). The research surrounding reflection, feedback, revision, metacognition, and executive functions repeatedly confirms that students who learn to think about their own **learning** and think about their **thinking** become more independent and engaged learners (Hammond, 2014). It is our hope that you are equipped with the reasons and strategies for intentionally arranging opportunities for students to reflect and make changes to their work.

In the following section, we take you back into the story of the *Outdoor Classroom* project in order to demonstrate how students can engage in reflection, feedback, and revision throughout the different phases of the project and for different reasons. It is through these experiences that the students began to understand the role they played in the learning process. You will see that young children can in fact learn to reflect, give, and receive feedback and revise in the areas of content, learning processes, and when developing products.

Table 7.3 Revision in PBL: Possible Topics and Strategies for Instruction

Content	Process	Products
• Teach students how to add details to a project. • Ask older students, like buddy classes, to provide specific feedback that can be acted upon through the revision process. • After a field experience, guest speaker, or in-class learning experience, ask the students to complete the following sentence frame: I used to think ____, but now I know___. • Teach students how to literally add to their picture or add words to their writing so they aren't starting over, but revising.	• Teach students how to look at something carefully. • Use language in the classroom that reminds students they aren't finished *yet*. • Use HighScope's plan-do-review process (Hohmann et al., 1995). • Model recording next steps in a project planner. • Set up conference times for revision or have set days when you plan to check-in with individuals and teams. • Use revision protocols like "Praise, Question, Suggest" Collaborative Critique, Compliment Circle (EL Education). • Coach students to look at their work with fresh eyes or from a different perspective to learn to consider how a peer, adult, etc. may be viewing their project.	• Ask students, "What do you want to change about this project?" (Juliani, 2018) • Use specific prompts: "How might you make this X?" (i.e., more stable, easier for the audience to read). • After exploring new materials or seeing authentic product examples, ask students to revise their work in light of their new learning. • Spend time coaching individual students through the revision process while others are engaged in choice time, independent work time, or centers. • Use analysis to identify what is missing from a draft. • Coach students to identify and determine what to add to a project and/or something they want to change.

The *Outdoor Classroom* Project: Reflection, Feedback, and Revision

Sara's initial plan did not actually include having students design original musical instruments; this was added into her project design only *after* the children suggested having a Music Area. Sara was pleased that an authentic addition to the project happened naturally (spontaneous integration) and was excited to leverage her students' interests by adding the music area into her lesson plans. Sara started thinking about what the class would need in order to create this area of the outdoor classroom. What instruments would they have? How would they learn about them? Where would they get them? As Sara planned the lessons and experiences that would culminate in the children's instrument designs, she knew she needed to build in specific times for children to think about what they already knew about instruments, how they felt about those instruments, and how they would go about designing their own. Sara recognized that if the instruments were going to work as the children had envisioned and be durable enough to last the whole school year, the children would need time to engage in project work over an extended period of time. Creating a Music Area for the outdoor classroom included the following student learning outcomes, with the phase of the learning process listed in parenthesis:

- identify and name what they already knew about instruments (experience)
- build additional knowledge about musical instruments (experience)
- explore different instruments and consider different characteristics (reflect)
- thoughtfully plan their instruments (experience)
- make the instruments (experience)
- let peers test the instruments and make suggestions (feedback, revision)
- make changes based on feedback and experimentation (revise, reflect)
- look back on their changes and process after garnering feedback (reflect)

Sara's intentional and thoughtful planning for **reflection, feedback**, and **revision** opportunities led her students to engage deeply with the content and provided students with a greater awareness about the role they play in the learning process. Designing instruments for a collective classroom space authentically drew the children into a shared ownership of learning. Weaving these processes throughout the different phases of just this one slice of the whole *Outdoor Classroom* project resulted in positive learning outcomes in both academic content and social emotional goals. By the end of the Music Area component of the project, the students felt supported by their peers and empowered in their own learning. They found success in the challenge of designing their own instruments, developing skills and strategies that would carry them forward with future project work.

As you read the story of the instrument design process below, look for ways in which Sara's students grew into more independent learners through intentional opportunities for reflection, feedback, and revision.

Exploring Instruments

Today we are going to have the chance to explore a lot of instruments that I borrowed from Mr. Malcolm, our music teacher. There are all different kinds – percussion, strings, woodwinds. While you are playing the instruments, think about what kind of instruments we should have for the Music Area of our Outdoor Classroom. I placed the instruments around the room. You can play them by yourself or with a partner.

Sara included a reflection opportunity on the very first day of this part of the project. *While* the students explored the musical instruments in the room, Sara asked direct, open-ended questions. These questions were not used to "quiz" children on what they saw or did. She wanted children to think about their experiences, make connections, and inspire new questions. As Sara circulated the room during that initial exploration, she jotted down the children's comments. Children shared that "drums were loud and made them feel excited or scared," and that they liked the feel of the ukulele strings because they were soft and "relaxing." The shape of a xylophone "looked like steps going up." Most of them favored an unusual instrument – a "thunder tube" – that sounded like a thunderclap and had a picture of a lightning bolt and rain on the outside.

In the middle of the lesson, Sara highlighted some of the ways in which children were playing with the instruments, and some of the observations children were making themselves. She had overheard a child comment about the thunder tube, "I wonder how they made this?" and then shared this thought with the class, hoping (and predicting) that other students would begin to become aware of what *they* were learning about the instruments. She wanted them to consider what they found interesting, how they felt when playing the instruments, and how they would begin to extend that new knowledge so that eventually they would be able to design and create their own.

After the children had rotated through all the instrument centers, Sara called her students to the rug. She placed all the instruments on a table at the front of the room, so that children could still see them as they began their discussion.

Sara created a T-chart where she listed what children said they *noticed* and what they *needed to know* to move forward with the process of designing instruments for their music area. Her goal of charting their thinking was to help make the reflection process visible for the learners. Sara made sure not to *tell* them that designing instruments was the next step and in fact, one child added his own question to the chart, "How will we design our own?" Although Sara had planned to design instruments (*intentional integration*), she also left space to see if any of the children would come up with the idea after an initial exploration (*spontaneous integration*). If the student hadn't mentioned it, then Sara would have waited to see if her line of questioning during the reflection meeting the next day prompted anyone to inquire about making their own instruments.

Through this initial reflection, the children were able to consolidate their learning about instruments, e.g., drums can be very, very loud and usually you hit them, instruments with strings often make you feel relaxed, and wind instruments can be hard to play because you sometimes have to blow really hard. Their initial reflections would lead them to broader knowledge about instruments: how to play them, their sound, shape, and volume. This reflection also introduced the connection between music and emotion which would later play a role in children's design decisions.

A Musician Visits

We've been learning a lot about instruments, so I thought it would be helpful to talk to someone who plays music for her job. This is Heather. She knows a lot about her instrument and other instruments. She is a musician and a composer. Has anyone heard those words before? A musician is someone who plays music, and a composer is someone who writes music – she makes up songs. Heather plays a cello and writes a special kind of music, called a score, for movies.

Through the initial exploration and Need to Know list, it was clear that there was ample student interest in learning more about instruments and making their own. Sara wanted to incorporate an authentic context into the project so that her students would see the relevance of music and instruments outside of the classroom. Having the opportunity to meet someone who worked in the music industry met that goal. A few days later, Sara invited Heather, a musician/composer into the classroom to share about her job, talk about her cello, and answer the students' questions. Prior to Heather's visit, Sara mentally modeled thinking through questions related to a guest or expert and then introduced the students to a protocol to help the children come up with their own questions to ask Heather and prepare for the visit. Sara shared a simple "Asking Our Visitor Questions" rubric (Figure 7.2) that included three elements: speaking loudly, speaking slowly, and looking directly at the visitor. The students evaluated Sara using the rubric so they were familiar with the expectations, could practice using the vocabulary of the rubric, and could internalize what was going to be expected of them the next day.

Sara then split the class into pairs. Children talked with a partner and came up with two questions (one apiece) they wanted to ask the composer.

Your Name_____

Your partner's name_____

Did your partner....

Speak loudly? 	Not yet	Yes!
Speak slowly? 	Not yet	Yes!
Look directly at the visitor? 	Not yet	Yes!

Figure 7.2 Visitor questions rubric

They drew pictures on sticky notes to help them remember their questions and practiced asking them to one another. Partners then gave a quick piece of feedback based on one of the three elements: slow pace, loud voice, looking at the speaker. Using a simple rubric, children circled a picture of each element if they thought their partner had successfully demonstrated and circled a question mark if they thought their partner had not.

When the composer visited, she played her cello and gave children an opportunity to play it. She also brought in videos of her orchestra playing a concert, so children could see the conductor and other musicians. Children then asked their questions, including, "How did you learn to play?" "What do you do at your job?" and "Is your cello heavy?" Some of the questions came from the pre-conversation, and some clearly were thought of on the spot. Following the visit, children drew a picture of something they saw, heard, or felt. Sara added words (dictated by the children) and bound all the pages into a book. At read-aloud that afternoon, Sara read the book *Story of Heather's Visit* to the class and children looked at the book independently during Quiet Time.

Initial Designs

Today during choice time, I noticed a lot of you were playing with Mr. Malcolm's instruments. Lily was the conductor, and I saw a few people were in the orchestra and a few others were watching the concert! It looked a lot like the video that Heather showed us of her orchestra and conductor yesterday when she visited. I know that one of our questions was how we could design our own instruments for our Music Area, so I was thinking: If we are going to add our own instruments to our Music Area, what types of instruments will they be? I was thinking maybe if we looked really closely at some of the instruments we have, we can learn about the things we should think about when we design our own.

During Project Work Time, Sara handed each small group of students a photo of a musical instrument they had already explored over the past few days during choice time. She asked the children to talk about what they knew about the instruments after having played them. She asked them to consider questions like: How were they played? Were they big or small? What they might be made of? Did they make loud or soft sounds? As the children discussed these questions in their groups, Sara listened in for key ideas that she might want repeated during the discussions. Sara organized a large chart paper according to how each instrument was played. Then, children looked at the chart and reflected on what they noticed, for example, "All the shakers were made of wood" and "The instruments that you plucked all had strings."

At this point, Sara was confident the children had started thinking about their own ideas and were probably ready to engage in the design process using an instrument design graphic organizer (see Figure 7.3). The students

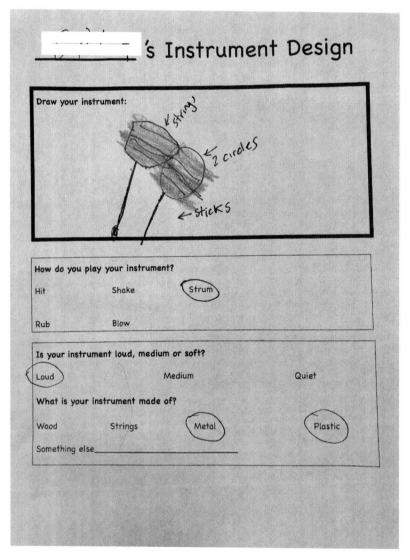

Figure 7.3 Initial instrument design before the music store visit

began planning their original idea later that day, when Sara arranged for one half of the class to be designing and the other half to be participating in choice time with puppets, borrowed instruments, and dramatic play. Sara worked with students one-on-one to help them compose their designs using shapes. The graphic organizer included:

1. space for a picture
2. space to articulate decisions about the shape
3. volume level
4. material of the instruments
5. ideas for how the instrument is played (hit, shake, strum, rub, or blow into)

In the small group, each child had a turn to describe their instrument, and receive feedback on the instrument design. Peers asked clarifying questions and responded with feedback based on the designer's response. Sara collected the children's written ideas and tucked them away for the time being. She knew she wanted children to have a chance to revise them before actually creating a 3-D model, so she opted to hold onto the original designs until they were needed.

A Visit to the Guitar Center

Do you remember that Ginnia suggested we go to a music store to learn more about instruments? Today we are going! We are going to visit a store called the Guitar Center. In a small group, you will walk around the store and look for specific instruments. To help you, I created a sheet with actual pictures of the instruments on it. You will carry your clipboard around the store and when you find a specific instrument on your sheet, circle it. I want you to focus on the shape, size, and material of different instruments, and also how different instruments are played, because they might inspire you as you design your own instrument. You will have time to draw some of the things you see on the back of your piece of paper. And if you'd like help writing down some words – things you saw or thought or questions you have that you want to remember – ask a grown-up who is with your group to write for you. When we come back from the visit, we will make at least one revision to our instruments. Maybe it means you will add something new or change one thing about it.

When the children arrived at the Guitar Center, they were greeted by the store manager. Sara had visited the store the week before to take photos of some of the instruments (to help guide and focus students on a "scavenger hunt") and to talk with the manager in preparation for the visit. Sara wanted to be sure that children would be able to touch, hold, and play the instruments. Sara made sure that she allotted time for the students to draw pictures of what they saw and/or make notes about any of their observations so that upon their return to school, they could use these notes to inform their own instrument designs. Prior to the trip, children had dictated questions they had for the store manager. It turned out that some of the questions were more appropriate for the music teachers who worked at the store, so the children asked those experts. The music teachers invited the children into the practice rooms to play pianos, guitars, and drums.

Immediately upon returning to the classroom, the children looked back at their original musical instrument designs and were prompted to "make at least one change or add at least one new part" based on what they had seen at the Guitar Center. Sara asked them to reflect on what they had seen or done, and to consider how their experience might help them to improve their own instrument design. The children made their revisions by drawing them, and they dictated the change to Sara so she could record and label any new additions or changes. For those who needed support, Sara suggested they consider changing the instrument's shape or material. Sara could have also invited one of the music teachers or the store manager into the classroom to look at the instrument designs, ask the students questions, and then provide feedback, but time was limited, so children revised based on the new knowledge obtained at the store (Figure 7.4).

Once Work Time began, one student changed the shape of her instrument from a square to a star because she had noticed a guitar shaped like a star at the store. Another child had spotted a guitar made entirely out of dimes and decided that his instrument would be made of coins instead of wood. Having built new knowledge on the trip, children were able to make better informed decisions when designing their instruments. Some children decided to name their instruments or add entirely new elements based on their observations and experiences on the trip. The expectation was that the students would discuss and write/draw their revision ideas as a step in the learning process ahead of creating an instrument.

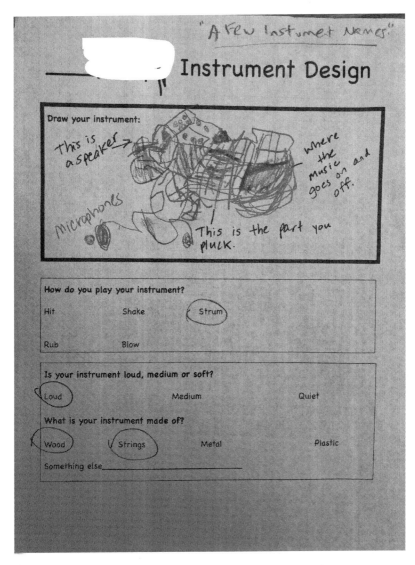

Figure 7.4 After a visit to the music store, a child returned and added microphones and additional details to his design

3-D Instrument Design

Yesterday, we took time to make changes to the drawings of our instrument designs. Today we get to make the real 3-D instruments! We have collected a lot of materials based on your initial plans. There is metal, wood, cardboard, string, plastic, and other materials. Think about what materials will work best for your design. Our art teacher, Ms. Andrea, is here to help too.

To support the children as they turned their designs into actual instruments, Sara enlisted the help of the art teacher, Ms. Andrea. About one week later, both Sara and Andrea worked one-on-one with children during choice time and during the class' art period to create their musical instruments (Figure 7.5). Sara often collaborated with specialists (art, music, P.E.) to plan the lessons she was going to teach in her classroom in addition to identifying project ideas they could tackle jointly. The art teacher was instrumental in providing one-on-one help because Sara needed to attend to other children in the class. Both teachers helped the children

Figure 7.5 Ms. Andrea, the art teacher, works with a student to create a 3-D model instrument from the initial 2-D design

choose appropriate materials and to realize their vision. Some children added details that were not present in their drawings. Some saw materials that were available (for example, some plastic Easter eggs) and decided to incorporate them into their designs.

Children took their time, carefully considering what they had envisioned and how the materials could make that vision come to life. Andrea and Sara supported the design process by helping the student to bend, shape, and mold the materials (cardboard, plastic, wire, metal) to their needs. Occasionally, as children experimented with the materials, they realized that some were better than others for their instruments. A child who designed an instrument that was a combination of a drum and a guitar initially chose wire and yarn for strings, but when he realized that the yarn was too quiet, he revised to include a combination of different widths and types of wire. A child who had imagined filling a rain stick with rice chose to include large beads instead for a louder sound. Children moved through a variety of emotions as they watched their instruments come off the page – at times expressing frustration, at times excitement, and in the end, a visible sense of pride.

At the end of the day, during Closing Circle, the children had a chance to share and play their instruments, first individually, and then together as a "band." Children took turns acting as the conductor, leading their friends in different volumes and speeds, just as they had watched people do in videos. Then Sara had the children individually reflect on the challenges they faced during the process of making their instruments. After the sharing circle ended, they placed their instruments in a large wicker basket which, for several weeks had been mostly empty, awaiting those instruments that finally made up the outdoor classroom Music Area.

Overcoming the Misconception

Over the course of a project, there are a variety of opportunities for students to learn and practice reflecting, giving/receiving feedback, and revising. While we might assume that this presents too great of a challenge for young children, if we stop and think about what each of these three elements of learning truly look like in practice, we discover that our young children *can* engage in reflection, giving/receiving feedback, and revision. Reflection is more than thinking about how something went or the choices made when the project is over. The inquiry cycle calls for us to repeatedly critique work and ideas, using feedback tools to ensure the comments are kind, specific, and helpful. Revision is the process of reflecting on the just-in-time feedback, and new learning, to make meaningful changes or additions to our work and our ideas. If we make the time to scaffold and support these emerging skills, our children will reap the benefits and apply this new learning to their daily lives outside of school. Experiencing these three parts of the learning process creates a greater sense of responsibility for our students and encourages them to take ownership over their learning.

References

Applefield, J. M., Huber, R., & Moallem, M. (2000). Constructivism in theory and practice: Toward a better understanding. *The High School Journal, 84*(2), 35–53.

Berger, R. (2014). *Leaders of their own learning: Transforming schools through student-engaged assessment.* San Francisco, CA: Jossey-Bass.

Boud, D., & Molloy, E. (2013). Rethinking models of feedback for learning: The challenge of design. *Assessment & Evaluation in Higher Education, 38*(6), 698–712. doi.org/10.1080/02602938.2012.691462.

Brookhart, S. M. (2017). *How to give effective feedback to your students* (2nd ed.). Alexandria, VA: ASCD.

Butler, D. L., & Winne, P. H. (1995). Feedback and self-regulated learning: A theoretical synthesis. *Review of Educational Research, 65*(3), 245–281. doi.org/10.3102/00346543065003245.

Carr, M. (2011). Young children reflecting on their learning: Teachers' conversation strategies. *Early Years, 31*(3), 257–270. doi.org/10.1080/09575146.2011.613805.

Driscoll, M. (2005). *Psychology of learning for instruction* (3rd ed.). New York, NY: Pearson.

Epstein, A. S. (2003). How planning and reflection develop young children's thinking skills. *Young Children, 58*(5), 28–36.

Frey, N., Fisher, D., & Smith, D. (2019). *All learning is social and emotional: Helping students develop essential skills for the classroom and beyond.* Alexandria, VA: ASCD.

Hall, P., & Simeral, A. (2015). *Teach, reflect, learn: Building your capacity for success in the classroom*. Alexandria, VA: ASCD.

Hammond, Z. (2014). *Culturally responsive teaching and the brain: Promoting authentic engagement and rigor among culturally and linguistically diverse students*. Thousand Oaks, CA: Corwin Press.

Hattie, J. (2012). Know thy impact. *Educational Leadership, 70*(1), 18–23.

Helm, H., & Katz, L. (2011). *Young investigators: The project approach in the early years* (2nd ed.). New York, NY: Teachers College Columbia University.

Hicks, T. (2017). *What research says about driving growth for writers with practice, feedback and revision*. Retrieved from: https://www.edsurge.com/news/2017-11-06-what-research-says-about-driving-growth-for-writers-with-practice-feedback-and-revision

Hohmann, M., Weikart, D. P., & Epstein, A. S. (1995). *Educating young children: Active learning practices for preschool and child care programs*. Ypsilanti, MI: High/Scope Press.

Jansen, A., Cooper, B., Vascellaro, S., & Wandless, P. (2017). Rough-draft talk in mathematics classrooms. *Mathematics Teaching in the Middle School, 22*(5), 304–307. doi:10.5951/mathteacmiddscho.22.5.0304.

Juliani, A. J. (2018). *The PBL playbook: A step-by-step guide to actually doing project-based learning*. United States of America: Write Nerdy Publishing.

Kolb, D. (2015). *Experiential learning: Experience as the source of learning and development*. Upper Saddle River, NJ: Pearson.

Kuby, C., Rucker, T., & Kirchhofer, J. (2015). "Go be a writer": Intra-activity with materials, time and space in literacy learning. *Journal of Early Childhood Literacy, 15*(3), 394–419. doi:10.1177/1468798414566702.

Larkin, S. (2010). *Metacognition in young children*. New York, NY: Routledge.

McDonald, J., Mohr, N., Dichter, A., & McDonald, E. (2003). *The power of protocols: An educator's guide to better practice*. New York, NY: Teachers College Press.

McDowell, M. (2017). *Rigorous PBL by design: Three shifts for developing confident and competent learners*. Thousand Oaks, CA: Corwin Press.

Peltier, J. W., Hay, A., & Drago, W. (2005). The reflective learning continuum: Reflecting on reflection. *Journal of Marketing Education, 27*(3), 250–263. doi:/10.1177/0273475305279657.

Sackstein, S., & Berkowicz, J. (2017). *Peer feedback in the classroom: Empowering students to be the experts*. Alexandria, VA: ASCD.

Saddler, B., Saddler, K., Befoorhooz, B., & Cuccio-Slichko, J. (2014). A national survey of revising practices in the primary classroom. *Learning Disabilities: A Contemporary Journal, 12*(2), 129–149.

Wiggins, G. (1993). *Assessing student performance: Exploring the purpose and limits of testing*. San Francisco, CA: Jossey-Bass Publishers.

Wiggins, G. (2012). 7 keys to effective feedback. *Educational Leadership, 70*(1), 10–16.

Willis, E., & Dinehart, L. H. (2014). Contemplative practices in early childhood: Implications for self-regulation skills and school readiness. *Early Child Development and Care, 184*(4), 487–499. doi:10.1080/03 004430.2013.804069.

Wilson, M. (2012). Look at my drawing. *Feedback for Learning, 70*(1), 52–56.

Zelazo, P. D. (2015). Executive function: Reflection, iterative reprocessing, complexity, and the developing brain. *Developmental Review, 38*, 55–68. doi.org/10.1016/j.dr.2015.07.001.

Sharing Our Learning
Assessment and Public Products in Early Childhood PBL

Assessments in PBL won't reliably measure my students' progress. And my children will be too nervous to get up in front of a big audience and present what they've learned.

Over the course of this book, we have discussed the constructivist philosophy that underpins Project Based Learning (PBL), we have described the learner-centered environment in which PBL takes place, and we have examined the aspects of projects themselves: content integration, research, literacy, social and emotional learning (SEL), along with reflection, feedback, and revision. What remains is for students to communicate what they have learned and what it means in a wider context. In PBL, this is accomplished through assessment and public products.

In our current educational landscape, testing and assessment practices heavily influence teachers' instructional decisions. Teachers are reticent to embrace Project Based Learning in this environment because they feel a sense of pressure to cover test-related content in order to prepare students for future grade levels. They might think that PBL lacks reliable assessments and they are unsure what high-quality assessments would even look like in PBL. With the push toward data-driven instruction and the sheer number of assessments teachers must administer throughout the year, teachers wonder how they can possibly add any more assessments, much less design them from scratch for a PBL unit. As they contemplate implementing PBL, teachers may wonder things like *How will I create an assessment that will adequately measure student learning? What evidence will there be that they understand key concepts? What happens if at the end of a project, the assessment data doesn't reflect student progress with the same accuracy as current testing practices?* These are important questions. We believe that the answers will inspire you to embrace PBL for the way in which it invites children to demonstrate their learning in meaningful ways.

Often, early childhood teachers resist attempting Project Based Learning because they feel overwhelmed by the assumption that every project must end with a formal culminating event attended by family members and school stakeholders. Teachers are intimidated by the prospect of organizing this (very) "public product" and worry that their young students will not be comfortable participating. They may fear that their students are not capable of standing up and speaking in front of an audience, might freeze on a stage, or can't effectively communicate their learning. But contrary to those beliefs, while PBL does require a public product as the culmination of the learning, the purpose of that product is to present a *relevant application of student learning*, and *not* to "put on a show." Rather than feeling pressure to have students "perform," what is most essential is that children have an authentic audience and a relevant context in which to share and apply their learning. When we talk about a culminating public product, we mean that students are demonstrating, for the public, the project's practical application in the world.

While assessment may seem like a barrier to implementing PBL, it is actually an invaluable teaching practice that informs our decisions throughout a project. And public products are an essential element to any quality PBL unit. It is a matter of identifying how you want students to exhibit their learning by sharing what they create with an audience beyond the classroom. In this final chapter, we explain assessments and public products, which are both effective and meaningful ways to understand what students have learned and what they can do as a result of that learning.

Reflect and Connect

As we discuss how assessment and public products capture students' learning, ask yourself:

- *How often do students use tools (such as rubrics) or strategies (like protocols) to gauge what they have learned or still need to learn?*
- *How might having students share their learning with others positively impact their project work?*

Part 1: Assessment in Early Childhood PBL

What Is the Purpose of Assessment?

It is widely known in the field of education that assessments fall into two primary categories, assessments *of* learning (summative) and assessments *for* learning (formative). Summative assessments are used to communicate what students know at the end of a unit while formative assessments are used to inform classroom instructional decisions. In many classroom scenarios, assessment feels static and burdensome for both students and teachers. Teachers pre-assess content or skill knowledge, use direct instruction to teach that specific content or skills, and then assess student mastery and "learning" by way of summative assessments. Tests, reports, or presentations concerning the learning that took place are typically used so teachers can check for "right" and "wrong" answers based on the content transmitted through a given unit. Teachers score the assessments based on how many questions the students answered correctly and often assign a grade. These types of assessments are becoming more and more common, even in early childhood classrooms (Blessing, 2019; Diamond, Grob, & Reitzes, 2015) because of the strong emphasis on measuring students' skill level on state and national standards and benchmarks.

A view of assessment that is heavily focused on obtaining scores and data points rather than collecting evidence of student learning runs counter to the beliefs that knowledge should be constructed (principle #5) and that children should share in the learning process (principle #2). In education, "assessment should not be separate from teaching, but should be a natural step within the teaching and learning process" (Brown, 1998, p. 60). We must use assessments to inform instruction, give feedback, and monitor student progress. When we think about regularly monitoring children's growth and development in academics and social and emotional learning, assessment becomes

> An innovative classroom is a place where you tend not to find things like grades and tests but instead meaningful assessment that's meant to make kids more excited about and proficient at wrestling with ideas that matter.
>
> (Kohn, 2013, p. 22)

meaningful and relevant. Formative assessments should support teachers with project planning and directly guide instructional decisions. Assessments should encourage students to improve and grow (Marzano, 2006; Tomlinson & Moon, 2013). This means that teachers must become adept at intentionally embedding assessments into all phases of a project. It also means teachers should find alternative ways to assess alongside assignments that can be used for numerical grades if it is a necessary requirement.

With PBL, content assessment is not enough on its own because the nature of the learning is more complex. Therefore, ongoing, timely, and meaningful assessments throughout the project, specifically during key moments called "Milestones" (pblworks.org) allow the teacher to make adjustments to lessons, check for understanding, and provide scaffolds and support to ensure all students achieve success with the learning goals of a project. Student learning is assessed frequently during a project to ensure that children are taking active roles in all aspects of the learning process. In PBL, teachers have a responsibility to ensure that assessments align not only with content, but with process, products, as well as social and emotional learning skills. Wiggins and McTighe (2011) recommend having learning goals, and assessments, for four areas of learning – knowledge, basic skills, understanding, and long-term transfer. Well-timed assessment practices communicate to young learners that we value the learning *process* as much as or even more than the end *product*.

Meaningful assessment communicates a sense of purpose for why and what students are learning. These practices are two-fold. In one sense, meaningful assessment practices ensure that we are gathering the information we need in a way that makes sense and informs instruction. This means that teachers determine the criteria for what will be assessed, who will do the assessing, when to assess, and how the results will be used in ways that drive project work forward and illuminate for students the content connections to the project work. In another sense, we want the work that we are asking students to engage in during an assessment to reflect the idea that knowledge is created and requires a level of rigor that is consistent with the type of thinking they have been doing throughout the project. The assessments should reveal what the students know and can do, not whether or not they can follow directions for how to carry out an assessment.

For early childhood teachers, concerns about developing and implementing additional high-quality assessments during a PBL unit are magnified because of how time-consuming assessments usually are with young learners. So many early childhood assessments are administered one-one-one, in small groups, and through conferences or observations. Teachers use informal checklists, running records, observations, and conferences as essential assessment strategies in an early childhood class-room because they allow the teacher to engage naturally with children in an authentic setting (Blessing, 2019). Many teachers wonder if those types of assessments can still be utilized in a project, and the answer, fortunately, is *yes*. Early childhood teachers are actually uniquely positioned to tackle assessment in Project Based Learning because they can administer content-rich one-on-one assessments as well as use their observation and conferring skills to layer in assessments geared toward learning processes and product development. Because of the young age of their students, early childhood teachers have to be innovative and creative with their assessment moves. That means they draw heavily on their observation skills, questioning strat-egies, and wait time (Duckor, 2014).

Since assessment is part of the learning process, it is important that we include even our youngest learners in assessment practices. In Project Based Learning, we encourage students to learn to self-assess as well as to take part in the broader classroom assessment practices. Students who are aware of their current level of understanding, and who are able to use feedback (from self, teacher, and peers) to help recognize what they are learning, set goals, and monitor progress, are on their way to becoming "assessment-capable" learners (Frey, Fisher, & Hattie, 2018). Project Based Learning provides opportunities for children to become assessment-capable learners in all four areas of learning: content, product development, final products, and processes. Wrestling with the content and ideas leads to assessment-capable students. Taking a risk to try something new and to monitor progress over time also involves students in the assessment pro-cess. Using reflection, feedback, and revision when working on a product draws students into the assessment process. Using rubrics to monitor pro-gress on different learning processes, observing and monitoring growth over time, and giving students the tools to recognize mistakes supports students as they develop their processing skills and dispositions. Students can also become assessment-capable by beginning to observe and under-stand their social and emotional growth as part of a project.

The right balance of assessments, administered at the right time, creates a full profile of the skills, knowledge, and dispositions of each learner and provides the teacher with invaluable information with which to plan instruction.

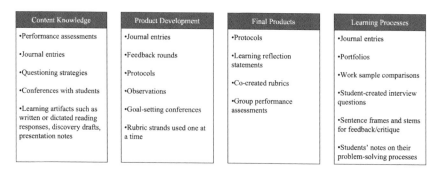

Content Knowledge	Product Development	Final Products	Learning Processes
•Performance assessments	•Journal entries	•Protocols	•Journal entries
•Journal entries	•Feedback rounds	•Learning reflection statements	•Portfolios
•Questioning strategies	•Protocols	•Co-created rubrics	•Work sample comparisons
•Conferences with students	•Observations	•Group performance assessments	•Student-created interview questions
•Learning artifacts such as written or dictated reading responses, discovery drafts, presentation notes	•Goal-setting conferences		•Sentence frames and stems for feedback/critique
	•Rubric strands used one at a time		•Students' notes on their problem-solving processes

Figure 8.1 Assessment types

This involves identifying some assessments before the project begins and layering in additional assessments as the project progresses. Different phases of the project will call for different types of assessments, depending upon the purpose and the public product(s). In Figure 8.1, we compiled a list of some of the most effective assessments for PBL in early childhood classrooms.

Assessment Types

A PBL lens for assessment means that teachers use familiar high-quality assessments as well as alternative approaches. In fact, we encourage you to identify assessments for learning that you have historically used if they can be incorporated into the learning process, in order to provide specific, timely, and helpful feedback, or to plan for instruction. For example, if you have used rubrics before, keep using them, but consider introducing the success criteria earlier in the project rather than withholding the rubric until the work is completed. Commonly used science journals can be used to document growth in learning processes related to observing and recording data when students engage in the inquiry process. As children keep a journal, they gradually add elements to each entry, beginning with simple drawings, then adding detailed diagrams, then labels, then questions. This might be included in a project portfolio which documents the learning process. All of these practices help create a richer picture of what our students know and can do within a project.

We recognize that you may have federal, state, district, and building assessment mandates to consider, and these are still important to implement alongside your project assessments. Many of these assessments are designed to measure learning differently and for different purposes. While, for instance, the grade level team may create a common formative assessment about specific content, teachers still have autonomy to use observations, anecdotal notes, and other assessment tools throughout project to monitor student learning. Perhaps you have some options for how to incorporate required assessments. Maybe you can alter assessment content, process, or timing to align with project goals. In the *Outdoor Classroom* project, Sara had a set grade level math assessment that included a geometry section. She administered that assessment at the end of the trimester, and *also* had a project-specific assessment for her students' puppet theater design which included being able to identify and name different shapes. She did an observational assessment of children's ability to describe character features on their puppet designs, and also conferred with children about the same topic during her guided reading groups and individual reading assessments.

We want to invite young children to take ownership over their own learning and develop a greater understanding of how their own knowledge and skills are constructed within the context of a project. Implementing meaningful, high quality assessments takes intentional planning. Learning to use data for the intended purposes comes with practice. To support you with this process, we return to the *Outdoor Classroom* project. In Sara's assessments (shown in Tables 8.1–8.6), you will notice (1) when the

Table 8.1 Social and Emotional Learning

Standards	Project Reference	Assessment Description	Assessment Type
PLF 5.1 SEL: Initiative In learning *Take greater initiative in making new discoveries, identifying new solutions, and persist in trying to figure things out*	Initial (whole class) outdoor classroom brainstorm Individual drawing of one idea for the classroom with dictated description recorded by Sara Idea Board	**A chart** with student names listed by the idea they shared allowed Sara to assess student sharing/taking initiative to suggest an idea **Teacher conference** where students described ideas using words or pointed to the key pieces to explain their ideas	***Learning process***

Table 8.2 English Language Arts

Standards	Project Reference	Assessment Description	Assessment Type
CCSS.ELA-LITERACY. SL.K. 1 **Speaking and listening: Comprehension and collaboration** *Participate in collaborative conversations with diverse partners about kindergarten topics* **CCSS.ELA-LITERACY. RL.K.3** **Literature:** *With prompting and support, identify characters, settings, and major events in a story.* **CCSS.ELA-LITERACY. SL.K.5** *Add drawings or other visual displays to descriptions as desired to provide additional detail.*	Classroom meetings and discussions	**Observations** of discussions about deciding on final plans for classroom and writing a letter to the principals Checklists of who participates and how many times Completed reflections after field experience **Puppet drawing** Children made a plan for an original puppet that included a drawing of the puppet character and labeled characteristics (i.e., funny, loves art).	*Learning process, product development* *Product development, content knowledge*
CCSS.ELA-LITERACY. RF.K.2 **Phonological awareness:** *Demonstrate understanding of spoken words, syllables, and sounds (phonemes).*	Choice of finger puppets and/ or instruments during the assessment of breaking words into syllables and identifying syllables in words	*Words their way* Syllable assessment **(one-on-one teacher conference)**	*Content knowledge*

208

Table 8.3 Math

Standards	Project Reference	Assessment Description	Assessment Type
PLF 1.0-2.1 **GEOMETRY** **CCSS.MATH.** **CONTENT** **K.G.A.1-6** *Children identify and use a variety of shapes in their everyday environment, combine different shapes to create a picture or design, expand their understanding of positions in space.*	Puppet theater collage	**Teacher observation/ conference** Students used either pre-cut shapes or self-cut shapes and glued on paper. They named shapes and described what the shapes are used for in the design (i.e., "The triangle is the roof. The square is the place the puppets hide behind. I used a rectangle for the curtain."). TERC/Investigations Curriculum – geometry **checklist** "Make a Shape, Build a Block"	*Product development* *content knowledge* *Content knowledge*

Table 8.4 Social Studies

Standards	Project Reference	Assessment Description	Assessment Type
SOCIAL STUDIES K.4 – *Students compare and contrast the locations of people, places, and environments and describe their characteristics (determine relative locations of objects using the terms near/far, left/right, behind/front).*	Individual floor plan	**Teacher observation/ conference** Children met with teacher and described (using the picture and actual classroom space) where each area would be.	*Product development, content knowledge content knowledge*

Table 8.5 Science

Standards	Project Reference	Assessment Description	Assessment Type
Next Generation Science Standards Engineering Design K-2-ETS1-2. *Develop a simple sketch, drawing, or physical model to illustrate how the shape of an object helps it function as needed to solve a given problem.*	Musical instrument design	Students drew individual **pictures** of 2-D instrument designs. They needed to complete a set of **rubric criteria** including instrument size, shape, material, and how the instrument would be played (plus one revision). Children constructed 3-D **models** using recycled materials.	*Content knowledge, product development, learning process*

Table 8.6 Speaking and Listening

Standards	Project Reference	Assessment Description	Assessment Type
PLF Language and Literacy (Listening and speaking) 1.0: Language use and conventions **CCSS.ELA-Literacy. SLK.4** Presentation of knowledge and ideas *Describe familiar people, places, things, and events and, with prompting and support, provide additional detail.*	Planned questions for visitor	**Peer-peer practice session** where children used a **rubric** to practice asking a visitor questions.	*Learning process*

(continued)

Table 8.6 Speaking and Listening (Continued)

Standards	Project Reference	Assessment Description	Assessment Type
CCSS.ELA-Literacy. SLK.6 *Speak audibly and express thoughts, feelings, and ideas clearly.*	Outdoor classroom tour with parents and guests	Children give a **parent tour** of the outdoor classroom, give them a map of the classroom, describe one area and what it is used for. Children share puppets and instruments with family and describe how they were made.	***Final product***

assessments were used, (2) who was doing the assessing, (3) what information was collected, and (4) how Sara used the data as a tool for encouraging learning. As you view the project through an assessment lens, we encourage you to turn back to the parts of the projects being referenced so you can better understand the varied nature of the assessments, the areas that were being assessed, and how students were involved in the assessments.

Developing and implementing assessments in PBL may look and feel very different than what you may be used to. Remember, there are many ways for children to demonstrate their understanding, and the ways we assess students should reflect those differences. The more frequently and intentionally you carry out assessments during a project, the more holistic a picture you paint of what students know or still need to know. The data we collect from assessments like observations, performance tasks, discussions, or peer-to-peer interactions give us insight into the skills, knowledge, abilities, and thoughts of our students. When learning is viewed as a process and assessment happens *throughout* a project, not just at the end, it becomes more than a single measurement of learning and we can celebrate with all of our learners just how much they grew during a project.

At the beginning of this chapter, we posed some common assessment questions related to PBL. We return to those questions here, offering you guiding questions and considerations as you begin planning your own project.

How will I create assessments that adequately measure student learning?

- Have you woven in assessments for content, learning processes, product development, and final product?

- Have you considered multiple ways for students to express their learning? (visual/illustrated, written, oral)

- What are some of the required assessments that could align with the project?

What evidence will there be that students understand key concepts?

- How often, and in what ways, are students keeping track of what they are learning and why that learning is important?

- Have you sprinkled in exit tickets throughout the project so students can routinely communicate what they are learning?

- Are you carrying out observations in students' natural learning environment?

- Are you documenting class conversations or individual conferences using photos, videos, and other technological aids?

What happens if the assessment data doesn't reflect student progress with the same accuracy as current testing practices?

- How often have you planned to assess for content in a variety of ways (rubrics, multiple choice, observations, conversations, etc.)?

- In what ways can students engage in assessments during the projects that mirror district- or school-mandated assessments?

Part 2: Public Products in Early Childhood PBL

When considering a public product, teachers need to take into account both the "public" and the "product." This involves more than just thinking about what the students will create and how they will share their learning with others. First, it is imperative that you align the public product to student learning goals and that you keep the authentic connections to *what* students create, *why* they create it, and *how* their creations demonstrate learning. Since students will be engaging in sustained inquiry throughout the project, the teacher must consider how the knowledge, skills, and dispositions the students are developing can be channeled toward the product. It is also helpful to identify how students' background knowledge and prior project experience might be leveraged throughout the project.

In the context of the Outdoor Classroom project, Sara sought to have a truly authentic public product. In addition to the completed outdoor classroom, she also had her students decide how they wanted to share their learning with families. They made a slideshow of photos and captions that documented the entire design process and shared it with their parents. Some students volunteered to speak in front of the whole group, describing the steps of the project. Then, all of the children gave their families a map (Figure 8.2), showed them around the space, and shared their puppets and instruments. The map served as a scaffold for children to remember where things were in the space and reminded them about the many steps of the design process. Then they celebrated by eating a family breakfast in the outdoor classroom, honoring all the children had accomplished.

It can be challenging to find just the right public product; one that aligns to learning goals is meaningful for students, achievable through sustained inquiry, and is developmentally appropriate. It can be equally challenging to find an authentic audience who is interested in your children's work and learning. Therefore, it may be valuable to ask your students for ideas on how they would like to share their learning. As you plan your public product, consider leaving some things undetermined so that students can have a say. Young children will have even more investment if they have a role in deciding some ways in which the public product is shared.

In the *Outdoor Classroom* project, Sara knew that there would be some type of tour. But she waited to see what her students specifically wanted to do in final planning. Sara was pleasantly surprised (and had not previously decided this) by her students' suggestion to decorate the classroom with balloons and colored lights for the tour. They also suggested telling their parents how they designed their instruments and decided they should play them for the guests. Even if you have already determined the type of product, you might guide your students in a way that makes them feel like they invented the plan. When teachers take the time to really think through the possibilities, they ensure that students are engaging in Project Based Learning in a deep and authentic way.

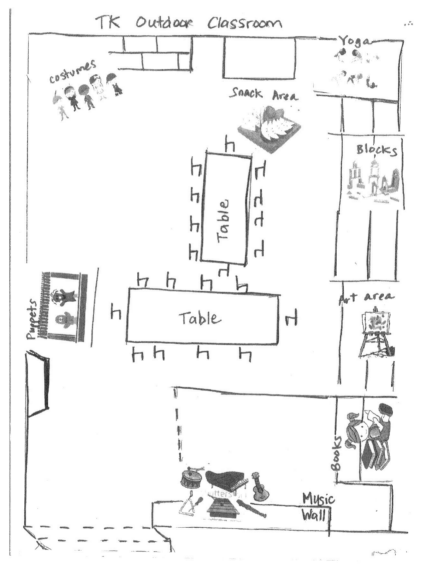

Figure 8.2 The outdoor classroom map

 The Product

Products must be aligned with student learning goals in order to keep the authentic connections to *what* is created, *why* it was created, and *how* this creation demonstrates content learning. Considering what type(s) of products would align best with the selected student learning goals goes hand-in-hand with how students will share their learning with a broader public. Teachers must consider how the things the students create help students answer the driving question. It is also important to think about the actual purposes and uses for a product to ensure that it mirrors the intended use in the world beyond the classroom as closely as possible. For example, if a project learning goal is to learn the design process (as with designing the outdoor classroom), children must use authentic tools (Idea Boards, measuring tape, floor plans) to actually design a space (a real-life context) as a professional designer might do. At its best, an authentic product makes a genuine impact on the world, as it did in the *Outdoor Classroom* project. In this case, the public product of the *Outdoor Classroom* project was indeed the classroom itself (to be used by students in TK as well as many other children at school), but also, the public celebration and mini "tour" the TK students gave their parents, who were also members of the school community and who might also be utilizing the space.

We recommend that you consider more than one idea for your public product during your initial planning. Brainstorming ideas from all the product categories – written, oral, media, art, technology, constructed and planning – prevents us from settling for the first idea that comes into our minds. Sometimes, a project results in multiple types of public products because of student needs and interests.

Once you have some ideas for a public product that you are considering, ask yourself the following questions:

- Is the public product *authentic* to the project learning goals?
- Is the work the students will need to do *developmentally appropriate*?
- Are there elements of the public product for both individuals *and* small groups?
- Would an adult use this product *in the same way* that I am asking the students to develop or use it?
- *Where* and *how* would the product be used?

- What support and help will my students need if they choose a certain product?

- How might students' identities, cultures and personal experiences enrich what they create?

The answers will help guide your next decision: How students will present this product to the public?

The Public

There are many options for teachers to choose from when deciding how to present the product(s) students create to the **public**. The "public" could be family members, a buddy classroom, or members of the school or local community. Sometimes, however, depending on the specific product selected for the project, you might not have an audience that appears all on a specific date, at a specific time. Students may, instead, share or display their work in community buildings or businesses, like a store, a nature center, or a historical building, and the public is comprised of people who live in, visit, or work in those spaces. Students could donate an original book to the school library, hang a large mural or map in the front walkway of the building, or create a public service announcement that is broadcast on a school web page. The product is still public, and while a formal "presentation" is not necessary, there should be an invitation for students to share what they learned and how they learned it with others outside of their classroom.

In this sense, then, making a product public is less about creating a presentation, or a showcase of work, and more about providing students an outlet to share learning in a meaningful way with an interested public. We mentioned in Chapter 7 that community members and experts can play an important role in a project by providing feedback that leads to reflection and revision. Sometimes those experts are interested in viewing the project when it is finished. If it is appropriate, consider inviting those who have played a part in the learning process to celebrate with your students. We encourage you, then, to be mindful of that "public" as you and students plan their celebration of learning.

In the following pages, we present a list of public product ideas and examples. It may be helpful to consider what type of public product would make the most sense for the project and then locate that section of the list. For example, if you are envisioning a written public product, then read through all of the suggestions for written products or consider coming up with your own. If you are thinking a public product that is constructed makes more sense, then read through the list of ideas in the constructed products.

Public Product Ideas and Examples for Early Childhood

Written products in early childhood classrooms can include drawings, illustrations, and dictation (i.e., an adult writes down a child's spoken words). If students are doing their own writing, do not feel the need to correct your students' emergent spelling skills. Sometimes their invented spelling adds to the authenticity of a project. Make sure you consider the purpose for the writing when selecting an audience.

- **Letters:** In early childhood classrooms, the teacher can use inter-active writing time or shared writing time to compose a class letter. As students become more proficient writers, they can progress from using a letter template to developing their own letters.

  Students write letters to a city leader offering suggestions of solutions for a local community issue.

- **Brochures:** Brochures can be created on various size pieces of paper and in various formats, including cutting out images and gluing them on, freehand drawings, and digital creations. Breaking up the different panels into mini-projects is a great way to help the students focus on one aspect of the project at a time and scaffold student teams.

  Students create a "Welcome to our School" brochure that gets placed in the front office to welcome visitors.

- **Scripts:** Students can create original plays, puppet shows, or video scripts in small groups or as a class. The script may or may not be performed for a live audience. Plays and puppet shows could be recorded and shown later or distributed via social media using private settings.

  Students design and put on a performance for other students of the expectations for different areas of the school, i.e., the hallways, cafeteria, or bathrooms.

- **Book review:** Children write book reviews or book recommendations for others, starting with books you've shared in your classroom.

> Students write book reviews that are "published" in a newspaper, magazine, or as a blog post. They could also be displayed in the school or public library.

- **Training manual:** Children can write informational texts ("How-To Books") teaching others how to do a particular job.

  > Students create trainings for next year's class on a variety of topics like checking out books, participating in class discussions, and doing classroom jobs.

- **Book:** Children can write and publish a book related to the content they are learning about and donate it to the school library.

  > Students write and illustrate an alphabet book about their school community. After learning about animal camouflage, the students might make a "look and find" book that combines art and animal adaptations.

- **Scientific study/Experiment report:** Children can plan and carry out an investigation, documenting their ideas, observations, successes, and challenges through words and pictures in a science journal.

  > Students' science journals could be used to develop another public product, e.g., a training manual or a book with labeled drawings.

- **Field guide:** Children can create a field guide, donate it to the nature center to give to visitors.

  > Students focus the field guides on topics such as identifying trees by their leaves and bark, field guide to birds through the seasons, field guide to butterflies (from egg to adult).

Oral presentation products[*] There are many ways to scaffold oral presentations. For example, you might use visual cards, realia, and plan for

---

[*] *If it makes sense for your project, embrace formal presentations and use the opportunity to support your students in developing their public speaking skills and self-efficacy. More than just developing confidence to "speak into a microphone," presentations help children to articulate what they have learned about a topic in an in-depth, conceptual way. Formal presentation preparation must include more than learning to look at an audience, speaking loudly, slowly, and clearly. It requires students to practice communicating their understanding of content, learning process, and product development. If you choose this option, keep in mind that there will be hiccups and imperfections, and this is all part of the learning process.*

many opportunities to rehearse before presenting. Sometimes it is helpful to record your students presenting so they can watch themselves and use their observations to revise and refine the presentation. Recording and showing a video of the oral presentation works well if there are additional components to a culminating event, or if your students are more comfortable having a video shown versus presenting live. For example, the presentations could be playing while parents are gathering for a poetry cafe or could be used as one of the learning stations if guests are visiting and learning about numerous things. If the presentation is a song or a dance and if your school has a music or performing arts teacher, you can enlist their help to support the project work by providing students with rehearsal time, feedback, or materials.

- **Speech:** After researching a topic and developing opinions, recommendations, or statements of fact, the teacher identifies a public platform for the children to share their work.
  Students give speeches at a rally for a community or school event.

- **Debate:** Self-select, or accept an assignment for one of the perspectives in which there is a topic to debate. After preparing for the debate throughout the project through research, analysis, and possibly a simulation, the children deliberate about the topic using an open forum approach.
  Students choose from topics like school lunches, recess options, getting a class pet.

- **Play, music, song or dance:** Create works of art using content from the project and the arts as a vehicle for educating or entertaining others.
  Presenting for a small audience, school-wide or community event.

- **Poetry slam or poetry cafe:** Share original poems in a small, intimate setting – could be for a buddy class, younger students, or parents.
  Students choose a subject for the poems from a specific concept or content area. The teacher may introduce students to many forms of poetry, including free verse; and after writing multiple pieces, the students select some to share at the event.

Media, art, and technology products. If your school has an art or media specialist, this is a wonderful opportunity to collaborate and brainstorm ideas to support the work your students are doing in the project.

- **Audio recording/Podcast:** Record original stories or a podcast.

    Students can easily incorporate fables, fairy tales, fractured fairy tales, or personal narratives.

- **Slideshow:** Take photos and create/present a slideshow to a small group of visitors/guests.

    Student products could incorporate the elements of art, what they are learning about cameras and digital photography, and all content area studies.

- **Drawing/Painting:** Create original artwork, art in the style of a famous artist, a class art piece, etc.

    Students' art can be displayed in a classroom, school, or local gallery. Children may or may not include artists' statements or stand by their pieces and share with visitors as they look at the art. Creating QR codes of the student artists talking about their pieces is another way to attach the artist comments with the work.

- **Video/Animation:** Write and animate their own cartoon story using the content or subject as the basis for their work.

    Students apply what they are learning about myths, fairy tales, or legends into digital storytelling.

- **Website:** Contribute content to the school website by showcasing their artwork, media productions, blog writing, or vlogs. Many public products can be adjusted for display on social media. Works in progress, as well as final products, should be considered.

    Students can keep others at school informed of their process on a project by writing a weekly blog update or posting pictures after a guest speaker or field experience. The students can develop the content all at once and then systematically release the content throughout a month or other time frame. For example, if the students are creating a public service announcement about a topic, and they are expected to write a script, then every Monday a different script could be included for X weeks, depending upon how many students are in the class.

- **Comic:** Create an original comic about the topic they are studying in during the project.

    Students can easily incorporate their learning from a variety of content areas like phases of the moon, a garden harvest, a trip to the orthodontist, or classroom visit from an expert into a comic.

Constructed Products

If you are able to enlist parent support, construction projects provide a great in-class learning opportunity. Ask parents who are handy, enjoy building, and have time to help out when building is taking place. Local tradespeople, students in industrial tech courses at the high school, and pre-service industrial tech teachers are also valuable resources.

- **Small scale model:** Use recycled material, clay or other material, to create a small-scale model.
   Students share an original toy design or a playhouse.
- **Consumer product:** Create products to sell in a school store.
   Students buy-in because they understand the goal is that they have an authentic purpose for raising funds, such as earning money to buy food for a class pet, donating to charity, purchasing supplies for recess, etc.
- **Device/Machine:** Develop/Build a machine or device to help someone do a particular job or solve a problem.
   Students could create a prototype, a design that is attempted on a 3-D printer, or anything the students design to actually work to solve the problem.
- **Invention:** Design and produce an invention.
   Students design an invention to help with inclement weather, classroom chores, or any other classroom problem.
- **Museum exhibit:** Create an exhibit for a designated section of a museum, adjusting their modality of representation to align with the type of museum, their personal strengths, or artistic visions.
   Students honor the heroes in their lives, famous people from their state or community, or a voice from a historical event, by making sculptures, using multimedia, creating a photo collage, etc.
- **Garden:** Plan and take care of a garden at school.
   Students should be involved in the majority of the decisions about which plants, where to put the plants, watering schedule, harvest schedule, recipes, etc.

Planning Products

- **Proposal:** Children can draft a proposal in words, images, scale drawings, etc.

Students present actual suggestions for how to add or change a space at their school, design their own classroom, or revise a school procedure.

- **Blueprint/Design:** Children are charged with developing design ideas for a real space at the school or to fulfill the need in a community.

  Students submit ideas for a mural on the playground or in the hallway, a structure to hold recess equipment closer to the playground, a space in the school that is being converted from a classroom to another usable area for children.

- **Event:** Children are tasked with planning an event for the class, the grade level, or the school.

  Students might be responsible for planning meaningful events like bike rodeos, field day, Meet the Teacher night, or poetry night.

Additional Ideas

- **Fashion show:** Depending upon the age of the students and the availability of resources, the students could create child-sized fashions or smaller versions that could be worn by action figures or dolls.

  Students model original clothing designs based on animal adaptations.

- **Obstacle course/Circuit:** Children can design and create an indoor movement experience for peers or other classes.

  Students could create the circuit or routine, teach it to their peers, and then have it available for use as brain breaks, indoor recess times, or rainy days.

- **Map:** Children can create a map of their school or classroom to hang in entryway of the school or to help guide visitors.

  Students could map routes to various places (like music room, cafeteria, gymnasium) from the classroom, or develop fire safety escape routes as authentic uses of map designs.

- **Simulation:** Simulations can be a good option for students if they are unable to participate in a fully authentic experience for any reason – that is, there is no opportunity for a particular audience, or if the true context is not readily available.

  Students design toy prototypes. They hold a simulated "Toy Show" where they display and promote their new toys to other students.

Students simulate applying for patents (presenting their patent applications and proposals for a committee of parents or teachers) after coming up with inventions to help people do their jobs.

Main categories for public products were adapted from *PBL Starter Kit: To-the-Point Advice, Tools and Tips for Your First Project in Middle or High School* (Larmer, Ross, & Mergendoller, 2009). Examples for using these public products in early childhood PBL units were developed by the authors.

 ## Overcoming the Misconception

When planning a project, we must consider how we can use ongoing, timely, and meaningful assessment opportunities to inform instruction and monitor student progress toward the creation of an authentic public product. This includes finding ways to assess students' knowledge and understanding of the content, their growth and development through the learning processes, and their skills to evaluate their own projects as well as those of their peers. Public products are meant to show children how their new knowledge and skills have relevance in the world, not to entertain. Assessments of learning are meant to guide our instruction and help children move their learning forward. Both of these aspects of Project Based Learning invite children to join in the learning process and as a result, they develop a greater understanding of who they are as learners.

References

Bear, D., Invernizzi, M., Johnston, F., & Templeton, S. (2018). *Words their way letter and picture sorts for emergent spellers* (3rd ed.). New York, NY: Pearson.

Blessing, A. (2019). Assessment in kindergarten: Meeting children where they are. *Young Children, 74*(3), 6–12.

Brown, J. D. (1998). *New ways of classroom assessment*. Alexandria, VA: Teachers of English to Speakers of Other Languages, Inc.

Diamond, J., Grob, B., & Reitzes, F. (2015). *Teaching kindergarten: Learner-centered classrooms for the 21st Century*. New York, NY: Teachers College Press.

Duckor, B. (2014). Formative assessment in seven good moves. *Educational Leadership, 71*(6), 28–32.

Frey, N., Fisher, D., & Hattie, J. (2018). Developing "assessment capable" learners. *Educational Leadership, 75*(5), 46–51.

Kohn, A. (2013). How to rock the boat: Do you think that just because you're a new teacher you can create meaningful changing your classroom? Alfie Kohn begs to differ. *Educational Horizons, 91*(4), 21–25.

Larmer, J., Ross, D., & Mergendoller, J. R. (2009). *PBL starter kit: To-the-point advice, tools and tips for your first project in middle or high school.* Novato, CA: Buck Institute for Education.

Marzano, R. J. (2006). *Classroom assessment & grading that work.* Alexandria, VA: ASCD.

TERC (2008). *Investigations in number, data, and space: Make a shape, build a block: 2-D and 3-D geometry, Unit 5, Grade K, teacher's guide.* Glenview, IL: Pearson Scott Foresman.

Tomlinson, C. A., & Moon, T. (2013). *Assessment and student success in a differentiated classroom.* Alexandria, VA: ASCD.

Wiggins, G., & McTighe, J. (2011). *The understanding by design guide to creating high quality units.* Alexandria, VA: ASCD.

Conclusion
Reaching Success

We know that assumptions and misconceptions often prevent early childhood teachers from believing that Project Based Learning (PBL) can be successfully implemented in their classrooms. While every chapter in this book grew out of a specific sentiment or misconception expressed or experienced by teachers across the country, all of them can easily be summed up into one primary belief: Project Based Learning won't work in an early childhood setting because the children are too young. As you read the story of the *Outdoor Classroom* project, you discovered that although Sara's children were "only" four and five years old, there was still much that they *could* do.

Sara wasn't concerned that her students couldn't read or write yet.

Instead, she knew that emergent literacy skills, including early phonemic awareness, representational drawings, and speaking and listening could all be purposefully integrated into any project.

Sara wasn't concerned that her students were too young to research on their own.

Instead, she knew that her children were naturally curious, and she would support students in formulating and articulating their questions, suggesting authentic ways to seek and find answers and share new knowledge.

Sara wasn't concerned that her students would need support working independently and with others.

Instead, she knew that children of all ages are developing social and emotional skills that are inextricably linked to academics, and Sara would take the time to explicitly teach and scaffold these skills both inside and outside of the project context.

Sara wasn't concerned that her students spoke many different languages, came from different cultural backgrounds, and varied in their prior school experiences.

Instead, she knew that she would need to make every aspect of the learning process accessible and differentiated. She knew that the emphasis of the final product would be about the learning process and that there were many ways to share learning and demonstrate understanding in a relevant context.

Sara wasn't concerned that her students would initially find it challenging to articulate their thoughts, reflect on their work, and make changes when needed.

Instead, she knew that reflection takes practice, and that there are many ways to ask children to add or change just one or two things to make work better. She knew that her students would appreciate giving and receiving feedback, especially in conversations where they could see how far they had come in their learning by comparing what they could do now with what they weren't able to do in the past. Through feedback, they would begin to notice their own growth and talk about what they really want to improve upon.

Reaching success in early childhood Project Based Learning is about acknowledging, honoring, and leveraging what children *can* do. It is believing that every young child who enters your classroom already possesses the foundational skills necessary to engage in PBL. It is about getting to know your students, finding out what is meaningful to them, what engages and excites them, and what connects them to one another.

As you embark on your Project Based Learning journey with young children, begin by holding these beliefs firm. Identify what your children know and wonder about, building on their interests. Place your students at the center – of your classroom environment, of your planning, and the community you seek to build. Intentionally weave together content where it makes sense and be open to surprises as the project unfolds. Develop children's emergent literacy by giving purpose and relevance to skills and build and sustain inquiry over time. Encourage students to collaborate with one another and make their voices heard as they work through challenges that arise. Inspire children to learn skills and knowledge toward the creation of an authentic public product. Listen, build relationships, scaffold, and support. Trust in your knowledge of how young children develop, communicate, and learn best. Commit to these practices and these values – the values that most likely led you to become an early childhood educator. For those are the values that will deeply impact the children whom you teach, and who will, in turn, teach you.

Appendix A
Project Planner

*Items in italics were added during the course of the project

1. Project Overview

Project Title	The Outdoor Classroom	**Public Product(s) (Individual and Team)**	**Individual:**
Driving Question	How can we create an outdoor classroom where we can play and learn?		• *Idea Boards* • *Puppet theater design and puppet character* • *Instrument design (2-D drawing and 3-D model)*
			Team:
Grade Level/ Subject	Transitional Kindergarten		• Whole class collaborative floor plan of classroom design • Small group presentation of one area of the classroom to parents and family members
Time Frame	6–8 weeks (depending on time dedicated to project)		
Project Summary	Students will design an outdoor classroom space. After meeting with a designer and learning about the design process, they will create plans for their new space. Children will collaborate to create all of the different areas which might include (based on student suggestions) a puppet theater, a painted mural, or a music area. Students design and create these spaces, integrating social studies (mapping skills), *science (engineering/design)*, math (geometry), literacy (phonemic awareness/ speaking and listening), and social and emotional skills (taking initiative and collaboration). They will present their new outdoor classroom to family members during a culminating celebration, sharing their floor plans/classroom maps as well as the different spaces they created, what they are used for, and how they were designed.		

2. Learning Goals

Standards	Preschool Learning Foundations:	Literacy Skills	Preschool Learning Foundations:
	• 5.1 SED: Initiative in Learning: Take greater initiative in making new discoveries, identifying new solutions, and persist in trying to figure things out. • 1.0–2.1 Geometry – Children identify and use a variety of shapes in their everyday environment, combine different shapes to create a picture or design, expand their understanding of positions in space. **Kindergarten Standards:** • _SOCIAL STUDIES K.4_ – Students compare and contrast the locations of people, places, and environments and describe their characteristics (determine relative locations of objects using the terms near/far, left/right, behind/front). • Geometry: _CCSS.MATH.CONTENT.K.G.A.1-6_ Identify and describe shapes. Analyze, compare, create, and compose shapes.		Language and Literacy (Listening and Speaking) 1.0: Language use and conventions **Kindergarten Standards:** Speaking and Listening: Comprehension and Collaboration _CCSS.ELA-LITERACY.SL.K. 1_ Participate in collaborative conversations with diverse partners about kindergarten topics. *Phonological Awareness:* _CCSS.ELA-LITERACY.RF.K.2_ _Demonstrate understanding of spoken words, syllables, and sounds (phonemes)._ *Literature:* _CCSS.ELA-LITERACY.RL.K.3_ _With prompting and support, identify characters, settings, and major events in a story._ Presentation of Knowledge and Ideas: _CCSS.ELA-LITERACY.SL.K.4_ Describe familiar people, places, things, and events and, with prompting and support, provide additional detail.

(continued)

2. Learning Goals (Continued)

*Science

- *K–2-ETS1-1 Ask questions, make observations, and gather information about a situation people want to change, to define a simple problem that can be solved through the development of a new or improved object or tool.*

<u>CCSS.ELA-LITERACY.SL.K.5</u>
Add drawings or other visual displays to descriptions as desired to provide additional detail.
<u>CCSS.ELA-LITERACY.SL.K.6</u>
Speak audibly and express thoughts, feelings, and ideas clearly.

Success Skills	Oral Communication (Presentation skills)
Rubric(s)	Visitor Questioning Rubric *Self-created project rubric for musical instrument design and model*
Key Vocabulary	**over/under** **left/right** **behind/in front** **design** *Idea Board* *puppeteer* *conductor* *composer* *syllable* *material* *volume* *instrument* *model* *character* *characteristics* *describe*

3. Project Milestones

This section is a high-level overview of the project. While Sara determined certain lessons and plans during her initial planning, she also left some things open to be filled in as she went along and as she saw what children were interested in. It is absolutely fine (and encouraged) to not have all the answers when you first sit down to plan your project. Have an overarching vision, clear learning goals, and a strong idea for your public product. Think about how content and SEL can be integrated throughout the project in authentic ways.

Milestone #1 Entry Event (2 days)	Milestone #2 (4 days)	Milestone #3 (3 days)	Milestone #4 (3 days)	Milestone #5 (5 days)	Milestone #6 Public Product (5 days)
Entry Event – Classroom Exploration, generation of ideas (with pictures) and Need to Know questions	Design plan, proposal to principals	*Mural*	*Puppet theater and original puppet characters*	*Musical Instrument designs (2-D and 3-D models)*	Presentation and celebration of learning

(continued)

3. Project Milestones (Continued)

Key Student Question	Key Student Question	Key Student Question	Key Student Question	Key Student Question	Key Student Question
What could we add to our outdoor classroom to make it a more fun place to learn and play?	How can we use pictures to show the areas we want and where they are located?	How can we work together to paint a mural to make our outdoor classroom more colorful?	How can we make a puppet theater and puppets that we can play with in our puppet theater?	How can we design our own instruments for our music area?	How will we share our learning and all the parts of our outdoor classroom with our families?
Formative Assessment(s)	**Formative Assessment(s)**	**Formative Assessment(s)**	**Formative Assessment(s)**	**Formative Assessment(s)**	**Summative Assessment(s)**
• Chart of student ideas, suggestions and questions • Chart student names next to their individual contributions • Drawing of one idea (Individual)	• *Individual Idea Boards* • *Floor plans* • *Student one-on-one conference describing the space (Individual)*	• *Completed murals (Team)*	• *Completed design using a variety of shapes (Individual)* • *Puppet character sketch with descriptions labeled (and completed sock puppet) (Individual)*	• *Scavenger hunt and observation sheet at field site (Team)* • *Completed instrument design on paper including revisions and completed 3-D model (Individual)*	• Small group presentation of areas of the outdoor classroom and individual puppets and instruments (Team)

4. Project Calendar

Driving Question: How can we design an outdoor classroom where we can play and learn?

Week: 1

2 days

Project Milestone #1: Entry Event-

Explore the outdoor classroom, generate a list of ideas of possible areas to be added, generate a list of questions students need to know in order to move forward with the design process.

Key Student Question(s): What could we add to our outdoor classroom to make it a more fun place to learn and play? What could we add to our outdoor classroom to make it a more fun place to learn and play?

Day 1:	Day 2:	Day 3:	Day 4:	Day 5:
LEARNING TARGET/ OUTCOME	**LEARNING TARGET/ OUTCOME**			
Students will generate a list of possible ideas for their classroom and choose one idea in which to draw/ represent and label (teacher dictation).	Students will generate a list of questions to help them move toward answering the driving question.			
LESSON STEPS	**LESSON STEPS**			
Invite children to explore the space, play with what is there, and then return. What would make this space more fun? What would you like to add? Chart student ideas.	Students review initial list of ideas (from Day 1) as well as pictures that were drawn. Generate a list of questions. Ask: What do we need to know in order to create an outdoor classroom where we can play and learn? Chart student "Need to Knows".			

(continued)

4. Project Calendar (Continued)

Day 1:	Day 2:	Day 3:	Day 4:	Day 5:
SCAFFOLDS	**SCAFFOLDS**			

Day 1:

SCAFFOLDS

- Do this lesson *in the* outdoor classroom space to provide context/visual cues for students who may need it.
- Model drawing or two ideas on the list (or choose something *not* on the list so that students are not tempted to copy teacher idea).
- Show students photos of other outdoor classroom spaces to help generate ideas or build context.

FORMATIVE ASSESSMENTS
Chart with student names listed alongside their suggested idea/comment. Individual representation of one area of the classroom that each student would like to create (teacher/student conference and student dictates a description of his/her idea).

Day 2:

SCAFFOLDS

- English language learners (EL) – review pictures/chart of ideas ahead of time (preview during designated EL time or other time of day).
- Introduce any new vocabulary with pictures or objects (e.g., "blocks" or "tables", photos, etc.).
- If students make a suggestion or observation rather than posing a question, use language to support adapting their statement into a question.

FORMATIVE ASSESSMENTS
Chart student questions with names next to each. Was each student able to formulate one question about what they observed?

REFLECTION
Whole Class Share: Which questions do you think are the most important? that is, which do students think we should answer first? If possible, write questions on individual index cards and prioritize to help determine which ideas should happen first. (This could be done in subsequent days).

Notes: Connect with any enrichment/specialist teachers to collaborate – for example, if students suggest painting, the art teacher may have ideas. In this project, our art teacher had great suggestions as to how to paint the cabinets/create a mural. Create a Project Wall to highlight driving question and student's initial list of ideas.

4. Project Calendar (Continued)

Driving Question: How can we design an outdoor classroom where we can play and learn?

Week: 2   **Project Milestone #2:** Classroom design, floor plan, proposal to principals

4 days

Key Student Question(s): How can we use pictures to show the areas we want and where they are located?

Day 1:	Day 2:	Day 3:	Day 4:	Day 5:
LEARNING TARGET/ OUTCOME Students will learn about the design process from an interior designer. **LESSON STEPS** 1. Interior designer visits and shares tools and process with the class. 2. After showing them an "Idea Board" samples, children work with boards and images (from Pinterest or other resource) to select and show their vision of what they would like in the outdoor classroom. 3. Designer offers feedback on initial Idea Boards. 4. Students begin to imagine the space and what might go where.	**LEARNING TARGET/ OUTCOME** Students will look at all the Idea Boards and collaborate to select final choices for the outdoor classroom floor plan. They will then draw their own plan (or use cut pictures) and place them on a "map" showing the areas where they want them to be. **LESSON STEPS** 1. Teacher facilitates a discussion around how to "compromise" and select one another's ideas. 2. Discuss "How can we listen to one another's ideas and look for common ground?" (Look for things that are the same/we can all agree on.)	**LEARNING TARGET/ OUTCOME** Students write a letter to school leaders proposing a design for their outdoor classroom. They practice presenting/ reading the letter and answering questions about it. **LESSON STEPS** 1. Whole Class Interactive Writing Session: "How can we ask our principals if we can design the outdoor classroom?"	**LEARNING TARGET/ OUTCOME** Students present their proposal/ letter and floor plan to principals for their approval. **LESSON STEPS** 1. Principals visit. Students (teacher helps as needed) read the letter, shows the floor plan and the outdoor classroom. 2. Students answer questions.	

(continued)

4. Project Calendar (Continued)

Day 1:	Day 2:	Day 3:	Day 4:	Day 5:
5. Students share Idea Boards with a partner. **SCAFFOLDS** • Pre-select and cut out a variety of images that come from the list of initial student ideas (i.e., if students suggested a snack area, find different sizes/shapes of tables and place them in a pile). • Expert or teacher can model selecting different ideas. • For academically advanced students, model labeling the individual images and encourage students to do the same. • Interactive Modeling: What do we do if two people want the same image and there are none left?	3. Teacher models having a conversation with a partner and looking for commonalities, with pre-cut images and a large poster/map. 4. Discuss what should be chosen and where it should go (use pre-cut images that correspond to the list of student ideas). 5. Teacher facilitates whole group discussion and helps student compromise/come to an agreement, creating one new large-scale map. 6. Teacher models for students how they can decide where elements should go using pre-cut images. **SCAFFOLDS** Facilitate this lesson in the outdoor classroom so students can walk around the space. This will help them envision where they want things to be, traffic patterns, etc.	2. Facilitate discussion of student suggestions – dictate into letter. 3. When letter is done, role-play being the principal asking questions and have kids answer the questions. **SCAFFOLDS** • Use pictures along with writing. • Academically Advanced: Ask to write letters or site words rather than initial consonants. • Introduce skills from PBLWorks Presentation Rubric. Can we practice some of these so that when the principals come we can convince them to design a new outdoor classroom?		

(continued)

4. Project Calendar (Continued)

Day 1:	Day 2:	Day 3:	Day 4:	Day 5:
FORMATIVE ASSESSMENTS Students share Idea Boards with a partner. **This could be done non-verbally if students wish by pointing or just holding up the board for a friend to see.** **REFLECTION** Whole Group: Was it hard to choose ideas? Why did you choose one idea or another?	**FORMATIVE ASSESSMENTS** Whole class picture of all of the areas they agree on for the outdoor classroom. Individual "floor plans" that show a sense of where things might be in the outdoor classroom.	**REFLECTION** Review some of the presentation skills. How do you feel about each one? (Thumbs up/side/down).		

Notes: Talk with the visitor ahead of time to discuss the plan and ask about hands-on tools he/she might bring. Before presenting any ideas, clear possibilities with campus admin so the answer will be "yes" to whatever kids suggest.

4. Project Calendar (Continued)

Driving Question: How can we design an outdoor classroom where we can play and learn?

Week: 3   **Project Milestone #3:** Mural

3 days

Key Student Question(s): How can we work together to paint a mural to make our outdoor classroom more colorful?

Day 1:	Day 2:	Day 3:	Day 4:	Day 5:
LEARNING TARGET/OUTCOME Students understand what it means to "collaborate." **LESSON STEPS** 1. Using the Teamwork Rubric (PBLWorks), explain what the word "collaboration" means. 2. Block Challenge Activity: In small groups, children will need to collaborate to build a building. The building must have a way in and a way to see out, and must have two floors. 3. Role-play/interactive model each of the collaboration (teamwork) skills. 4. Groups build the buildings and share out. **FORMATIVE ASSESSMENT** Self-Assessment: Thumbs up/side/down when reflecting on how each person did when working as a team.	**LEARNING TARGET/ OUTCOME** Students learn about different artists and his/her style. **LESSON STEPS** Children plan their mural designs.	**LEARNING TARGET/ OUTCOME** Students paint their collaborative mural.		

Notes:

4. Project Calendar (Continued)

Driving Question: How can we create an outdoor classroom where we can play and learn?

Week: 4   **Project Milestone #4:** *Puppet theater and original puppet characters*

5 days

Key Student Question(s): *How can we make a puppet theater and puppets that we can play with in our puppet theater?*

Day 1:	Day 2:	Day 3:	Day 4:	Day 5:
LEARNING TARGET/ OUTCOME	**LEARNING TARGET/ OUTCOME**	**LEARNING TARGET/ OUTCOME**	**LEARNING TARGET/ OUTCOME**	**LEARNING TARGET/ OUTCOME**
Students will create puppet theater designs made of pre-cut shapes.	Students help to build puppet theater using pre-cut pieces of wood.	Children will understand what a "character" is and review some of their favorite characters from familiar storybooks.	Children learn about puppetry and puppets from a professional puppeteer. They learn how puppets can be made and how to act out stories with them in their puppet theater.	Children create puppets based on their original drawings/designs. These can be made of different materials but socks are an easy base adding things like feathers, googly eyes, fabric and yarn.
LESSON STEPS	**LESSON STEPS**	**LESSON STEPS**	**LESSON STEPS**	**LESSON STEPS**
1. Students look at original puppet theater designs.	1. Children look at the wood pieces, name the shapes, and share what they notice.	1. Mini-Lesson: What is a character? Who are some of our favorite main characters? If we learn about characters and how to describe them, can we then create our own puppet characters to play with?	1. A puppeteer visits the classroom with his puppets and shares a bit about his process and how we might make puppets. He demonstrates how to maneuver the puppets.	1. Each student creates a sock puppet based on their drawn designs.
2. Discuss: What do you notice? What shapes do you see?	2. To the degree possible, children help put pieces together – nailing or holding or at minimum observing an adult do the building.	2. Children discuss characters and describe them. Focus on the different characteristics (inside vs. outside characteristics).		2. Children experiment with character tone of voice, movement, and dialogue.
3. Teacher models using the shapes to design own puppet theater.				

(continued)

4. Project Calendar (Continued)

Day 1:	Day 2:	Day 3:	Day 4:	Day 5:
4. Students choose shapes to design their own theater on paper. **SCAFFOLDS** • Some children can cut their own shapes, some will use pre-cut shapes. **FORMATIVE ASSESSMENT** Check-in (conferring) - "What shapes did you use? Can you tell me about your design?" **REFLECTION** Children share designs with a partner or in small group.	3. If painting the theater is an option, children can decide on colors and help with that. **SCAFFOLDS** **REFLECTION** What shapes did we use to build our theater? How is it the same or different from our designs?	3. Teacher models drawing how to draw a character and label with different features – for example, "loves to smell the flowers" or "has a silly laugh." 4. Children choose one character (from a book, from their imagination, or from real life) and draw a picture of the character. 5. They then think about at least three characteristics of that character and dictate or write them down. This serves as a model for their puppet design. **SCAFFOLDS** • ELL preview of different books, vocabulary "character" and "describe."	2. Students get a chance to use his puppets and practice. 3. Children ask questions about what they need to know to create puppet characters. **REFLECTION** Children make thank-you cards for the puppeteer, drawing a picture of the visit and sharing something they learned.	3. Children have opportunities to put on puppet shows in small groups. 4. Puppets are placed in a box near the puppet theater. **SCAFFOLDS** If art teacher or parent volunteers are available, ask for support to help students build their puppets in small groups or 1:1.

Notes: **During this week, each day read one or two different read-alouds that highlight strong characters. Ideas could include: Any *Elephant and Piggie* book (Mo Willems), *Stand Tall, Molly Lou Melon* (Patty Lovell), *Amazing Grace* (Mary Hoffman), *The Story of Ferdinand* (Munro Leaf). By Day 3, students should have a repertoire of beloved characters to draw from when designing their puppet.**

4. Project Calendar (Continued)

Driving Question: How can we design an outdoor classroom where we can play and learn?

Week: 5　　**Project Milestone #5:** *Instrument Designs*

5 days

Key Student Question(s): *How can we design our own instruments for our music area?*

Day 1:	Day 2:	Day 3:	Day 4:	Day 5: *This may take more than one session.*
LEARNING TARGET/ OUTCOME	**LEARNING TARGET/ OUTCOME**	**LEARNING TARGET/ OUTCOME**	**LEARNING TARGET/ OUTCOME**	**LEARNING TARGET/ OUTCOME**
Students will explore a variety of instruments, considering volume, material, shape, size, and how they are played.	A composer/ musician visits the class. Children learn about a job related to music as well as a specific instrument, its characteristics, the materials it's made of, and how it is cared for. They have the chance to ask questions to learn more about instruments.	Children design an original instrument	Children visit a music store and identify, compare, and contrast different instruments. They also have a chance to play a variety of instruments.	Children work with the art teacher in small groups to build a 3-D model of their instruments. They place their instruments in the basket in our music area in the outdoor classroom.
LESSON STEPS		**LESSON STEPS**	*Before Trip:* Visit the music store, take photos, talk with manager and music teacher to clarify expectations.	**LESSON STEPS**
1. Group Mini-Lesson: What instruments do you know? Children brainstorm a list of instruments.		1. How can we design our own instruments for our music area? Children consider all of the features they have learned about.	**LESSON STEPS**	1. After returning from the music store, children revise their instruments.
2. Children explore a variety of instruments.		2. Teacher models thinking about each element and filling out a design sheet (see below).	Students visit the music store.	2. They must add or change at least two details based on what they learned.
		3. Work Time Centers:Teacher meets with 2–3 students at a time while other students participate in Work Time Centers. Centers might include:	1. In small groups, children explore the store, instruments.	*(continued)*
		a. quiet instrument play	2. Manager talks to students and they have a chance to ask questions.	

4. Project Calendar (Continued)

Day 1:	Day 2:	Day 3:	Day 4:	Day 5: *This may take more than one session.
3. In partners, children share observations about each instrument. 4. Together chart similarities and differences between the explored instruments. **SCAFFOLDS** • EL students – pre-teach names of instruments and other vocabulary like "shake," "strum," "hit," "pluck." **REFLECTION** Which instrument was your favorite? Why? Which was your least favorite? Why? OR What feelings do you feel when you hear different instruments?	**LESSON STEPS** 1. A composer visits and describes his/her work and talks to them about how s/he learned to play his/her instrument. 2. Children play their instruments with the musician and ask questions. (Question asking is scaffolded by use of a rubric and practice/ peer feedback). **FORMATIVE ASSESSMENT/ REFLECTION** Children write/draw a page for a book about the visit.	b. listening center (different musical genres on headphones c. sheet music creation or exploration (using stickers, stencils, or self-created) d. looking through nonfiction books about instruments **SCAFFOLDS** • Teacher reads "Instrument design sheet" to students and helps them think through each choice (after they draw the initial picture). • Help with labeling pictures of different parts of the instrument. **FORMATIVE ASSESSMENT** Student design on paper **REFLECTION** Students share one or two details of their design with whole group.	3. Students visit the practice rooms/meet music teacher and ask questions. **SCAFFOLDS** • Teacher-selected groups of no more than three children. • Scavenger Hunt: Before trip, make a T-chart asking students: What do we think we will see? What do we wonder? **FORMATIVE ASSESSMENT** Children revise their instruments on paper, adding or changing at least one thing. **REFLECTION** Chart Responses To: What did we see? What did we learn? Later: Teacher shares photos of the trip, and students sequence them and dictate captions. Make this into a class book to reread and keep in the class library.	3. When this is done, they may work with art teacher and/or teacher to create a 3-D model of their instrument. 4. Children consider size, shape, material, and how the instrument is played. 5. Instruments are placed in the music area. **SCAFFOLDS** Support some students with tracing shapes and/or cutting. **FORMATIVE ASSESSMENT** 3-D instrument design **REFLECTION** Children share and play original instruments together. Possible Reflection Topics: What was challenging about making it? What did you do when you faced that challenge? What part of the instrument are you most proud of?

Notes: **Visit the music store ahead of time. Take photos of instruments to show students ahead of time/possible group scavenger hunt or just "look for" these instruments. For the 3-D instrument model, begin collecting materials early in the week.**

4. Project Calendar (Continued)

Driving Question: How can we design an outdoor classroom where we can play and learn?

Week: 6 **Project Milestone #6:** Celebration and Outdoor Classroom tour

5 days

Key Student Question(s): How can we share our learning and all of the parts of our outdoor classroom with our families?

Day 1:	Day 2: *This may take more than one session.*	Day 3:	Day 4:	Day 5:
LEARNING TARGET/ OUTCOME	**LEARNING TARGET/ OUTCOME**	**LEARNING TARGET/ OUTCOME**	**PUBLIC PRODUCT**	**REFLECTION**
Students decide how they would like to share their outdoor classroom by charting a list of ideas.	Children plan what they will say when they give their tour of the outdoor classroom.	Students practice for their presentation (PBLWorks Presentation Rubric)	*Celebration/ Outdoor Classroom Tour** (This can be revised based on student ideas)	Students reflect on their project, what they learned and how they learned.
LESSON STEPS	**LESSON STEPS**	**LESSON STEPS**	1. Parents and families arrive.	Quadrant Chart:
Meeting Topic:	1. Teachers may write it down in script form, or children can stand and practice.	1. Review PBLWorks Presentation Rubric and role-play as necessary. Teacher and students give targeted feedback using the "Two Stars and One Wish" protocol.	2. Share photo slideshow and student captions.	(see chart below)
How do you want to share our learning and everything in our outdoor classroom?*	2. Teams of two or three practice giving a tour of the space and sharing their work. The group decides which areas they will talk about and in what order.	2. Brainstorm a list of questions we think parents might ask and chart responses.	3. Student volunteers share overall process.	Circle: What was your favorite part of sharing your learning with your families?
		3. Give feedback on presentation skills using rubric.		

Quadrant Chart:

What we did	What worked
What needs work	Ideas for next time

(continued)

4. Project Calendar (Continued)

Day 1:	Day 2: *This may take more than one session.*	Day 3:	Day 4:	Day 5:
*This can be a predetermined plan, or can be open to student input. 1. Students make suggestions but there are also teacher-predetermined ideas. Include: • Inviting parents to come, and in small groups, children show them around the space. • Students also share with parents their floor plans, instruments and puppets. 2. Interactive writing – students create an invitation for parents. **SCAFFOLDS** • Include pictures and gestures for interactive writing piece. • Children use alphabet chart to come up and write initial consonants of the words in the letter.	3. Slide Show: Students dictate one line of a slideshow of photos documenting outdoor classroom process. 4. A few student volunteers share the larger project (practice saying it in front of the group). **SCAFFOLDS** • Pre-made notes on what students might say (EL/Special Needs) **FORMATIVE ASSESSMENT** Teacher observation – all students (in small groups) practice sharing their puppets, instruments and floor plan. Each student offers one line of text for the slide show.	**SCAFFOLDS** • EL students can use script or can also point to work/areas if more comfortable. Alternatively, a native English speaker can be in the same group to help or support. **REFLECTION** Circle With Talking Piece: What can we do if we feel nervous presenting to our families?	4. Students break up into groups of two or three and give their parents classroom floor plan, and walk them around different areas of the space and describe what the space is used for and why we wanted to have it. 5. Children share their puppets and instruments, describing the design process of each, along with their initial designs.	

Notes:

**A blank version of this planner can be found at pblworks.org.

Appendix B
Additional Resources

Learner-Centered Instruction

Alexander, P. A., & Murphy, P. K. (1998). The research base for APA's learner-centered psychological principles. *How students learn: Reforming schools through learner-centered education*, 25–60. Retrieved from: https://www.researchgate.net/profile/Patricia_Alexander4/publication/232541621_The_Research_Base_for_APA's_Learner-Centered_Psychological_Principles/links/56a97a9d08aef6e05df2b84f/The-Research-Base-for-APAs-Learner-Centered-Psychological-Principles.pdf

American Psychological Association (APA), Learner-Centered Principles Work Group (1997). *Learner-centered psychological principles: A framework for school reform and redesign*. Retrieved from: https://www.apa.org/ed/governance/bea/learner-centered.pdf

McCombs, B., & Miller, L. (2007). *Learner-centered classroom practices and assessments: Maximizing student motivation, learning, and achievement*. Thousand Oaks, CA: Corwin Press.

McCombs, B. L. (2003). A framework for the redesign of K-12 education in the context of current educational reform. *Theory Into Practice, 42*(2), 93–101.

Wood, C. (2015). *Yardsticks for elementary school: Children in the classroom ages* (3rd ed., pp. 4–14). Turner Falls, MA: Center for Responsive Classroom, Inc.

Integration

Campbell, D. M., & Harris, L. S. (2001). *Collaborative theme building: How teachers write integrated curriculum*. Needham Heights, MA: Allyn & Bacon.

Drake, S. M., & Burns, R. C. (2004). *Meeting standards through integrated curriculum*. Thousand Oaks, CA: ASCD.

Gehrke, N. J. (1998). A look at curriculum integration from the bridge. *Curriculum Journal, 9*(2), 247–260. doi:10.1080/0958517970090209.

Hattie, J. (2012). *Visible learning for teachers: Maximizing impact on learning*. New York, NY: Routledge.

Loepp, F. L. (1999). Models of curriculum integration. *The Journal of Technology Studies, 25*(2), 21–25.

Mallory, B., & New, R. (1994). Social constructivist theory and inclusion: Challenges for early childhood special education. *The Journal of Special Education, 28*(3), 322–337. doi:10.1177/002246699402800307.

Perkins, D. H. (1989). Selecting fertile themes for integrated learning. In H. H. Jacobs (Ed.), *Interdisciplinary curriculum: Design and implementation* (pp. 67–76). Alexandria, VA: ASCD.

Literacy and Choice Time

Bennett, S. (2007). *That workshop book*. Portsmouth, NH: Heinemann.

Flynn, E. E. (2016). Language-rich early childhood classroom: Simple but powerful beginnings. *The Reading Teacher, 70*(2), 159–166.

Fountas, I., & Pinnell, G. (1994). *Literacy beginnings: A prekindergarten handbook*. Portsmouth, NH: Heinemann.

Opal School ~ opalschool.org

Social and Emotional Learning

Anderson, M. (2015). Social-emotional learning and academics: Better together. *Educational Leadership, 73*(2). Retrieved from: http://www.ascd.org/publications/educational-leadership/oct15/vol73/num02/toc.aspx

Bailey, R., Stickle, L., Brion-Meisels, G., & Jones, S. M. (2019). Re-imagining social-emotional learning: Findings from a strategy-based approach. *Phi Delta Kappan, 100*(5), 53–58. doi:10.1177/0031721719827549.

CASEL ~ www.casel.org

Costello, B. (2009). *Restorative practices handbook for teachers, disciplinarians and administrators.* Bethlehem, PA: International Institute for Restorative Practices.

Durlak, J., Weissberg, R., Dymnicki, A., Taylor, R., & Schellinger, K. (2011). The impact of enhancing students' social and emotional learning: A meta-analysis of school-based universal interventions. *Child Development, 82*(1), 405–432. doi.org/10.1111/j.1467-8624.2010.01564.

Dweck, C. (2006). *Mindset: The new psychology of success.* New York, NY: Random House.

Elias, M., Parker, S., Kash, V., & Dunkeblau, E. (2007). Social-emotional learning and character and moral education in children: Synergy or fundamental divergence in our schools? *Journal of Character Education, 5*(2), 167–181.

Johnson, D. W., & Johnson, R. T. (2009). An educational psychology success story: Social interdependence theory and cooperative learning. *Educational Researcher, 38*(5), 365–379. doi.org/10.3102/0013189X09339057.

Kozar, O. (2010). Towards better group work: Seeing the difference between cooperation and collaboration. *English Teaching Forum, 48*(2), 16–23.

Krachman, S. B., LaRocca, R., & Gabrieli, C. (2018). Accounting for the whole child. *Educational Leadership, 75*(5), 28–34.

Mind Up Curriculum ~ https://mindup.org

PBLworks.org

- K–2 Teamwork Rubric https://my.pblworks.org/resource/document/k_2_teamwork_rubric
- 3–5 Collaboration Rubric https://my.pblworks.org/resource/document/3_5_collaboration_rubric_ccss_aligned

Responsive Classroom ~ https://responsiveclassroom.org

Restorative Practices ~ http://schottfoundation.org/restorative-practices

Second Step ~ https://www.secondstep.org

SEE Learning Program ~ https://seelearning.emory.edu/resources-research

Zin, J., & Elias, M. (2007). Social and emotional learning: Promoting students. *Journal of Educational and Psychological Consultation*, *17*(2–3), 233–255.

Reflection, Feedback, and Revision

Chappius, J. (2012). How am I doing? *Educational Leadership 70*(1), 36–40.

Hattie, J., & Timperley, H. (2007). The power of feedback. *Review of Educational Research*, *77*(1), 81–112. doi:10.3102/003465430298487.

Tovani, C. (2012). Feedback is a two-way street. *Educational Leadership*, *70*(1), 48–51.

Van Gelderen, A. (1997). Elementary students' skills in revising: Integrating quantitative and qualitative analysis. *Written Communication*, *14*(3), 360–397. doi:10.1177/0741088397014003003.

Wiliam, D. (2012). Feedback: Part of a system. *Educational Leadership*, *70*(1), 30–34.

Wilson, M. (2012). Look at my drawing. *Educational Leadership*, *70*(1), 52–56.

Assessment

Catlett, C., & Soukakou, E. (2019). Assessing opportunities to support each child: 12 practices for quality inclusion. *Young Children*, *74*(3), 34–43.

Fisher, D., & Frey, N. (2007). *Checking for understanding: Formative assessment techniques for your classroom.* Alexandria, VA: ASCD.

Hess, K. (2018). *A local assessment toolkit to promote deeper learning: Transforming research into practice.* Thousand Oaks, CA: Corwin Press.

Himmele, W., & Himmel, P. (2012). How to know what students know. *Educational Leadership*, *70*(1), 58–62.

McTighe, J. (2018). Three key questions on measuring learning. *Educational Leadership*, *75*(5), 14–20.

Protocols for Promoting Positive Student-Student Interactions and Enhancing Learning

EL Education ~ https://eleducation.org

Hollie, S. (2017). *Culturally and linguistically responsive teaching and learning: Classroom practices for student success* (2nd ed.). Huntington Beach, CA: Shell Education.

Kagan, S., Kagan, M., & Kagan, L. (2015). *59 Kagan structures*. San Clemente, CA: Kagan Publishing.

Making Thinking Visible http://www.visiblethinkingpz.org/VisibleThinking_html_files/03_ThinkingRoutines/03a_ThinkingRoutines.html

National School Reform Faculty ~ https://nsrfharmony.org

Rothstein, D., & Santana, L. (2011) *Make just one change: Teach students to ask their own questions*. Cambridge, MA: Harvard Education Press.

School Reform Initiative ~ https://www.schoolreforminitiative.org

Wright, T. S., & Gotwals, A. W. (2017). Supporting kindergartners' science talk in the context of an integrated science and disciplinary literacy curriculum. *The Elementary School Journal, 117*(3), 513–537. doi:10.1086/690273.

Facebook Groups

Early Childhood Project Based Learning

PBLWorks Community

Project Based Learning Community

Elementary Project Based Learning

Professional Learning Opportunities

Early Childhood Project Based Learning ~ earlychildhoodpbl.com

Culturally Responsive Teaching and the Brain ~ https://crtandthebrain.com

Responsive Classroom ~ https://www.responsiveclassroom.org

PBLWorks ~ https://www.pblworks.org

The Right Question Institute ~ https://rightquestion.org

International Institute for Restorative Practices ~ https://www.iirp.edu

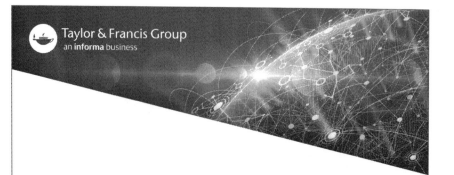